D0403060

The
New
Sexual
Revolution

Published in Association with Prometheus Books

# The

## NEW

## SEXUAL

## REVOLUTION

EDITED BY LESTER A. KIRKENDALL
*and* ROBERT N. WHITEHURST

With a Preface by Paul Kurtz

DONALD W. BROWN INC.
*New York*

# Acknowledgments

"Sterilization: Accepting the Irrevocable" by Garrett Hardin, was originally published in THE JOURNAL OF MARRIAGE AND THE FAMILY, May, 1969, and is reprinted by permission.

The following articles originally appeared in THE HUMANIST and are reprinted by permission. Rustum and Della Roy, "Is Monogamy Outdated?" March/April 1970. Albert Ellis, "Rationality in Sexual Morality," September/October 1970. Edward Sagarin, "An Essay on Obscenity and Pornography: Pardon Me Sir, But Your Asterisk is Missing," July/August 1969. Alice Taylor Day, "Population Control and Personal Freedom: Are They Compatible?" November/December 1968. Donald J. Cantor, "The Homosexual Revolution: A Status Report," November/December 1967.

Lester A. Kirkendall, "Developing Human Sexuality" is adapted from the author's article "Sex Education: A Reappraisal," spring 1965. Several paragraphs are also adapted from an article published in PASTORAL PSYCHOLOGY, November 1970.

To ABRAHAM MASLOW,
whose work in self-actualization
continues to provide insight and leadership.

# Contents

## Preface: Humanism and the Sexual Revolution

A revolution in sex is occurring and a new morality is emerging. This morality demands liberation and freedom for the individual to realize his own potentialities and satisfy his own needs, desires, and tastes as he sees fit, with a minimum of intolerant social rules and regulations. This revolution is basically a *humanist* revolution; for it is committed to the propositions that *human* happiness is the end of man, that sexual enjoyment is a significant part of the life well-lived, and that it is not to be approached with fear or guilt but with openness and receptiveness.

But, we may ask, is contemporary man—who is now equipped with critical scientific intelligence—able to rid himself fully of an alien religious legacy based upon mythology and illusion? Is man willing to take himself for what he is? Can he see that absolute moral codes of "righteousness" that seem to go contrary to his most basic biological drives are profoundly immoral? This is the option that now faces man: can human beings rediscover the sources of eudaemonia, and will they develop the courage to accept their animality, finding it positive and good? Those who defend the new morality answer in the affirmative.

Yet in opting for moral freedom, an essential qualification must enter. For although the proper demand for sexual liberation is part of the contemporary demand for justice, still this does not mean that there should be no rules or self-regulatory principles governing the expression of sexual drives. It is one thing to recognize that obsolete and deadening moral restrictions should be overthrown and that morality should not be legislated; it is another to argue that there should be *no* rules and/or that complete anarchy and permissiveness should prevail. The problem is to replace authoritarian standards, allegedly sanctified from on high, with rules intelligently developed from within human experience in terms of actual human needs and desires. Sexual liberation insists that we be emancipated from the Puritan-Catholic theology of repression and that we develop more realistic attitudes toward sexuality. This also means that we need to develop a mutual respect and understanding for the varieties of human enjoyment. Yet any reflective person recognizes that life without some rules would be impossible. Thus the challenge facing the sexual libertarian who is a humanist is whether the human being who frees himself from the dead hand of arbitrary rules, can at the same time, accept the responsibility for his own freedom. If frustrated sexuality can provide, the seeds of sickness and despair, so may utter abandon and promiscuity lead to misery and unhappiness. The life of the fleshpot, Plato observed, is like a leaking pitcher; it can never be filled or satiated. The quest for vicarious thrill and feeling at any moment and in any place without any controlling principles would make individual life chaotic and social life impossible; for, insensitive to the requirements of reflection, one would be buffeted by random choice. Human beings should learn to appreciate and savor the immediacy of the Now; but most people find even greater enjoyment by maximizing their creative self-fulfillment and enjoyment in the long run and over a full life. To forfeit one's life always to the dictates of the immediate present is to make a complete life, well-lived, nigh impossible.

Thus, one can argue that human beings should not necessarily satisfy all of their sexual urges indiscriminately, and a mature person is able to understand this. However, human beings should always be open to a wider range of sexual experience and be willing to experiment with different ways of enjoyment. The point to be reiterated is that any limitations that emerge must emerge from within human experience, not be forced on people from without. Also they must be appropriate to the needs and desires of human beings.

The questions then are: can man once sexually liberated from false restrictions accept his new freedom with responsibility; can he rediscover his natural biological sexuality—so often made impotent by social existence—and lead an active sex life, learning to love and appreciate others, to enjoy and share sex with them, and to find beauty and delight? Civilization at its best need not be repressive; in its higher forms of development it should involve genuine toleration and respect for the sexual capacities, needs, desires, and tastes of others.

The humanist then is committed to the sexual revolution. But this means that there is a need to develop some sense of individual responsibility about sexuality—one's own and others. A civilized person surely should not thrive on repressing others: a repressive person or society is not civilized but cruel and barbaric. Rather, civilized humans learn to recognize and accept what is within them and also to accept what is within others.

Humanists concerned with furthering the sexual revolution have worked hard for reform of laws against abortion, adultery, prostitution, homosexuality, and the liberalization of the divorce laws; sexuality between consenting adults should be out of the range of the law. However, humanists are also concerned with the question of sexual responsibility; all the more since the new morality is gathering speed on many fronts—as witnessed by the more tolerant attitudes of the young toward sex and of changes in social attitudes in literature, the arts, the mass media, and everyday life about nudity, obscenity, and pornography.

It is to the possibility of both sexual freedom and sexual responsibility for contemporary man that the authors of this volume have addressed themselves. This book grew out of an invitation to Lester A. Kirkendall, professor of family life, and the sociologist, Robert N. Whitehurst, by *The Humanist* magazine to commission a series of essays on the meaning of "the new sexual revolution."

The essays in this collection were written by eminent authorities in their fields. Most of them were written especially for this book; and some of the articles have already appeared in *The Humanist*. The authors were motivated by a common concern to evaluate human sexuality in the contemporary world and to provide some direction for those who demand a new sexual "bill of rights." It is our hope that this book will point to some guidelines that responsible people will recognize as reasonable and as worthy of intelligent commitment and support.

PAUL KURTZ
Editor, *The Humanist*

# Introduction

R O B E R T   N.   W H I T E H U R S T

Western man now appears to find himself in a new kind of struggle, a bit different from any of his other intrepid adventures in his unfolding saga. At the time we have become most free of the exigencies of labor and the stringencies of environment, we have become less and less able to deal with our freedom constructively and in truly humanizing ways. What we say we have always longed for is now within our grasp. Freedom to be, to explore the parameters of meaning aside from daily struggle, has left us even more bewildered than before. This book becomes one more document in the account of that struggle to clarify meanings; hopefully, it will provide one of the bases for more rational discourse and dialogue in an era we are coming to characterize as post-industrial, post-Freudian, and post-Christian.

What seems to be universal among all the people who write as though man is now emerging into a new age (and isn't he always?) is the new dimension of the struggle: the struggle for meaning and significance. Perhaps it is merely a function of the post-industrial era that we now have time and leisure to ferret out meanings, whereas our ancestors of necessity struggled for survival at levels not allowing such philosophical luxuries. We seem to be embroiled in self-defense against the monster machine we have contrived to make things for us (and now machines to make and run the other machines); we are attempting to marshall our human resources and capacities to forestall further mechanization *and dehumanization.*

Whatever the underlying causes or factors leading us into our new era of deep ambivalence about our freedoms, we can be much more sure of our facts than of our interpretations of them. It is the hope of the editors of this book that facts have not been pre-selected to suit certain biases of the authors. We know of course that all professionals incur their own sets of blinders in the process of socialization into their professions—variously called the illusion of centrality, occupational psychosis, and other such uncomplimentary terms, even megalomania. On balance, we hope to avoid the major errors implied by professional narrowness and enable the reader to exercise more fully his own critical evaluations. The sets of facts herein presented are broadly conceived to be consonant with the assumptions made by humanists. To evaluate them or interpret them in another context would lead to other errors. We hope that you will give the humanist framework of the book consideration before interpreting the materials in it. Only in the perspective provided by humanism can the facts be developed in terms of their full potential for humans struggling with the meaning of sexuality for man in the last years of the twentieth century.

If the meaning of the humanist perspective is kept to the fore, the book becomes less sexual and more an effort to place sex in the context of the total gestalt of man in his total lifespan. In some respects, western man has experienced repression, has painfully become aware of the costs involved in reactions to repression, the costs of behaving in sexually irresponsible ways, and now is at a stage where sexual freedom with responsibility can more fully emerge. It is toward this goal that humanistic dialogue encouraged by this book may be helpful.

Havelock Ellis is purported once in his later years to have suggested that man seeks, not simply sex, but a more total sense of involvement and completion of the self in those significant sexual others he encounters in his life. Eric Berne's transactional analytic therapy experience has led him to note the levels of involvement that modern Americans experience. What we all say we want is fully developed intimacy with significant others, but what we actually achieve are highly superficial and stilted forms of interaction with others. Real intimacy is much more than sexual and probably the most rare of all human experiences. Some of the means open to modern man to maximize this human potential are explored in these pages.

Our multi-disciplinary approach does not provide instant

truth, fully integrating man as sexual from the materials of the diverse (but hopefully unified) viewpoints in this book. It does, however, provide a broader possibility of making the intellectual excursion into our sexual no-man's-land more comprehensible. Toward that end, we have represented among our writers all of the social sciences, law, medicine, and some of the physical sciences that deal with human sexual problems.

A book with nineteen authors runs some risk of confusing, alienating, or otherwise disconcerting its readers (to say nothing of boring or insulting them). Attempting to get some order and coherence is no mean task in a volume of this variety. It is the editors' feeling that most readers will find flashes of real insight and go away after having finished this book wanting to tell friends of new ideas they have uncovered. If, in the process of discussions emanating from exposure to the ideas herein presented, readers are compelled to assess anew these old problems with fresh insights and perspectives, we shall consider ourselves successful. As humanists we hold that not only where there is life there is hope, but that man has the possibility of creating new forms more closely related to his goals today. Tradition has had its day; let us now proceed to more thoroughly examine the goals of contemporary man in the context of his need, his knowledge, and the means now used. If we find new adaptations that seem potentially more suitable, let us perform in that honored western way of experimentation, honest reappraisal, and reintegration in good faith with our fellows.

# PART I

# Background

## 1. *American Sexophobia*

ROBERT N. WHITEHURST

A basic supposition to be examined involves an assumption that Americans still experience some fears of sex which have multiple roots in historical events. Admittedly, a highly complex pattern of cultural events has brought us to this present state of affairs, but I will try to lend some clarification by stressing some of the important facets in the developing contemporary situation. Specifically, this chapter will deal with the impact of religious expression as it has affected several developing motifs recognizable in the Western conception of sex. Although forces other than religious ones are responsible for the development of our contemporary sexual attitudes, it is clearly possible to trace a good part of our orientation directly to religious origins. The historical trends to be discussed involve the development of several motifs historically. Among these, the most important to understand are: first, the loss of a naturalist philosophy in regard to sexual expression; second, the nearly universal subjugation of females in Western society; third, the development of dualistic philosophies in Western thought, which have tended to view things of the body and things of the mind or spirit as in separate realms. This tendency throughout our history has lead to an asceticism which has definitely denied sexual expression as a legitimate and important part of human activity. Fourth, as an extension of this developing dualism and asceticism, a Western body taboo has emerged which remains extremely strong. A fifth motif in Western society involves a long-existing sexual underground, which has had a varying impact on the sex lives of many people, but has rarely lent itself to reasonable expression of sex needs in any rational sense.

As a result of this complex set of social forces, we find ourselves living in a sexually polarized society. On the one hand it seems sexually obsessed, tending by indirect and subtle means to give sexual messages, while on the other hand it is often sex-denying in terms of formal socialization procedures.

Considering the nature of the human sex drive, it is reasonable to assume that Americans would have arrived at some state of complex confusion, since our highly technological and rational society has given us a level of individual choice and freedom unknown to other people in the history of human society. Since individuals are less closely tied to the church, the family, and sources of social control in the community than formerly, these authoritative organizations have lost a significant portion of their control over the bodily actions of people, especially females. The church has traditionally been a repository of traditional, double-standard values throughout history. Mary Daly contends in *The Church and the Second Sex* that the girl of *Playboy* (the bunny) which epitomizes contemporary American ideals of femininity (at least for some males) and the "eternal woman" of Catholic literature are one and the same in terms of types of females; both are passive, both understand their subservient role in history as compared to the really important roles and functions of men.[1] This intense little book bares the double standard in all its inequality in a scathing manner. The legacy of the long-standing double standard of treatment and special consideration given to women has created some peculiar dysfunctions in Western society which do not accord with other levels of scientific and technological reasoning. I will view the problem as a traditional fear of females, which may be characterized as "femiphobia" rather than "sexophobia"—a form that suggests that males fear sex when in reality, I suggest, the fear of women, and especially the fear of women gaining power over men, may be much closer to the heart of the problem.

To understand further how the five motifs came to be woven into the fabric of contemporary Western life, it may

be well to begin with the Greeks. A short review of the sex
and love habits of the early Greeks and Romans, the Hebrews,
the early Christians and Christian philosophers, later Christians and the Reformation leaders, as well as a discussion of
other European influences, will provide a background to
clarify these trends and provide some focus for better com-
prehension of our present sexual period.

### Sex, Love, and Marriage in Greece:

The Greeks not only had a low opinion of females, but
they also held marriage in low esteem. Greek children were
threatened by bogeys, all of which were female. They heard
about Pandora, source of all human ills, and Helen, cause
of the terrible Trojan War. A popular Greek saying was that
there was a woman behind every war. Plato noted the inferiority of women, as did Aristotle. In his *Republic,* Plato
appeared to liberate females, but in reality, he made of womankind a kind of collective pool of depersonalized fertility,
which might be interpreted as the fantasy of a man who had
no interest in close relationships with females. Thus, although
describing a kind of democracy, Plato still subjugated females
and left them in a depersonalized and impersonal position in
his society. Aristotle described women as suffering from a
"sort of natural deficiency" and felt that women should love
husbands more than husbands should love their wives, as a
compensation for feminine inferiority.

The Greeks did pursue the worlds of love with a sensitivity
unknown to the world before, but they did not add much to
the real possibility of making women fully participating members of the human race. The most perfect form of love was
the love of a man for a young boy.

The best Greek attempt to humanize women probably
appeared in a form of prostitution involving the *hetaerae,*
which included well-born females of Athenian citizenship,
trained in the arts in order to be mentally and sexually
stimulating companions of intelligent men. Hetaerae were
much higher in status than wives. Wives were held in mixed
contempt and regard, for their wants were apparently insatiable. Although the Greeks spent much time in the con-
templative life, they also lived active sex and love lives.
Their contributions to a Western conception of sex, love, and
marriage was noted by quoting Hunt.

And so the Greeks, though they invented love, neither connected it with marriage nor endowed it with genuine ethical value, and hence never solved the dilemmas it presented them with. For they found love either a sensuous amusement that faded all too soon, or a god-sent affliction that seemed to last all too long; they yearned for inspiration and found it only in immature, impermanent boyhood, or longed for the love of woman and found it only in the arms of whores.[2]

## The Hebrews:

Hebrew life is often seen as romantic and inspired, but many bits of evidence create a mixed view of the nature of the heritage given Western society by this religious-cultural group. The Hebrew emphasis on having sons, the fear of having one's family line die out, and a naturalistic interpretation of sex led to an unrepressed sex life for males, but conspired to make females something less than equals. The *Talmud* says:

A daughter is a vain treasure to her father. From anxiety about her he does not sleep at night; during her early years lest she be seduced, in her adolescence lest she go astray, in her marriageable years lest she does not find a husband, when she is married lest she be childless, and when she is old lest she practice witchcraft.

This seems to point up the need for males to subjugate, control, and keep women in an inferior position. The Jewish tradition embodies some fears of female functions, and tends to preclude female participation in a variety of traditional ceremonies, relegating women to important but inferior social positions.

Frumkin claims that later Hebrew developments added even more complications to the sex lives of Hebrews.[3] He indicates that the Hebrew male saw it as imperative that his bride be a virgin so that his sons were assured to be his own. This overriding desire to produce sons, to continue the family line, tended to give the Hebrew male utter control over the sexuality of his wife. Since the chief purpose of life was to perpetuate the family line through sons, the end (of achieving sons) legitimized almost any means. Concubinage, polygamy, and prostitution were all approved at some level. From the beginning of Hebrew history, man has had the upper hand in sexual interaction, a salient historical fact that has not as yet changed significantly.

The Hebrew conception of sex, however, was naturalistic; since sex was a part of man's heritage from God, man believed that it should be enjoyed and enjoyed lustily. Even a casual reading of the Old Testament supports the idea that our Hebrews forebears were not at all squeamish in the exercise of their sexual proclivity. The intrusion of some Eastern philosophies and of Christianity had the effect of changing the naturalistic concept of sex into a dualist philosophy carried over even into the later Christian period.

### Jesus and the Early Christians:

Eastern philosophies and Western ideals appeared to merge in a kind of syncretism that amounted to the blending of two civilizations into the culture of the Hellenistic age. Philosophical ideas fostering a dualistic interpretation of life were in evidence in the Middle East at about the time of Jesus. The Zoroastrian religion is one example giving impetus to dualistic philosophy. In this religion, the gods of darkness and light were in opposition, with the final outcome of the struggle between them in doubt. Zoroastrianism, characterized as it was by the dichotomous struggle of good and evil forces, came to be expressed in the early Christian era. Cole claims that an emerging and new goal of life in the early Christian era could be summed up in the word *ataraxia*, meaning detachment and freedom from passion. There apparently was no major philosophical school or religious cult at this time which was not importantly dualistic. Manichaean dualism emphasized the polarity of darkness and light, the struggle between the gods of good and evil, which later became part of the philosophical underpinnings of some Christian thought.

The dualistic nature of the thought of the earlier followers of Jesus conflicted with the old Hebrew naturalistic notions of sexual expression. Sex became involved partly because of the feeling of the imminence of the second coming of Christ. If a believer was to prepare for this event by some form of denial, what better way was there than to deny the pleasure of the flesh? In time, sex came to be associated with evil due to these historical processes. Denial and hardship seem to lend themselves to an increased sense of commitment in a minority group and to create solidarity for the marginal participant in such a group. A short review of the history of Methodists, Mormons, or Salvation Army members would be enough to remind the reader of this fact.

Jesus, as a Palestinian Jew, probably had little contact with the dualistic, Hellenistic philosophy which subordinated the body to things of the spirit. Rather, Jesus was, in all respects, brought up in the old Hebrew naturalist tradition, believing that all was of God and therefore good. On the basis of his very few pronouncements about sex, it is extremely difficult to present any full interpretation of sex from the teachings of Jesus. Cole makes three observations about the message and mission of Jesus: First, in his conviction that all behavior is symptomatic, that as a man thinketh within himself, so he is, Jesus seems less interested in what men do than in what they are, looking behind the act itself to the meaning and the motive in a framework, especially in terms of innner attitude. Secondly, in his teaching the central focus is on the law of love, striking at the legalism of the Pharisees. Third, his ministry is characterized by a therapeutic and redemptive outlook which is so familiar in his dealings with individuals. Instead of applying the universal principles of law, he placed the welfare of individuals above legal abstractions. His violation of Sabbath laws would be an example of this kind of orientation. Jesus sought the spirit of the law and de-emphasized the letter.

Sensuality, in the eyes of Jesus, was a minor vice when compared to the enormity of the sin of spiritual pride of the scribes and the Pharisees. In his encounter with these types, his essentially naturalistic attitude towards sex is inescapable. The norm by which men's sexual relations are to be judged, according to Jesus, adheres less in the letter of the law than in the inward meaning.

## St. Paul:

Paul is often seen as the villain in the sexual tragedy that befell Christianity after the time of Jesus. Paul, although far removed from the Hellenistic categories of thought regarding dualism, was at least concerned with man's constant choice between God and idols. The great apostle to the Gentiles seemed to mark the transition point between the naturalism of the Hebrews, characterized by a healthy attitude toward bodily pleasures, and the negative dualistic approach which came after Jesus and increased through time in the Christian thought of the next two or three centuries. Paul was very inconsistent in his interpretations of sex, for at one point he declared that in Christ the distinctions of sex had been transcended. At another point, he suggested that, since woman was created from man, she was distinctly inferior, subject to her husband, who is her head. His male arrogance was not unqualified, however, as husbands were bound to honor and protect their wives. He counseled celibacy but seemed to understand the need for marital sex; in fact he advised against too long periods of continence. Paul saw marriage not as an inherently evil thing, but rather as secondary to the really crucial task of preparing for salvation. His famous dictum "It is better to marry than to burn," is currently often interpreted to mean that Paul felt that those who could not abstain from illicit sexual intercourse should marry to prevent this worse evil befalling them.

Paul has often been misunderstood and misquoted, for his dualism is not completely rigid. He does not admonish man to struggle to the end with the sexual forces in an effort to make the spirit the utter master of the body. Paul's preachments were at best inconsistent, but he can be understood in terms of his own experiences: He was a Jew raised in a naturalistic tradition who was captivated by Jesus, who preached the message of love, and was convinced that God goes beneath the surface of the man and finds the inner motive. He was not in reality a Hellenistic dualist who regarded matter as evil, or the spirit as the only pure thing in man, for he allowed sexual outlets for those strongly desirous. His cosmopolitanism led him to prefer celibacy, a Hellenistic bias which was contrary to his Hebrew upbringing. Possibly his own sexual problems (some feel this was the "thorn in his side") contributed to his definitions.

### Roman Influences:

The excesses of pagan eroticism had begun to decrease as Christianity gained a stronger foothold in Roman civilization. Some Roman, non-Christian philosophers began to sound more like Christians, as Stoics and Neo-Platonists advocated varying styles of asceticism. The Christian influence in sex and love was thus less a revolution than an alliance with other

forces. With the apparent end of a pattern of Roman sex behavior which seemed to be self-exhausting, Christians began
to displace Graeco-Roman patterns of sexuality. The Old
Testament was revived and used as a source of explanation
and justification for subordination of females and to provide
a rationale for the celibate life: since woman was the villain
in the Garden of Eden, and sensual shame was sometimes
seen as one of the results of the verdant transgression, God
himself set man against woman. It was not until after Paul
that the Temptation, Original Sin, and the Fall were seen as
the central tragedy of mankind and Eve's guilt seemed so
great that it justified woman's subordinate place in life. In
the second and third centuries of the Christian era, the followers of Jesus developed a fanatical fixation about virginity,
the evils of woman and sexual connection, and the spiritual
merit of denying the flesh and repudiating human love. Sex
and sin became synonymous, a burden irrationally born of
historical accidents and misinterpretation. It is still borne by
the succeeding generations of Christians who know that who-
ever mentions sin is really talking about sex. The difficult
position of the Christians in the Roman Empire, their anticipation of the imminent second coming of Christ, their relative poverty, and their struggles to survive as a very small
minority in the Roman Empire may all have contributed
something to the development of this anti-sexual attitude
which has prevailed so long beyond the original development
of the philosophy. Although virtually none of the original
reasons or functions of this philosophy remain, the philosophy
itself tends to hang on tenaciously in Western society.

In the meantime in the Roman world, the experiences of
this far-flung empire began to cut loose a series of forces
which we are also still experiencing today in some respects:
the beginning struggles for the emancipation of women from
the absolute power of men. What began in the Roman Empire as a struggle by women to exercise the right to wear gold
ornaments and vari-colored garments in time led to the refusal
to have children, the right to free divorce and to hold property, and a host of other freedoms which are deeply implicated in social change throughout the time of the later
Roman Empire. In part, these great changes in the power of
Roman women can be seen as an outcome of Rome's constant
involvement in war throughout its history. The Punic Wars

especially provide a model for understanding the beginning
of greater freedom for females. Although wars are not the
only variable to be considered in changing female roles and
privileges, it is apparent that all wars add to the possibility
of increasing strength for feminism and women's rights.

Roman sexuality can be partly understood from the writings of Ovid, who seems to have encouraged adultery and
made an attempt to revive what he felt were the lost arts of
love. Homosexuality was imported from older Greek periods,
but the love element was apparently lost on the Romans,
who often prostituted young boys, sold them into sexual
slavery, and in general were involved in norms at variance
from the developing Christian mores. Homosexuality was
essentially a sexual evil because it did not have as its goal
reproduction, the essence of the sex act to Christians. The
detachment of love from marriage, the refusal of Roman
women to bear children, high abortion rates, and a host of
other non-sexual problems appear to have conspired in the
downfall of Rome. The thing of importance is to note that
Roman moralists and Christian reformers alike were busily
attacking the symptoms while history marched on. Rome fell,
and our ancestry was in some measure determined by these
established trends.

### Manichaeism and the Later Christians:

The Manichaeistic philosophy appears to have developed
in some interdependent ways with Christianity in the third
and fourth centuries A.D. The Manichaeans equated good with
light and evil with darkness to form a religious system involving the knowledge of nature and her elements, redemption
consisting in a process of freeing the element of light from
darkness. In this strongly dualistic religion, darkness is a
spiritual kingdom also conceived of as a spiritual and feminine
personification. This provides one more focus for Christianity's
concern with the vision of females as evil. In terms of the
creation of man, Adam was associated with Satan in conjunc-
tion with "sin," "cupidity," and "desire." Adam, to the Manichaeans, was a discordant being, created in the image of
Satan, but carrying within him a stronger spark of light than
did Eve. Eve was seductively sensuous, even though she had
in her a small spark of light. The glorious bright spirits took
these original characters under their care from the outset,

however, and sent down aeons, who instructed them regarding their nature, and in particular, warned Adam against sensuality. This first man fell under the temptation of sexual desire, and the illness of darkness (perceived as yielding to the sins of bodily desire) fell upon women, since they had less light than did men. There is little doubt that the strongly ascetic forces developed in Manichaeistic philosophy extended over into early Christianity and exerted forces that influenced such church philosophers as St. Augustine and others.

The Church adjusted itself to the new conditions of life as darkness fell on the continent. St. Thomas Aquinas looms large in the history of the Church as his system came to be officially sanctioned by Catholicism. The synthesis of Thomas, wrought by his understanding of Aristotle and Augustine, was to have far-reaching effects. Despite his attitude that sex involved "the inferior appetite" which should be controlled by the intellect, he saw procreation as part of the divine plan. While Thomas followed Augustine's interpretation of sex and marriage with less suspicion of bodily pleasure and more naturalism, he still stressed the life of reason and contemplation.

Neither Paul, Aquinas, nor Augustine was married—all shared roughly the same view that sex and marriage were to be avoided if at all possible so as to maximize the life of the spirit and contemplation. They all shared a fear of the passions involved in sex. They were not altogether dualistic in their interpretations of sex; but elements of their disgust and fear kept cropping up, so as to maintain in Christianity a heavy sanction against sex and, in some lesser instances, marriage. In this latter state, procreation and "rendering the [sexual] debt" were tolerated, but never seen as a positive element in the entire scheme of life as given by God. Obviously, these early Christians strayed far from the Hebrew naturalistic view of sex and the essence of the teachings of Jesus.

### Luther, Calvin, and the Protestant Reformation:

The history of the Church in the first millennium of Christianity is replete with examples of the struggle against lust. The gap between prescribed behavior and actual conduct grew, appalling many of the faithful. Luther, who found the Bishop of Brandenburg and his indulgence-hawker Tetzel repulsive, went to the Pope for redress. When the Pope failed

to correct what Luther felt were serious errors, Luther, un-
daunted, pursued his course of action with vigor. Luther's
married life at home was apparently tinged with a healthy
naturalism and an earthy sense of humor befitting the times.
Theologically he differed little from Aquinas, but he stressed
the following as the results of sin: shame at nakedness and
all things sexual, the burning of lust, the subjection of woman
to man, the pangs of childbirth, and the heartaches of parenthood. He felt these were only symptoms of sin, however, and
the effects of an inner condition of depravity rather than being
the disease itself. Luther looked on matrimony (despite his
own marriage) and sex as somehow an unhappy necessity; he
did maintain a slightly more realistic view of divorce and the
necessity of sex than did most of his predecessors and con-
temporaries. Luther tended more to give advice and opinions,
not commands, about the nature of what he saw as God's will.
He firmly believed in man's exercising restraint and recognizing
the obligations in Christian freedoms.

Calvin's theology differed mainly in emphasis from the
work of Luther. Growing out of Calvinist theology, an early
offshoot, Puritanism, came to stress the dualism inherent in all
Christian ideologies. Calvin, although he affirmed sex and
marriage as facts of creation, also stressed a kind of asceticism
which in effect created a heavy emphasis on bodily denial, a
new kind of dualism. He summarized Paul's teachings in three
articles. First, he conceded the superiority of celibacy, since
the unmarried could devote more time to God. Second, however, no requirement of celibacy must be imposed by the
Church; men must be free to marry if they felt the need. Third,
marriage is a divinely appointed remedy to be used by all who
have not been blessed with the gift of continence. Calvin
appeared to share the fear of sexual pleasure but sanctioned
marriage as a means of avoiding more serious sin. The outgrowth was a Puritan ethic describing sexual joy as a very
great evil to be avoided. Since children were highly valued
(in part as evidence that God had found favor—as a sign that
one must therefore be among the elect to go heavenward),
this does seem to pose something of a dilemma. Ellis considers
the problem of the true sexual nature of the Puritans in
America and suggests that actual behavior then may have
been little different from that of today.[4]

Calvin seemed to feel that Satan's trap was a sexual one.

If the problem was not one of abstinence and handling the sex problem delicately, one must cope with the problem of modesty. He admitted that the punishment afforded in Deuteronomy 25:11-12 for the female who accidentally touched the man's genitals was overly severe (cutting off the offending hand). He regarded it as an "inexcusable effrontery" to touch that part of a man's body "from the sight and touch of which all chaste women naturally recoil."[5] Only holy matrimony can draw the veil over the sin of sex, and then only under the properly genteel conditions. That Christianity, through the Calvinistic doctrine, came to be less rather than more liberated in terms of the exercise of sex can be little doubted by looking at the outcomes of Puritanism and the American Calvinistic sexual ethics.

## England and America:

In the meantime, early English sex customs had developed in ways that created an especially heavy burden for females. Women's status had reached new lows in history as women became property, prostitution flourished, and chastity became something of a marketable commodity. For the man, sexual freedom amounted to a problem more involving economics than moral principles. A clear double standard was in existence in England similar to the old Hebrew norm, but with Anglo-Saxon influence the penalties became very severe for the female who violated the rule of chastity. The desire to transmit feudal estates to legitimate children tended to make chastity one of woman's chief virtues. The value of women has virtually never involved their personhood, but rather has involved their being used as a means to achieve valued economic ends. It is probably no accident that the Church came to support the virtue of chastity inordinately for women. As bearers of children, feudal social organization focused upon the children produced by women rather than on either the marital relationship or the value of women as persons. Women sometimes were seen almost as chattel, and the economic basis for marriage remained well into the days of chivalry and the rise of the European middle-class, which created some alternative possibilities for women. Even with the appearance of troubadours and knights in the days of chivalry, an intensification of the double standard occurred. Ladies of high status were treated with great respect, but those of low estate were treated with scorn and cruelty. Large cities had their official brothels, sometimes controlled by the Church. The beginning of romantic love thus has had a complicated effect on later sex practices; some see it as an expression of our dualism, some as a means to achieve democracy for the female, and yet another view has it that romantic love is a functional necessity in a budding industrial society which traps the unwary into marriage when other social control forces have failed.

As a result of a variety of forces affecting life from the sixteenth to the nineteenth centuries, there arose a polarization of sexual writings, expression, and attitudes. On the one hand, the Church became more repressive as Calvinistic Puritanism gained strength and fervor in sexual repression; on the other, a sexual underground arose on a firm footing to counteract the religious forces of that day.

Probably the most important single force in American history relating to our own style of sexophobic development is to be seen in the rise of Puritanism. The American Puritans were intensely conscious of their covenant with God in their new country. This contract involved the assumption on the part of the Puritans that, if they (the Puritans) upheld their part of the religious bargain with God, kept themselves pure, chaste, and did His bidding, then God would favor their establishment in the New World. The conditions of life in America, the Puritan covenant with God, the exaggeration of Calvinism, and the necessity of controlling the people in the New England society, all conspired to constrict sexual freedoms and served to enhance the notion of this-worldly asceticism in America. The denial of bodily pleasures was an overriding and ever-present fear. Although the Protestant ethic apparently has made Americans rich and affluent beyond dreams of other nations, it seems to have left us with a sexual legacy very much out of touch with the reality of the contemporary social situation. Throughout history, man seems to have polarized sexual expression. Either it is suppressed and denied, with those activities which come to attention severely punished, or it is sanctified to the point where it cannot be discussed or dealt with realistically. In either case, heavily repressed or distorted variable expressions of sexuality often manifest themselves in obsessive concern with the subject. Obviously, healthful integration of sex into normal life becomes almost impossible. That some people manage to achieve a workable solution to this problem is a tribute to the resilience and flexibility of the human being.

To summarize, evidence from the development of Christianity leads inevitably to the conclusion that a loss of the naturalistic philosophy of the old Hebrews occurred through misinterpretation and historical accident, in combination with other social forces. The double standard which appears very early in the recorded history of mankind, has continued by and large unabated throughout history. It has operated, and still does, in many ways to subjugate the female. While some current discussions and data suggest that the double standard now is breathing its last in American society, the recent resurgence of militant feminism seems to refute this view. Perhaps history will record present developments in clearer detail than we now perceive, but surely much work is still necessary to clarify the many ways women are even yet subjugated and kept inferior. In many ways being female prevents a woman from dealing forthrightly and honestly, in the same way a man does, with issues affecting her. But it must also be said in passing that often women are their own worst enemies in the perpetuation of the double standard. In any event female subjugation will linger for a long time, even in modern America.

With the loss of naturalism as an approach to the expression of sexuality, the developing dualism that was so obvious in Manicheanistic philosophy in the early Christian era led to a kind of ascetic denial of all bodily pleasures. Thus the loss of the naturalist idea, the development of the double standard, the impact of dualism, and the increasing asceticism of the early Christians have also led to a norm which strongly prevails in Western society—the body taboo. Our fears of bodily contact are deeply embedded in cultural patterns of long standing, and only in very recent times has their persistence caused their rationality to come under close scrutiny. Although historically the failure of naturalism, the double standard, dualism and asceticism, and the development of the body taboo cannot be traced in an unbroken sequence, the body taboo is doubtless closely related to earlier Christian fears that once the taboo is broken, one is likely to be overpowered by his sexuality.

Unlike many Europeans, Americans suffer inordinately from fears of same-sex physical contacts. The homosexual implications of males kissing or embracing each other in American society is extremely obvious to cultural outsiders. Thus body contact in America poses a double threat: on the one hand the fear of sexual involvement with members of the opposite sex not one's marital partner, and on the other hand fears of homosexual tendencies or involvement. These forces together appear to have created a complex set of contradictory responses to sexuality in modern America. We have developed in our culture only the barest outline of the future possibilities of a sexually pluralistic society. The sexual underground persists and provides outlets for those whose activities cannot be accepted openly. We have not yet developed the social basis for the exercise of sexual pluralism in any real sense. Although we pride ourselves on dialogue, rational discourse to solve social problems, and the use of scientific data to inform ourselves about the nature of social problems, we change very slowly in this realm.

If we are to recognize the nature of truly democratic alternatives, not only must we recognize the historically derived errors of the past, but we must recognize the potential for a more adequate future. It is at this point that the perspectives of humanism as an approach to human problems can be of service. They can help citizens become better informed and able to strive toward more rational goals. We are all implicated as human participants in the great social drama of the culture. It is easiest to accept without question the definitions given by our institutions, but we must go far beyond this. As humanists, we should critically evaluate and analytically determine whether in fact our society is headed in a direction which is reasonable, necessary and promises fulfillment. When the humanist perspective is employed, man finds himself faced with accepting responsibility for his actions as well as for shaping his own future. It is time we recognize the potential for reviewing history, understanding the present, and acting toward a better future.

### Notes to Chapter 1

1. Mary Daly, *The Church and the Second Sex,* New York, Harper & Row, Inc., 1968, p. 128.
2. Morton M. Hunt, *The Natural History of Love,* New York, Knopf, 1959, p. 27.
3. Robert M. Frumkin, "Early English and American Sex Cus-

Let us consider some variations in sexual behavior that allow human beings to engage in those behaviors which will meet the need for being close. Courtship ceremonies may be conducted without the couples exchanging a single word during the whole process, or through a Polynesian custom of night-crawling where the young men slip into the houses of willing girls and engage in sexual intercourse while her parents are sound asleep. In the Mayan system the girl herself has little to say about the choice of her mate, the process is so involved with marriage broker, priest, father of the boy and father of the girl, that the whole of her society supports the new family unit. Courtship among Russian youth may not have all the trappings of an American ritual, but Wright Miller has described it as characterized by "truth-to-feeling. Their emotions flow out, warmly and passionately. They accept their emotions naturally. This gives them a vitality, a joy in living, that positively vibrates. It gives them also when their emotions are negative, a capacity for blank despair."[1] The Andaman Islanders are capable of this full range of emotional expression and can summon tears at will to express sentiment.

In many societies the exchange of gifts serves the purpose of expressing pleasure or appeasing the recipient to win his or her favor. There is a basic human need for approval, and different societies have different ways of expressing this need. In southern India a band of servants or slaves of the gods, called "devi-dasis," assist at all public ceremonies with dancing and merry song, then retire to their cells to perform temple prostitution. They are not coerced into this, though sometimes parents agree to devote an unborn child to this cause and the child is raised with this goal in mind. The practice of the levirate is another expression of this need. A woman whose husband has died is made to feel a sense of worth by immediately being made the wife of her husband's brother. This custom was practiced not only in Biblical days (Deuteronomy 25:5), but is practiced now by the New Caledonians, the Mongols, the Afghans, the Abyssinians, the Tongas of Siberia, the Nuer, and certain American Indian tribes. The word in the Nuer language for the condition of being co-wife is also the word for jealousy. The whole system of polygamous marriage functions to alleviate the lack of a sufficient number of men to marry the available women and provide for all women both companionship and sexual expression. The question arises: how long will it be before the surplus of American women grows enough for our laws to be revised to allow polygamous marriages? Among the Auca Indians of South America, because of the excess of women, men are allowed to have more than one wife, and often it is the village which decides by consensus that a man can take care of another woman.

The need to feel fulfilled is now being recognized by many of our most astute observers of human behavior (Maslow 1942, Rogers 1956, Jourard 1964). Increasingly, sexual fulfillment is recognized as a major component of this need, not as sufficient in and of itself, but rather as a means of expressing love. Ashley Montagu states in his book *On Being Human*, "The biological basis of love consists in the organism's drive to satisfy its basic needs in a particular manner, in a manner which is emotionally as well as physically satisfying."[2] Landis feels that "a satisfying sex relationship is one of the positive elements contributing to the well-being of each partner. . . ."[3] While Landis would limit this sex satisfaction to married couples only, René Guyon, in *Sex Life and Sex Ethics,* contends that our nature as human beings is such that we gain "specific pleasure, very vivid and at its height very intense" from physiological exercise of our sexual organs and that a distortion in values has made the morality of sexual acts dependent upon socially approved relationships (i.e., marriage).[4]

If two people, be they two males, two females, male and female, parent and child, teacher and child, or whatever, are in a relationship of caring, any physical touch between them is a legitimate means of expressing tender recognition of mutual satisfaction in each other's presence. Fortunately, most cultures allow expressions of physical feelings between the foregoing without tabooing touch as we do in much of Western culture. Thus Montagu points out "that the young of many animals, including man, react favorably and healthfully (in terms of better digestion and circulation, for instance) to gentle touching, stroking and comforting; sensuous stimulation is structurally linked to total creature health, and the emotion of love therefore draws its power from the instinct of self-preservation, the most basic of them all."[5]

The question is raised, then, as to how various taboos, such as homosexuality, masturbation, nudity and incest arose. Let us look at the incest taboo, which is almost universal. If the natural order of things is to allow stroking and touch, particularly of one's offspring, what occurred in the evolution of man to prohibit this phenomenon?

Apparently the theorists are not at all in agreement with respect to the rise of this taboo, nor are they in agreement with respect to the physical problems alleged to be the product of its violations. Lindzey contends that biologically the groups that have survived are those which have enforced this taboo. He states, "It seems unlikely that there would have been universal selection in favor of such a taboo if there were not rather widespread impulses toward expression of the prohibited act. Cultures seldom focus upon the inhibition of behavior which few individuals feel compelled to display."[6] We shall cite some examples of cultures in which incest existed.

North American Indians were "notorious sexual exploiters of children, using very young children—boys or girls indifferently—for their pleasure."[7] Masters' statement is supported by William Graham Sumner, who tells of the Indians of Sierra Madre, Mexico, who have daily occurrences of incest between father and daughter, which are associated with the agricultural, economic interests of the tribe. "The Indian tills small bits of land scattered in the hills. He cannot exist without a woman to grind corn for him. When he goes to a distant patch he takes his daughter with him. He has but one blanket and the nights are cold. If he has no daughter he must take another woman, but then he must share his crop with her."[8]

While some tribes proscribe endogamy, with death for those breaking the taboo, violations still occur. In fact, Murdock, who tabulated the number of cultures which prohibit endogamy stated, "the data from our 250 societies reveal not a single instance in which sexual intercourse or marriage is generally permissible between mother and son, father and daughter, or brother and sister."[9] Thus, its very prohibition is an indicator of the widespread impulse.

Stephens, after reviewing a number of theories on the subject, concludes by saying, "As a matter of fact, we do not know the reasons for the origin and prevalence of incest taboos."[10]

It has long been believed that when incest does occur in Western society, it is confined to lower-class families; but recent studies indicate that it occurs at all class levels and, like other "crimes," is more detectable at the lower-class levels because of welfare investigations and other intrusions into the privacy of such homes.

Guyon suggests that if we could look dispassionately and rationally at the principle of sexual pleasure without the arbitrary principles and conventional prohibitions, this behavior would not be condemned but would be tolerated as an extension of "the legitimate exercise of the sexual sense for its own ends . . . and the thing itself [as] ethically indifferent. Thus in time the community itself will cease to be interested in this out-of-date taboo, will no longer demand punishment for those who transgress it, and will eventually tend to disregard it altogether."[11] That such a view will prevail seems unlikely, particularly as one studies the structural-functional method which derives its typology from existing data of the elements of the community structure. While Mogey states, "In some societies incest is a fairly regular and acceptable occurrence,"[12] he goes on to show that community formation can only occur where "rules of exogamy or endogamy create community or society boundaries," and where norms (including the incest avoidance) operate, serving to restrict behavior. Parsons developed a theory of incest which attempts to show that incest is incompatible with a stable society.

Perhaps a day will come when the behavior of a given person will be judged not according to arbitrary rules but on the nature and quality of the relationship that exists. One of the persistent myths concerning incest is that the resulant inbreeding would be biologically harmful. Malinowski states, "to clear the ground it will be well to remember that biologists are in agreement on the point that there is no detrimental effect produced upon the species by incestuous unions."[13] Lindzey contends otherwise, saying that while inbreeding may produce an improved single characteristic it regularly results in a "general loss of fitness."[14]

That some children have been traumatized by brutal sexual assaults is a tragic truth, yet other children have looked back on early sexual experiences with high regard for the gentle and tender initiation to sexuality. We must avoid the judgments that speak of incest as "universally forbidden, by even the most backward peoples,"[15] when in fact it is not. One may convincingly argue that this taboo contributes to the integrity of the family only by ignoring the strength of the

Ptolemies of Egypt or the Incas of Peru. We have based our judgments largely on anthropological studies of kinship and court records of persons convicted of this "crime." Perhaps we should withhold judgment until we can gather data from families which have experienced this behavior but have never been studied with respect to its effect on the development of personality. Some data are becoming available in autobiographical materials being written by middle-class and upper-class college students.

Yet another need is to learn about one's self. At first we are content to learn all about man, hence our preoccupation with history and anthropology. But eventually we want to know more about our own particular origins. The British Museum has an entire section devoted to archives of genealogy, and these records are sought by persons around the world inquiring into their family origins. This interest in genealogy, however, does not represent the totality of our desire to know "who am I?" There has been an increasing demand for psychoanalysis in which a person explores the roots of all his feelings, the kinds of interactional experiences and their meanings, as well as the tabooed feelings long repressed concerning mother and father.

Anthropology has given us insights into possible origins of our behavior by showing people in earlier stages of development and thus giving us a chance to look back at ourselves in the mirror of time. Thus, when Levi-Strauss explores the Nambikwara or the Munde of Brazil and shows photographs of affectionate frolics and the naked joyousness of conjugal felicity, we can begin to understand some of our own needs which have been sterilized by too much covering; by the process of civilized socialization we have lost much of the spontaneity of interpersonal relations. It is perhaps significant that one of the newer approaches to psychotherapy includes the nude marathons or the baths at Esalen.

Perhaps our examination of premarital sexual behavior will give us clues to some of these interactional needs. From a humanistic point of view we should be able to examine them without the ethnocentricity of Western cultural values. Levi-Strauss tells of the "special relationship that exists between those children whose degree of cousinage is such that they are allowed to call one another 'husband' and 'wife.' Sometimes they behave like a real married couple and, at nightfall, they leave the family circle, take a few warm logs into the corner of the camp and light a fire, after which they 'set up house' and demonstrate their affections, insofar as they can, just as their elders do; the grown-ups glance their way in amusement."[16] Since the "search in science is for universal laws,"[17] perhaps we should be classifying human behavior on a much broader scale than we have used in the past and then we could see what *is*, not what somebody thinks it should be. There are many cultures which permit no coital activity until marriage. One such primitive culture is the Dyaks of Iban, Borneo. The value placed on virginity varies widely, and even in our culture different classes and sub-cultures place different values on it. The Dyaks mete out severe punishments to girls who try to fool men into thinking they are virgins when they are not. Often proof is offered, such as hanging the bedclothes out for public inspection of the bloody spots. Among the Brahui of Baluchistan the village selected a jury of matrons to inspect the girls' garments and certify as to the authenticity of the bloody stains. Other societies "consider a woman more desirable as a marriage partner once her fertility has been demonstrated by a premarital pregnancy."[18]

Scott, in his volume *Curious Customs of Sex and Marriage*, gives some interesting data on this: "Don Ulloa records that the ancient inhabitants of Peru would not, except in ignorance, marry virgins, and if it were discovered that any girl had failed to disclose the fact before marriage, the man considered he had been cheated." Similarly, in Tibet a virgin was thought to be unfit to become a wife. Westermarck mentions that the men of the Akamba tribe in British East Africa (now Kenya), consider a pregnant girl to be "a most eligible spouse"; while the Chibchas and Caribs of America, writes Sir Richard Burton, were accustomed to look upon "virginity as a reproach, proving that the maiden had never inspired love."[19] In certain African tribes (Nandi, Nuer, etc.) everyone may be having some kind of an affair by the time he is in his tenth year. The institution of sygraynet (men's house) allows the male to live apart from his parents and thus have freedom to experiment with girls who stay with their "other mother." They have a good deal of freedom and usually find their lovers without any particular interference from their respective families. Frisbie, a writer, trader, and navigator who lived in the South Seas, wrote, "A Puka-Pukan seldom marries his first love—

or his second, third, or twentieth, for that matter; but when he does marry, it is almost invariably successful."[20]

Sometimes the premarital sex was a ritual done by the gods (and through their emissaries, the priests). In tribes where virginity was sacred this service was performed for a fee, and if the girl could not afford temple deflowering she might grow to spinsterhood, since no one would marry someone who was not deflowered by the temple. A vestige of this rite lasted into fairly recent times when *jus primae noctis* (the right of the first night) was that of the lord of the manor.

Kinsey notes some anthropological data by Gorer which states, "sexual activity (of the Lepchas of Sikkim, a Himalayan state) is practically divorced from emotion; it is pleasant and amusing experience, and as much a necessity as food and drink; and like food and drink it does not matter from whom you receive it, as long as you get it, although you are grateful to the people who provide you with either regularly."[21]

Hegeler and Hegeler, two Danish psychologists, state, "As far as is known, approximately 5% of Danish women are virgins on their wedding day."[22] Swedish studies indicate a somewhat greater percentage (38% to 15% in a study done by Professor Carlson of the University of Uppsala).[23] Zetterberg found that 98% of the married population of Sweden had had premarital intercourse. A study done in East Germany by Dr. Rennert indicates that 83% of the unmarried males and 71% of the unmarried females had had sexual intercourse by the time they were twenty-five.[24]

Kinsey, in *Sexual Behavior of the Human Female*, reported, "Between the ages of sixteen and twenty, 38 percent of the grade school group and 32 percent of the high school group were having coitus as against 17 to 19 percent of the college-educated group."[25] Further, "Among the females who were not married by age twenty-three, almost the same percentages (about 30%) were having premarital coitus, irrespective of the occupational classes from which they had come."[26] Vance Packard's data from 644 males and 688 females who were in their junior and senior year in U.S. colleges reports coitus for 58% of the males and 43% of the females; however, if non-coital sexual experience is included (petting of girl's breast, 90% and 78% respectively; petting below the waist of the girl under her clothing, 81% of the males and 61% of the females; and genital petting of both man and girl, 63% and 58%

respectively), then by far the majority of American college students are experiencing some form of sexual gratification.[27] Winston Ehrmann found that "over one-half of the males and between one-quarter and one-third of the females were experiencing some form of genital activity, either manual-genital or genital-genital, at the time of the study."[28] Kinsey's data on the male in the same age bracket (college) indicates that 55% of the city boys and 47% of the rural boys have some premarital intercourse.[29]

It would appear that society's stated norms (no sexual intercourse until marriage) are honored more in the breach than in the observance, and yet the moral philosophers continue to exert pressure for the young to accept these stated norms despite the adverse effects of such attempted observance. The amount of guilt that is engendered and its concomitant anxiety in the adolescent who is striving to become an independent being is the cause of a great deal of the teen-age rebellion. The vast number of women who are sexually frigid or unresponsive long after the wedding indicates that their sexual nature was "armored" (to use a Reichian term) in dysfunctional ways. Kinsey notes, "Many of them [women with no sexual outlet] were sexually responsive enough, but they were inhibited, chiefly by their moral training, and had not allowed themselves to respond to the point of orgasm. Many of them had been psychologically disturbed as a result of this blockage of their sexual responses."[30] Since masturbation has also been disparaged as an acceptable behavior, many persons feel guilty about this method of sex-tension reduction. Again Kinsey notes that "pre-marital experience in masturbation may actually contribute to the female's capacity to respond in her coital relations in marriage."[31] Further, "If she has reached orgasm in her pre-marital petting, there is a much better chance that she will respond in all or nearly all of her marital intercourse during the early years of her marriage and also in the later years of her marriage."[32] In those cultures which permit relatively free sexual expression, the evidence indicates little mental disease, no psychosomatic disorders, and greater harmony in interpersonal relations. Since the form of conditioning is "culturally determined" it is possible to use rationality to change the norms in ways more consistent with human needs. That our youth are in the process of such change is evident from a study done in a Southern university where students were asked if sexual behavior was a moral and public issue or a person's own business; by far the majority (85% of the males and 75% of the females) felt it was personal and a good many felt that it was not sinful behavior.[33]

If the need to learn about one's self in relation to others and the need to have in-depth interaction could be satisfied without reference to laws on adultery and fornication there would be no need even to discuss this area. However, almost all societies have regulations concerning extra-marital relations, and regardless of the degree of enforcement there is always some social disapproval except in the institutionalized ways of cohabiting as at totem festivals, Mardi Gras, and May Pole Festivals.

The causes of extra-marital sex are varied, among them unresponsive spouse, boredom, desire for variety, social expectation (businessmen at a convention), desire for sexual activity which is disapproved of or thought perverted by spouse (oral-genital, fetish, sado-masochistic, etc.), desire to hurt the spouse for real or imagined hurts, impotence, and general non-monogamous desires that are felt by large segments of our own society as well as many other societies throughout the world. The degree to which a society penalizes a person for social deviance could be graphically pictured on our continuum of sexual permissiveness. Evans includes the wife-lending practices of the Eskimos, the pre-Christian natives of the Hawaiian Islands, and certain groups in Central Africa as one of the variants of extra-marital sexual behavior. Blood states, "Even when adultery is socially permitted, it is supervised to minimize the marital instability it would otherwise create."[34] Not unrelated to social regulation is the varying power of the social classes. During the Middle Ages "adultery was a social diversion among the upper classes."[35] Harry Elmer Barnes in his comprehensive volume *Society in Transition*, makes the point that only the most naive person believes we have "any complete prevalence of monogamy. Polygamy of a surreptitious sort is perhaps as prevalent among the upper American urban bourgeoisie—at least in periods of prosperity and a bull market —as its institutionalized form ever was in any Muslim land at any time in history."[36] Cuber and Harroff confirmed this in their study of *The Significant Americans*,[37] which came out in paperback as *Sex and the Significant Americans*. "Infidelity . . . occurs in most of the five types [of marriages]." While it has been thought that the upper classes are less inclined to deviant behavior inimical to marriage and the lower classes are more unrestrained in their sexual behavior, we know now that the difference is only with respect to actually getting a divorce, not the behavior that would lead to it. "At all social levels there are appreciable numbers of people whose conduct is not consistent with the expectations of the monolithic code. . . ."[38] But we are not alone in hypocrisy regarding extramarital sex. "In fourteen societies (of my sample of 39) there is a rule against adultery which is ineffective and 'honored in the breach.' Among the Subanom, adultery may be punished by a rather stiff fine; yet all but two men questioned . . . admitted having adulterous affairs."[39] "In India the licentiousness and vanity of the rich outruled all self-denial and spiritual affection. . . . Eastern potentates have been notorious for their teeming seraglios."[40] There seems to be some agreement among anthropologists, family sociologists, and other observers of human affairs that sexual conduct is a source of social problems and that feelings of possessiveness and sexual jealousy are present even in those societies which allow adultery. The exceptions are those societies which have institutionalized polygamy, such as in East Africa where the wife of a prosperous man will insist that her husband buy another, preferably young, wife. If he won't, she feels mistreated, for there is no one to help the older woman with the chores of grubbing the brush, planting the corn, and protecting the farm against the jungle beasts. Stephens cites a variety of societies which permit adultery: Baiga, Copper Eskimo, Fiji, Kwoma, Lepcha, Lesu, Marquesas, Morngin, Puka-Puka, Siriono, Siwai, and Toda. Sometimes it is limited to a special situation or occasion such as a ceremonial time, or the visit of a friendly tribesman, or is sanctioned in accordance with the previously mentioned wife-lending practices. The custom in Jaunswar Bawar, India, is polyandry; and it has an economic basis, for the people must till tiny, terraced fields and balance the meager food supply against the needs of the growing family. By having the younger son share the wife of the eldest son they avoid dividing the fields into smaller lots; and for some reason as yet unknown, polyandry reduces the fertility of wives and produces a ratio of more males than females. However, pressure is being put on the system by both the government of India and by the women who are changing status from ranty (a woman who lives with several husbands) to dhyanty (a woman who has several lovers). The quality of the relationship is part of the reason for this change, for the woman does not want to be considered the property of several brothers.

Much could be written about the variety of ways that various societies handle extra-marital sexual relations. Much has been omitted with respect to such sexual practices as masturbation, homosexuality, bestiality, and other forms of sexual activity. The point is that human sexual behavior is varied, regulated according to superstitions prevailing, controlled by religious institutions for a variety of purposes (e.g., belief in celibacy as a spiritual value, to pragmatic considerations of family structure); and often economic factors influence what behavior is condoned or condemned. In a pluralistic society no one standard can be fully accepted by the whole of the society, for differing levels (social classes, if you will) have differing values. It behooves us to make more judicious inquiry into the reasons for the behavior before we arrest, try, and convict a person of a "crime" (i.e., incest) which in fact may be a useful experience to the other person. With the increased freedom to conduct behavioral studies of premarital sex we may be moving in a direction of more rational solutions to adolescent needs. No one would advocate sexual anarchy as a viable solution, but certainly if socialization has any meaning at all we could socialize our youth to behavior which is both physically releasing and emotionally fulfilling. The direction of more openness and trust suggested in Kirkendall's *Premarital Intercourse and Interpersonal Relations* would move us toward self-actualization. A rational society would not imprison a male of 18 who had sexual intercourse with a female of 16 who freely consented; yet almost every state in the U.S. has statutory rape laws which dictate just that. Often such laws are used only when it is convenient to use them and ignored when the affluent have the means to manipulate the legal machinery.

If educational institutions were to be more honest with young people and tell them that premarital coitus may lead either to more "openness and trust between a couple" or to the risk of "distrust and separation," then they would have a legitimate choice; but when the great bulk of writers imply that only low-class, selfish, or unsocialized persons indulge in premarital sexual relations, the guilt feelings they subtly reinforce are of no real value in helping a relationship of trust to grow. Complete lack of sexual inhibition is not the antidote, but certainly enabling youth to relate to the opposite sex in meaningful ways would strengthen the interaction between them and provide sound experiences for future mate selection.

Nor is it suggested that we obliterate our cultural heritage or deny each group the right to express its values in ways productive for itself; instead, we would allow a wider variety of views to be expressed and consequently make available a wider choice of alternatives of behavior. We would think in terms of the needs of each of those involved in sexual behavior and judge (if judgment be needed) on the basis of the problem and the rationale of its solution. We would then move out of the nineteenth century with its repressive antisexuality into the twentieth century with its pro-life affirmation. Instead of assuming that "neuroses are the price humanity has to pay for cultural development,"[41] we can allow humanity to express its humanity without creating a conflict between cultural values and individual needs. To do this in a pluralistic society would be a marvelous display of democracy on the most personal level. It is possible, if we can learn from others in other lands and practice those values which we claim as our birthright . . . justice, tolerance, and human love.

## Notes to Chapter 2

1. David and Vera Mace, *The Soviet Family Garden,* Garden City, New York, Doubleday & Co., 1963, p. 118.
2. Ashley Montagu, *On Being Human,* New York, Hawthorn Books, Inc., 1966, p. 98.
3. Judson T. and Mary G. Landis, *Building a Successful Marriage,* Englewood Cliffs, N.J., Prentice-Hall, Inc., 4th Edition, 1963, p. 325.
4. Rene Guyon, *Sex Life and Sex Ethics,* London, John Lane, The Bodley Head Ltd., 1933, Chap. 4, "The Morality of Sexual Acts."
5. Morton M. Hunt, *The Natural History of Love,* Funk and Wagnalls, 1959, p. 396.
6. Jeffrey K. Hadden and Marie L. Borgatta, *Marriage and the Family: A Comprehensive Reader,* Itasca, Illinois, F. E. Peacock Publisher, 1969, (article by Lindzey, "Some Remarks Concerning Incest and Incest Taboo," pp. 37, 40-41).

7. R.E.L. Masters, *Forbidden Sexual Behavior and Morality*, New York, Matrix House Publishers, 1966, p. 379.
8. William Graham Sumner, *Folkways*, New York, Mentor Books, The New American Library, (originally published 1906), Reprinted 1960, pp. 407-8.
9. George Peter Murdock, *Social Structure*, New York, The Macmillan Co., 1949 Chapter 10.
10. William N. Stephens, *The Family in Cross-Cultural Perspective*, New York, Holt Rinehart and Winston, 1963, p. 265.
11. Guyon, pp. 309-10.
12. Harold T. Christensen, *Handbook of Marriage and the Family*, Chicago, Rand, McNally & Co., 1964, Chap. 13, "Family and Community in Urban-Industrial Societies," John Mogey, p. 503.
13. Bronislaw Malinowski, *Sex and Repression in Savage Society*, Cleveland and New York, The World Publishing Co., 5th Printing 1961. First Published 1927, p. 210.
14. Hadden and Borgatta, p. 40.
15. Ruth Cavan, *The American Family*, New York, Thomas Y. Crowell Co., 4th Ed., 1969, p. 352.
16. Claude Levi-Strauss, *A World on the Wane*, New York, Criterion Books, 1961, p. 276.
17. Richard A. and Patty Jo Watson, *Man and Nature: An Anthropological Essay in Human Ecology*, New York, Harcourt Brace and World, 1969, p. 159.
18. Quoted from *Coming of Age in Samoa* by Margaret Mead, Chap. 9, "Sexual Attitudes, Norms, and Practices in Cross-Cultural Perspective," David K. Evans, p. 169.
19. George Ryley Scott, *Curious Customs of Sex and Marriage*, New York, Key Publishing Co., 1960, p. 37.
20. Horace Knowles, ed., *Gentlemen, Scholars and Scoundrels*, New York, Harper & Brothers, 1958. Article by Robert Dean Frisbie, "The Sex Taboo at Puka-Puka," p. 177.
21. Alfred C. Kinsey, Wardell B. Pomeroy, Clyde E. Martin, Paul H. Gebhard, *Sexual Behavior in the Human Female*, Philadelphia, W. B. Saunders Co., 1953. Quotations from Pocket Books editions, p. 413.
22. Sten and Inge Hegeler, *An ABZ of Love*, New York, Medical Press, 1963 p. 286.
23. William Edward Mann, "Sexual Standards and Trends in Sweden," *Journal of Sex Research*, August, 1967.
24. *Sexology Magazine*, May 1969, p. 675.
25. Kinsey, p. 295.
26. *Ibid.*, p. 296.
27. Vance Packard, *The Sexual Wilderness*, New York, David McKay Co., Inc., 1968, p. 185.

28. Winston Ehrmann, *Premarital Dating Behavior,* New York, Henry Holt Co., 1959, p. 61.
29. Kinsey, p. 455.
30. *Ibid.,* p. 526.
31. *Ibid.,* p. 172.
32. *Ibid.,* p. 389.
33. *The Family Coordinator,* April 1968, pp. 119-123.
34. Robert O. Blood, Jr., *Marriage,* 2nd Ed., New York, The Free Press, 1969, p. 386.
35. Richard Lewinsohn, *A History of Sexual Customs,* New York, Bell Publishing Co., 1958, p. 136.
36. Harry Elmer Barnes, *Society in Transition,* New York, Prentice-Hall, 1939, pp. 388-9.
37. John F. Cuber and Peggy B. Harroff, *Sex and the Significant Americans,* Baltimore, Penguin Books Inc., 1966, pp. 62, 152, 193.
38. *Ibid.,* p. 198.
39. Stephens, p. 253.
40. Allen Edwardes, *The Jewel in the Lotus,* New York, The Julian Press Inc., 1964, pp. 34-5.
41. Thomas E. Lasswell, John H. Burma, Sidney H. Aranson, *Life in Society,* Scott, Foresman and Co., 1963. "How Culture Changes," George P. Murdock, p. 52; "Culture and Neurosis," Karen Horney, p. 609.

## 3. *Evolving Sexual Ethics Within a Democratic Society*

The traditional sex morality in America was sharply challenged by Kinsey's findings in 1948, which revealed that a considerable disparity existed between people's professed beliefs and actual behavior in matters of sexual conduct.

Since Kinsey and his colleagues were not studying sexual standards, any interpretations from their findings were hazardous. However, the problem of sex standards has since been scientifically studied by Ira L. Reiss, a sociologist from the University of Iowa. What Reiss did was to gather data on premarital sexual standards from a representative adult national sample. His findings suggest that in addition to the traditional sexual morality, there are other evolving sexual standards apparently stemming from a new sexual ethic.

Before setting forth those sexual standards documented by Reiss, I shall discuss certain factors that have been an integral part of the traditional sex morality. This will serve as a framework for examining in detail some of the forces both undermining the traditional morality and, at the same time, giving impetus to a new sexual ethic. In addition, I hope to point out how a traditional sex morality, based on the cooperation of certain institutions, would change as those institutions also changed.

By and large, the two institutions of church and family

33

have been the mainstay of traditional sex morality. That is, until recent times. For example, Bell points out that "until the beginning of the twentieth century, the institutions of Protestantism and the patriarchal family supported each other in defining, and ensuring high conformity to a conservative dogma of sexual morality."[1] The strength of adherence to this morality by society seems directly related to the extent in which church and family served each other's needs.

Although the church, at a later date, had considerable influence in supporting the concept of premarital chastity, the idea apparently was initially born out of property considerations rather than from a religious perspective. In any event, one of the mutually reinforcing factors in the relationship between church and family was the required adherence to a code of premarital chastity. Kinsey, in referring to this, states: "The demand that the female be virgin at the time of her marriage was comparable to the demand that cattle or other goods that he bought should be perfect. . . . Our moral judgments of premarital coitus for the female are, however, still affected by this economic principle which developed among the Chaldeans and other ancient peoples, three or four thousand years ago."[2]

Contrary to the "economic" principle ostensibly supporting chastity, David and Vera Mace offer a different interpretation. They state: "One factor in fitness for marriage was emphasized above all others—the chastity of the bride. . . . The explanation is simple when we remember the all-important function of the woman—to give her husband sons. A man wanted sons above all else, but he wanted his *own* sons, not those of some other man!"

Although the belief that it was the male who created life, while the woman provided the womb for it to grow in, was a mistaken one, it does reveal the strong male bias inherent in the patriarchal family. Also, the idea of insuring that a child belonged to the father by requiring chastity of the woman was a male-defined sex ethic.

The concept "chastity," then, was primarily a concern of the male as a proponent of the patriarchal family. Religion, at a later date, seemed to offer an additional way of strengthening that concern. Noting this kind of relationship between family and church apparently led Becker and Hill to conclude: "During the entire Colonial period the American family was first and foremost a property institution, despite the religious cloak that was flung about marriage."[3]

A traditional sex morality more concerned with property rights vested in the male, rather than the way the male used sex, spawned the notorious double standard. It works this way: A man was expected, if not actually encouraged, to enjoy sex relations before and outside of marriage. Both men and women believed that a *respectable* woman would have sex relations only within the marital bonds.

The problem with such a standard is that it perpetuated the false notion that sex was not a normal and enjoyable aspect of the marital relationship. Though marriage has slowly undergone change from an institutional to a companionship type, it could be argued that the attitudes generated from the double standard have hindered and retarded such change.

The impact of the double standard is seen in still another light by Atkinson who states: "The double standard imposes an inferior status on women, whether by artificially protecting the respectable many or by sexually exploiting the disreputable few. It feeds the attitudes which perpetuate it, making it difficult for men to have sexual relationships with women they respect, and restricts the opportunities of respectable women for sexual enjoyment."[4]

Actually, the double standard did not impose an inferior status on woman; it only reflected what her status already was in the patriarchal family. Furthermore, as mentioned above, the male at one time in the dim past had the mistaken notion that he was producing life while the woman simply provided the place for it to grow. Thus, there was no intended discrimination according to the male's understanding of his role in the reproductive process.

As long as the patriarchal family could control and perpetuate its own structure it seemed secure from any contrary influence within that arrangement. Only forces beyond its immediate control could possibly change this family system. Becker and Hill list those factors which helped to accelerate the process of change from a patriarchal to a more equalitarian or democratic type family. Obviously, no one could have foreseen such a change. "Yet, at the dawn of the nineteenth century, deep-moving forces were at work undermining father-power and the whole system of domestic industry on which the family was based. Most powerful among these forces were: (1) the frontier movement; and (2) the rise and rapid development of capitalistic industry. Hardly secondary in importance as influences shaping the modern family were: (1) the spread of democratic ideas; (2) the growth of science and the scientific spirit, with the corresponding decline of dogmatic religion; (3) the increase in economic independence for women, an outgrowth of industrialism; (4) the intellectual education of women, followed by their struggle for equal rights in the family and in society."[5]

Those who seemed to benefit most from these historical changes were the ones who had the least to begin with in rights, privileges, and power. They were, of course, women and children.

The patriarchal family structure, then, underwent considerable change, particularly as the Industrial Revolution took the man off the land and out of the home. This was perhaps the single most important historical event in undermining the man's authority and, thereby, hastening a more balanced power-structured relationship between husband and wife. One important outcome in this reduction of the man's authority was that he had less to say about the woman's world. This was the essence of the process which made impossible the continuance of the patriarchal family.

Not until woman had gained a status in the home nearly equal to that of man could she possibly be in a position to redefine a sex morality that would be concerned with the welfare of both sexes and would favor neither. Such a sexual ethic, however, would have to wait until powerful forces had gained momentum and combined to offer woman the degree of freedom that man had traditionally reserved for himself.

Thus, with the ushering in of the Industrial Revolution, a way was opened for woman to escape from the built-in dependency relationship she has had with man since the dawn of human history. She now had a way to support herself economically and still be considered respectable. This was a real change in woman's personal freedom. Thus, "for the first time in their lives spinsters and poor widows living in dependence on relatives, no less than young unmarried women, tasted the satisfactions of financial independence."[6]

The critical juncture, then, at which family structure began to change most noticeably was when women were freed from their historical dependency on some male for their survival.

This has been put aptly by Bell who advances the notion that "freedom and equality for the woman means a weakening of the patriarchal traditions. Sex equality and patriarchal values are in contradiction and can rarely exist within the same social group."[7]

With the family structure shifting from a patriarchal to an equalitarian type, traditional roles of husband and wife not only changed, but the property and family ideas connected with virginity slowly began to lose significance. Chastity for the bride was on the wane because one could choose one's own mate based on "love" rather than on economic or family values. Despite this amazingly significant change in family structure, there was no comparable change in the church's structure. Where the church once had a "supporting" role in the maintenance of the patriarchal family, it now stood awkwardly alone as the primary institution defining a sex morality for a family structure which no longer existed in purpose or in fact.

The family now changed from a cohesive unit with its primary concern on the status of the male, to one where the family is loosely held together. Bell interprets this change in the following vein: "This has meant that the impact of family influence on the attitudes of the individual has declined and, therefore, the traditional values of the family no longer have the same significance."[8]

Rather than family members supporting and strengthening the family, as once was the case, these same members now view the family as being there to serve the individual. Where individuals become delinquents, misfits, and problematic to society, the family is seen as having "failed" in its duty. Yet, because of influences related to employment away from home, education at schools, and commercialized recreation, the family has been stripped of its traditional functions and built-in controls. While responsibility is believed to reside within the family, the authority and wherewithal for rearing and training children has been diluted and undermined by such forces within the society.

One result of these varied and conflicting forces has been the achievement of relative freedom for the individual. The attainment of this freedom implies that no one group, including the family, has sole control over the socialization process of the individual. Furthermore, the individual is now torn in his loyalties to: family, peer group, school, state, and other competing organizations such as Boy Scouts, Y.M.C.A. and church groups. When seen in this perspective, the role of the modern family pales as an influential factor, much less a controlling force, in the life of the individual. One could easily argue that the "freedom" the individual has may be traced to the failure of the family and other "groups" to obtain his exclusive allegiance and, thereby, their failure to dominate and control his behavior.

The relative freedom now experienced by the individual is not of recent occurrence. In fact, Erich Fromm contends that the seeds of his ascendance and present freedom were planted several centuries ago. "European and American history since the end of the Middle Ages is the history of the full emergence of the individual. It is a process which started in Italy, in the Renaissance, and which only now seems to have come to climax. It took over four hundred years to break down the medieval world and to free people from the most apparent restraints."[9]

This quotation from Erich Fromm's *Escape From Freedom* provides an additional insight into the relationship between freedom and the individual. In a very real sense the freedom gained by woman has "passed beyond her" and has engulfed the entire society. Therefore, according to Fromm, it is the individual who has been freed; the woman is an example. Thus, the problem is not simply a gain in freedom for woman, as important as that is, but for everyone. That's the real issue.

This concept, "freedom," as written in the Declaration of Independence, has come ultimately to be accepted and applied by individuals in terms of "personal freedom." For instance, when an individual senses that he is free to choose, and circumstances warrant a choice, freedom then becomes a relevant personal experience in the life of the individual. As experiences of choosing accumulate, over a period of time, it could be expected that they would influence the directing of one's behavior when a decision must be made within a sexual context. Any *a priori* rules designed to inhibit an individual's behavior would probably have little effect when the logic of it boils down to whether "authority" or "self-direction" will be governing the decision-making process.

The term "freedom" also seems to have had an earlier connotation related to the idea of escaping from oppressive conditions. Religious freedom perhaps would be an example. In recent times, however, freedom has become equated with "autonomy" in making choices concerning an individual's personal welfare. Being free, then, implies autonomous behavior of independent individuals in a democratic society.

When the attainment of personal freedom tends to bring about equality between man and woman, a traditional sex morality favoring the male is no longer applicable, and perhaps for that reason more than any other, it becomes inevitable that a "push" toward a more relevant and equitable sexual ethic will evolve. Anything else would be a denial of the individual freedom experienced by the two sexes and the relative equality which has obtained between them in recent times.

Out of the innumerable changes which have occurred within this society, the concept "freedom," then, seems to be most potent as an explanatory factor. Moreover, as used here, it seems to have both unifying and explicative powers in accounting for what has happened in this society. For example, industrialization *freed* man from his association with the land; it also *freed* woman so that she might be economically independent; the change in family structure *freed* the individual from patriarchal control; and the decline of religious influence *freed* the individual to act more in harmony with his own inner convictions and conscience. From this freedom the individual has acquired an autonomy and independence to complement this situation. Rather than being controlled by some authority, he must now continually make choices in harmony with a rational decision-making process.

Factors enhancing autonomous behavior are the ability to control conception, to choose one's spouse, to move about the country, and to choose one's future occupation. While the ideology of freedom seems to be a most potent force in guiding an individual's behavior, however, technology, science, and the forces of education also have been powerful in shaping and giving meaning to the concept "freedom." Yet, Bossard, a sociologist, sees such changes in this light: "The great changes in human history occur, not in the mechanical gadgets which men use, nor in the institutionalized arrangements by which they live, but in their attitudes and in the values they accept. The revolutions of the past which have had great meaning for mankind are those which have taken place in the minds of men."[10]

For most people, ideas like truth, justice, and liberty remain as high-level abstractions throughout their lives. In contrast to this, "freedom" is something that is personally experienced day by day by the majority of people. Freedom implies choice, and, if anything, man is burdened by the choices he faces. Thus, his freedom is real and his choices seem infinite.

In a free-choice society where a traditional sex ethic prohibits a choice of action, such an ethic seems incongruent and hypocritical to those who are imbued with the concept "freedom" and are placed in a position to make such choices. The ingredients of this traditional sex morality are: authority, fear, sin, and punishment. Finally, it should be re-emphasized that this sex morality was originally conceived to protect property rights of the family (as exemplified by the requirement of chastity) and to perpetuate a patriarchal family organization. In a democratic society where individuals are considered free agents, able to choose and function as such, then it should not be surprising that these same people would begin the painful process of rejecting what appears to them as an impersonal and inhumane sex morality.

Because the traditional sex morality lingers on long after it has served its purpose, confusion reigns when people view present-day society from that vantage point. Some writers have tried to explain and describe what is happening. For example:

The rising concern over sexual conduct and standards results from many circumstances. Almost unlimited opportunities for the free association of unmarried men and women, the virtual disappearance of the chaperone, the decline of parental and religious authority, the freedom to acknowledge sex and sexual feelings, the near-collapse of a moral code based upon fears of pregnancy, disease, and social ostracism, the availability of automobiles, contraceptives, and general knowledge and information about sex—these conditions mean that young people encounter situations which pose problems their parents and grandparents never faced.[11]

Faced with rapid social change in a complex society, the individual is left in a quandary when situations arise in which there simply are no appropriate guidelines for arriving at a decision concerning his sexual conduct. A morality which fails to account for these changes soon loses significance as people discover that it does not work. When this happens there is a heightened conscious awareness by the individual of need for an ethic which can have relevance for him.

An example of a situation which has come about, and which is involving more young people than ever before, is the lengthened period needed for education in this age of specialization. The sexual problem they are faced with is that large numbers of males and females come freely into contact with one another, develop "love relationships," but find that it is impractical to marry for several years. Yet, they need and desire intimate relations which would have been satisfied had they not continued their education; i.e., they could have married.

Furthermore, when individuals live in a fast-moving world where their environment produces a dehumanizing effect, this in turn creates a counter-need for identity, belonging, and appreciation. Thus, when a complex industrialized society such as America's appears indifferent to human needs and dignity, a traditional morality which supports this indifference is not very reassuring to the individual. This point is clarified by Lawrence Frank who argues that "traditional morality is primarily an attempt to maintain social order with little concern for what that morality does to and for human personalities."[12] Where a morality served the patriarchal family, it now is obvious that the same morality lacks application for individuals.

Up to this point the terms "morality" and "ethic" have been used interchangeably. Because each term has a somewhat different connotation, a distinction should be made between them. Morality seems to have the connotation of being impersonal rules which are religiously based. Ethics, on the other hand, appear to be concerned with man's problems as a human being and are secular in origin. Morality, then, seems simplistic, general, and dogmatic, while ethics attend to the complex, are specifc, and are concerned with the betterment of the individual rather than the upholding of rules for their own sake.

Lawrence Frank, in his book, *The Conduct of Sex,* attempts to contrast the concepts of morality and ethics and to indicate why they are essentially different in their application. He states: "Initially, we may say that the ethical orientation is not primarily for the maintenance of social order by invoking obedience to authority and reliance upon fear of punishment. Rather, an ethical approach is concerned with discovering the meaning and significance of any human action, especially human relations, for both the actor and the person or persons who will be affected by that actor. This marks a shift in the individual's concern and orientation. The moral concern is an almost exclusive preoccupation with the role or code, what it permits, like looking over one's shoulder to the statements engraved on a wall, statements which define, without exception or equivocation, what you can and cannot, what you must and must not do. Thus, the moral concern is with the rightness and wrongness of an action according to pre-existing standards maintained by sanctions and a fear of punishment as these have been formulated by our predecessors."[13]

Other writers[14] have grappled with the problems of relating traditional morality to contemporary American life. From their writings, the idea of a "new morality" has emerged. All their views are essentially concerned with fulfillment of the individual's potential as a human being rather than simplistic lists of rules which assume all persons to be alike in their responses to the varying situations in which they find themselves.

One of the "new morality" writers, Pangborn, focuses on the traditional sex morality and contrasts that with a more comprehensive sex ethic geared to the needs of the individual.

The rubble strewn by legalistic traditionalists consists essentially of a sadly limited definition of sex, one divorced from appreciation of the pervasive and creative nature of sexuality as a dimension of being. . . . The new morality . . . calls for an end to the isolation of sex as a set of external acts and an integration of enriched notions of sexuality into our view of what comprises wholeness, complete personhood.[15]

The chief services performed by spokesmen of the "new morality" have been to trace some of the dilemmas and difficulties inherent in the traditional sex morality. For example, Frank clearly reveals that

the crux of a sex ethic is that each individual recognizes what he or she may do to another person by any attempted or proposed sex relation. Also, a sex ethic emphasizes what a sex relation does to the individual personality of the actor. By contrast, sex morality demands acceptance of certain regulations of sex activity, as in marriage, but exhibits little or no concern for what that permitted marital sex relation does to the individual, especially to the wife. In other words, one may be moral, obeying the code and respecting the commandments against unauthorized sex relations, but be ethically destructive to the sex partner and especially to one's own personality. On the other side, some extra-marital sex relations, considered as immoral, may be, and often are, ethically desirable and humanly fulfilling.[16]

Ira L. Reiss, in his article, "How and Why America's Sex Standards Are Changing," supports this paper's contention that sexual standards are evolving within a framework in which the young people themselves will be concerned.

What *has* been happening recently is that our young people have been assuming more responsibility for their own sexual standards and behavior. The influence of their parents has been progressively declining. The greater independence given to the young has long been evident in other fields—employment, spending, and prestige, to name three. The parallel change in sexual behavior patterns would have been evident if similar research had been made in this area. . . . In short, today's more permissive sexual standards represent not revolution but evolution, not anomie but normality.[17]

With new sex standards emerging, another writer, J. Richard Udry, contends that there are two basic patterns around which decisions are made concerning premarital sexuality.

The first pattern is simply to accept premarital chastity as an ultimate value, a good thing in life that does not have to be defended because it has more desirable consequences than some alternate choice, but because it is good in itself. . . . The second pattern establishes the meaning of sexual relations in the social context, and the meaning of sex determines its appropriateness in particular premarital settings.[18]

The sex standards which are evolving are viewed by Reiss as a positive change. He says:

For the first time in thousands of years, we have sexual standards which tend to unify rather than divide men and women. Especially in permissiveness with affection, coitus is no longer forbidden, and the motivation to deceive the opposite sex in order to obtain pleasure is greatly reduced. For the first time in many millenniums, Western society is evolving sexual standards which will tend to make men and women better able to understand and live with each other.[19]

Furthermore, Reiss had identified what he believes to be the four sexual standards which have evolved in America. Most people adhere to one of the following four standards, although some undoubtedly embrace more than one standard:

1) *Abstinence*—Premarital intercourse is wrong for both men and women, regardless of circumstances.
2) *Permissiveness with Affection*—Premarital intercourse is right for both men and women under certain conditions when a stable relationship with engagement, love, or strong affection is present.
3) *Permissiveness without Affection*—Premarital intercourse is right for both men and women regardless of the amount of affection or stability present, providing there is physical attraction.
4) *Double Standard*—Premarital intercourse is acceptable for men, but it is wrong and unacceptable for women.[20]

With four identified sexual standards one can appreciate the confusion and concern that exists among young people today. However, the double standard, with its exploitative male-prerogative, continues. Also, while the standard of complete abstinence seems to be a better alternative to the double standard, it, at the same time, suggests a complete denial of sexuality. The remaining two standards indicate (1) an acceptance of sex as a normal aspect of a heterosexual relationship, and (2) the development of criteria such as engagement, love, or affection as requisites to premarital sexual relations. Implicit within this latter standard is a responsible concern for sexual behavior as based on criteria relevant to the couple.

A sexual ethic which helps individuals treat sex in a responsible, mature manner seems to be emerging in our democratic society. Unshackled by traditional morality with its espousal of chastity as a means of protecting family and property rights, young people have begun to assume personal responsibility for their own sexual conduct. Moreover, they appear to have begun to define sex as a normal, healthy aspect of man-woman relationships. To that end the evolving sexual ethics reflects an intelligent approach which is in harmony with the dignity of rational man.

In a free-choice society where everyone is expected to become independent and autonomous in his behavior, such expectations find no exceptions in the area of sexual conduct. The process of individual freedom and its resultant autonomy have led to a sexual ethic which reflects this condition in this society. Moreover, when one considers that the American society encourages its young people to "freely" date, court, and marry with little, if any, family control in the total process, a sexual ethic which evolves out of this situation can then be easily understood.

## Notes to Chapter 3

1. Bell, Robert R. *Premarital Sex In a Changing Society*. New Jersey: Prentice-Hall, Inc. (A Spectrum Book), 1966, 182 pp., p. 13.
2. Kinsey, Alfred C., *et al.*, *Sexual Behavior in the Human Female*. Pocket Books, New York: 3rd printing, 1967, p. 322, 323.
3. Howard Becker and Hill, Reuben (Eds.) *Marriage and the Family*. Boston: D. C. Heath & Company, 1942, 663 pp., p. 72.
4. Atkinson, Ronald. *Sexual Morality*. New York: Harcourt, Brace & World, Inc., 1965, p. 105.
5. Hill, Reuben and Howard Becker, *op. cit.*, p. 86-87.
6. *Ibid.*, p. 89.
7. Bell, Robert R. *Marriage and Family Interaction*. New York: The Dorsey Press, 1967, 535 pp., p. 174.
8. *Ibid.*, p. 174.
9. Fromm, Erich. *Escape From Freedom*. New York: Avon Books, 1968, 333 pp., p. 52.
10. Bossard, James H. S. *Marriage and the Child*. Philadelphia, Pa.: University of Pennsylvania Press, 1940, 178 pp., p. 29.
11. Kirkendall, Lester A. *Premarital Intercourse and Interpersonal Relationships*. New York: Matrix House, Ltd. (An Agora Softback), 1966, 302 pp., p. 4.
12. Frank, Lawrence K. *The Conduct of Sex*. New York: Grove Press, Inc. (Black Cat Book), 1963, 160 pp., p. 113.
13. *Ibid.*, p. 119-120.
14. Fletcher, Joseph. *Moral Responsibility*: *Situation Ethics At Work*. Philadelphia: The Westminster Press, 1967, 256 pp.; Kirkendall, Lester A. "Interpersonal Morality." In: *Sex In America*. Edited by Henry Anatole Grunwald, New York: Bantam Books, Inc., 1964, 311 pp.; Pang-

born, Cyrus R. "Sex and the Single Standard," *The Christian Century,* 84:648-650, May 17, 1967.

15. Pangborn, p. 648.
16. Frank, p. 126.
17. Reiss, Ira L. "How & Why America's Sex Standards Are Changing." In: *Perspectives in Marriage and the Family.* Edited by J. Ross Eshleman. Boston: Allyn and Bacon, Inc., 1969, 770 pp., p. 398.
18. Udry, J. Richard. *The Social Context of Marriage.* New York: J. B. Lippincott Company, 1966, 580 pp., p. 169-170.
19. Reiss, Ira L. "The Four Sexual Standards." In: *Sex In America.* Edited by Henry Anatole Grunwald, New York: Bantam Books, Inc., 1964, 311 pp., p. 101.
20. *Ibid.,* p. 92-93.

# PART II

# Sex and Morality

## 4. *A Rational Sexual Morality*

ALBERT ELLIS

What constitutes a rational approach to sexual morality? Obviously, an entire book could be devoted to answering this question; and the present chapter, because of its brevity, will merely summarily try to answer it.

Rational, according to the dictionary, means based on or derived from reasoning. More specifically, an argument is rational when (a) it takes into account the facts of reality, is based on empirical evidence, and is not merely rooted in fantasy and wishful thinking; and (b) it is logically consistent with its own basic premises. As applied to human affairs, rational does not mean rationalistic: for rational*ism* is the doctrine of accepting reason as the *only* or *absolute* authority in determining one's opinions or course of action, and it is the belief that reason *rather than* the senses is the true source of knowledge. Rationalism, because of its dogmatism and absolutism, can actually be—as it is, for example, in the philosophy of Ayn Rand—an irrational, religious creed. Rationality, on the other hand, includes reasonableness, practicality, moderation, open-mindedness, provision for change, no allegiance to supernaturalism, and lack of condemnation of individuals who have opposing views.

The main thesis of this chapter will be that if sexual morality is to be rational it would better be a consistent subheading under the main heading of general morality. Sexual behavior is only an *aspect* of human behavior; and although it is an important aspect, it is not unique, special, and all-important. Indeed, it usually cannot be divorced from social-izing, relating, communicating, and various other forms of human contact and collaboration. Consequently, a sex act be-comes immoral, unethical, or irrational not merely because it *is* sexual, but because it is also in some respect nonsexually wrong, mistaken, or inefficient. Even rape, which is almost always immoral by practically any code one can devise, is not wrong because it involves intercourse but because it consists of forceful, freedom-depriving, injurious intercourse, and it is its breach of human consent rather than its sexuality which constitutes its wrongness.

What are the main principles of humanistic ethics, from which principles of sexual ethics can be logically derived? No one seems to know (nor perhaps will ever know) for sure, since invariant and absolute ethical ideals do not seem to be achievable; nor are they particularly *human*. Utopias, as recent sociological thinkers have been pointing out, are unrealistic and unattainable, because one of the main characteristics of men and their societies is that they distinctly change over the years, so that today's meat is tomorrow's synthetic. None-theless, like the other intrepid authors of this volume, I shall now attempt to establish some general ethical postulates which I believe are rational—meaning reasonable—and humanistic today, and which are even likely to have some relevance for the near, and perhaps even more distant, future.

In stating these "rational" moral postulates I shall try to abide by a principle which seems to me to be based upon em-pirical evidence and logical reasoning: namely, the principle of duality or plurality. Man tends to think in monolithic, one-sided ways, to look for absolute rules, for certainty. But few, if any, propositions (except those that are definitional or tau-tological) fall into an all-or-nothing schema; instead, prac-tically every idea or answer seems to have at least a two-sided, and often a many-faceted, aspect. Thus, human behavior is adequately explained by both heredity and environment; per-sonality includes cognition and emotion; sexual happiness stems from stable and varietist relationships; people would better be concerned with here and now experience as well as with future pains and pleasures. To understand what makes individuals tick without examining and taking into account the variegated influences upon them is to arrive at a narrow and unrealistic view of what they are and could be.

It is my thesis that a dualistic or many-sided point of view can be applied to the ticklish and still highly unresolved problem of human morality. It is also my thesis that moral codes generally emphasize the highly important issue of an individual's harming others, but that they almost totally ignore the equally important question of his defeating his own best interests and forget that he is just as unethical in the latter as in the former instance. In the following attempt at stating moral principles, I shall therefore include propositions which (a) concern themselves with self-defeatism as well as social sabotage and (b) consider a two-sided or pluralistic approach to "right" and "wrong." Using this kind of framework, I would hypothesize that an ethical code that includes the following rational ideas would hardly be perfect but that it would be more practical than various other codes that have been more dogmatically iterated over the centuries:

1. An individual would better strive primarily for his own welfare (usually, for continued existence and 'for maximum satisfaction and minimum pain); but since he almost invariably lives in a social group and his satisfactions and annoyances are importantly bound up with group living, he'd better also refrain from unduly interfering with the welfare of others.

2. A person would better try to live in the here and now and to enthusiastically enjoy many immediate or short-range pursuits; but he'd also better keep an eye on tomorrow and give up some immediate gains for longer-range, future satisfactions.

3. A moral code would better be constructed on the basis of as much empirical evidence about human beings and their functioning as it is possible for the morals-makers to obtain; but they'd better face the fact that, in the final analysis, morality is also based on a value system or set of assumptions: such as the assumptions that pleasure is "good" and pain is "bad."

4. There probably cannot ever be any absolutely correct or proper rules of morality, since people and conditions change over the years and what is "right" today may be "wrong" tomorrow. Sane ethics, therefore, are relativistic and situational. However, the nature of human beings and their environment is, and is likely to continue to be for some time to

come, so ordered that a few moral rules are almost invariant and will probably remain fairly stable for most groups under most circumstances. For example, "do not kill, lest you be killed," "love begets love," and "work hard to change the obnoxious conditions that you can change but gracefully lump those that are inevitable," are likely to retain some degree of truth for decades or eons to come.

5. It is generally better for one to follow the customs and laws of his social group the flaunting of which will bring real and noxious penalties. But to some degree one would better determine in his own mind what customs he thinks are insane and what laws he considers unjust and try to change or avoid them, even at the risk of some penalty.

6. No person, group, or thing is holy, sacred, all-important, or godly; nor is any person, group, or thing totally villainous, demoniacal, worthless, or hellish. But many things are more valuable for certain purposes than are other things. Thus, freedom and justice are not utterly necessary; and slavery and injustice are not completely horrible. But for most of the people most of the time freedom and justice are important, desirable conditions.

7. Moral codes would better be democratically applied to all individuals and groups within a given community; but discriminative morality, which is differentially enforced on elite and non-elite groups, may have advantages as well as disadvantages and need not be entirely bad.

8. In a well-ordered and reasonably fair society, the citizens would better resort to verbal protest, to the ballot box, and to peaceful demonstrations in order to try to effect desired changes in social processes; but in an unfair or ill-ordered society, resort to force, violence, or mob rule may sometimes help bring about progressive change.

9. Man would better base his morality on humanistic precepts: on the nature of man and his desires (rather than the assumed nature of supernatural gods and their supposed desires) and on the fulfilling of these desires in the present, near-future, and more distant future. But man also has the power to significantly change some of his "nature," some of his "desires," and some of his "humanity." It is "natural" and "human," for example, for man to be hostile, destructive, and warlike; and a rational ethical code may therefore include, as

one of its purposes, the goal of trying to teach him to be less "natural" and "human" in these respects, so that he thereby may be more "natural" and "human" in other, more collaborative respects.

10. Humanistic ethics include the primacy of human over sub-human goals, desires, and satisfactions: so that cattle, for example, can ethically be raised and slaughtered for human food. But man would also better be duly humane and uncruel to animals because in being needlessly brutal to them he also tends to become callous to human suffering and slaughter.

11. Rational ethics include provision for slight and serious modification of virtually all moral codes, especially as environmental conditions change and perhaps the biological nature of man changes too. But the alteration of ethical postulates would better be carefully approached, with considerable concomitant fact-finding and discussion, since more harm than good may easily be wrought in the changing process.

12. Immorality would better not be defined in terms of an individual's harming or acting unfairly toward another, but in terms of his *needlessly* or *gratuitously* injuring this other. For in the normal course of social living and consequent competition for jobs, sporting victories, sweethearts, or status, it is impossible for a person not to harm another—unless, of course, he is always a loser. However, in determining whether *A* necessarily and therefore justifiably harmed *B* (as, for example, when he ran off with the most desirable girl at a party when *B* very much wanted this girl for himself) or whether *A* needlessly and unjustifiably harmed *B* (as when he ran off with *B*'s girlfriend, even though he already had one of his own), it is frequently difficult to decide exactly what is and is not necessary to *A*'s happiness. *A* could contend that he "needed" the girl *B* wanted in both these instances; and if he were actually madly in love with *B*'s girl even when he already had a perfectly "satisfactory" girl of his own, many objective observers would uphold his "need." So although it is easy to say that one individual is immoral when he "needlessly" and "gratuitously" and "unfairly" injures or deprives another, it is difficult to give exact and invariant meanings to these modifying terms; so that "true" immorality is often most difficult to determine or measure.

13. A major concern of humanistic ethics would better be

the facilitation of interpersonal relationships. As Kirkendall and Avery (1956) have noted, "Whenever thought and choice regarding behavior and conduct are possible, those acts are morally good which create trust, and confidence, and a capacity among people to work together cooperatively." But man does not live by interpersonal relationships alone. His intracommunications are an integral part of his intercommunications; and he can enjoyably relate to and become absorbed in nonhuman organisms and things. Ethics includes his whole range of activity and not only his relationships with others. I-Thou relationships, as Buber has pointed out, are highly desirable and uniquely human; but they arise out of and are experienced in the context of I-It relations. As Buber himself states: "In all the seriousness of truth, hear this: without *It* man cannot live. . . . The communal life of man can no more than man himself dispense with the world of *It,* over which the presence of the *Thou* moves like the spirit upon the face of the waters."

14. Man is to some degree individually responsible for his actions. Theoretically, he has a measure of so-called free will and can, at least if he works very hard at thinking and acting, choose to perform or not to perform certain intrapersonal and interpersonal acts. But he is also powerfully influenced by his inherited biological tendencies and the social environment in which he is reared; consequently, although he is partly responsible for, or causes, his own behavior, he is never entirely accountable for it.

15. When an individual commits a wrong, mistaken, inefficient, self-defeating, or antisocial act, he may justifiably be termed a wrongdoer or—more accurately—a person who has performed this or that incorrect deed. As long, however, as he is a fallible human, it is an unscientific overgeneralization to say that he is an evil or bad person, because this statement implies (a) that he was born to be more immoral than the vast majority of other people; (b) that he will inevitably continue to be wrong; (c) that he deserves to be severely punished or damned as a total human being for being mistaken; and (d) that if there were some kind of life after death, he should be eternally consigned to the tortures of hell for having committed misdeeds. Of course, these statements cannot be empirically validated.

Assuming that the foregoing general rules of ethics have

some degree of validity, what are their correlatives in terms of more specific rules of sexual morality? As far as I can see, they are along the following lines:

1. An individual would better strive primarily for his own sex-love satisfaction; but since he lives in a social community and is going to be importantly affected by the sexual pleasures and annoyances of others, he'd better also refrain from unduly interfering with the sex-love welfare of these others. This means, negatively speaking, that he'd better not be dishonest with his potential or actual sex partners; that he'd better not take advantage of minors or incompetents merely for his own satisfaction; that he is immoral if he coerces unwilling individuals to have relations with him; and that it is generally wise for him to follow the sex laws of his community if these are actually enforced with harsh penalties. On the more positive side, it would be better if (a) he fully and freely expressed his feelings to his sex-love partners; (b) he was genuinely interested in their satisfactions as well as his own; (c) he sincerely tried to help them with their general and sexual problems, including their puritanism, sex phobias, compulsiveness, and inability to relate; and (d) he tried in some ways to help create the kind of a world in which other people were sexually alive, unblocked, and ethical.

This does *not* mean that the moral individual would necessarily go along with and bolster the prolongation of others' sex-love guilt, shame, and self-deprecation, as many puritans urge him to do. He might not, for example, "respect" a female's virginity, or her tendency to feel terribly hurt if he first loved and then left her, or her horror of his using "dirty" words. In these instances, he might either decide to stay away from her and look for less disturbed partners; or he might decide, keeping in mind her own good as well as his possible satisfactions with her, to help depropagandize her, induce her to surrender her sex-love hangups, and enable her to widen her potentialities for living. In these "seduction" attempts, he would take the same attitude as he would take in trying to influence or "seduce" another individual to change his or her conservative political, economic, or religious views and to become more liberal.

2. A person would better try to have sex-love relations in the here and now and to enthusiastically enjoy many immediate or short-range sexual pursuits; but he'd also better keep

an eye on tomorrow and give up some immediate sex-love gains for longer-range, future satisfactions. This means that, first, the individual is often wiser if he gives up present erotic pleasures for future erotic pleasures. Thus, he may (a) refrain from having intercourse with a minimum of foreplay in order to enjoy longer-lasting and deeper gratifications by employing more foreplay; (b) forego some amount of sex today because prolonged participation (and lack of sleep) may knock him out sexually for several days to come; (c) resist going to bed with an easily available girl because he might enjoy himself much more thoroughly with one who is not that easily bedded; (d) forbear having mere sex relations in favor of sex that is combined with companionship, love, or other values.

This means that, second, the individual is often a saner, long-range hedonist if he gives up present sex-love pleasures for future nonsexual gains. Thus, he may (a) leave his girlfriend relatively early in the evening because he has an important test to take or conference to attend the next morning; (b) choose to live with $X$ rather than $Y$ because, although she is not as good a sex partner as $Y$, she is much easier to get along with domestically; (c) decide that love relationships with women take up too much time in his very busy life and therefore refrain entirely from having affairs or honestly enter only casual sex relationships with females.

3. A code of sexual morality would better be constructed on the basis of as much empirical evidence about human beings and their functioning as it is possible for the morals-makers to obtain. Thus, historical, anthropological, and psychological studies of human beings tend to indicate that (a) they are quite varietist or non-monogamic in their sex desires; (b) they are easily attracted to each other sexually on very short notice, but their vital interest significantly wanes after prolonged sexual contact and shared domesticity, at least in many instances; (c) that, like intense sexual attraction but to a less notable degree, passionate romantic love between two people rarely outlasts a few years of living together; (d) that people who lust after each other sexually may detest each other in many nonsexual ways and that those who have notable nonsexual compatibility may lust for one another minimally; and (e) that large numbers of people can sexually desire and even be intensely, amatively attached to two or more members of the other sex simultaneously. If these are

common sex-love realities, then certain ethical codes, such as once-in-a-lifetime devotion and sexual fidelity to a single member of the other sex are, although advantageous in some respects, almost impossible for the average individual to achieve; and they would better be significantly altered or made preferential rather than mandatory.

When all is said and done, sexual morality still has to be related to some underlying value system that is not completely determined by empirical findings. Thus, some typical values that a humanist assumes in his sex codes are (a) that human life and its survival are good; (b) that pleasure is better than pain, self-acceptance better than self-deprecation, tolerance better than bigotry, societal change better than inflexibility and stasis; and that (c) human beings are more important than lower animals, than external objects, and than assumed gods. Given these assumptions, and also given the known and probable facts about people and their social relations, a fairly consistent and "rational" code of sex ethics can be constructed. But if other assumptions are made—such as the premise that people will be rewarded in some kind of afterlife if they meekly bear pain and deprecate themselves during their earthly existence—a quite different sexual code might logically follow.

4. There probably cannot ever be any absolutely correct or proper rules of sex morality, since people and conditions change over the years and what is "right" today may be "wrong" tomorrow. Under ancient conditions, when man lived in an agrarian-pastoral society, where contraception was virtually unknown, young people married in their early teens, and where there were no good medical methods for combatting venereal diseases, it may well have been wise to interdict premarital intercourse and adultery. Today, when socio-economic and medical conditions have changed considerably, it may be equally idiotic to ban these forms of sex.

At the same time, considering what the nature of human beings is and is likely to continue to be for a considerable time to come, it is unlikely that rape, sexual murder, or an adult's taking advantage of a young child will be considered a perfectly justifiable and ethical act. Nor is it likely that, from the standpoint of ethical self-interest, extreme sexual dissipation or the individual's neurotically and rigidly sticking to a single limited form of sex activity—for example, his only permitting himself to become aroused when he is copulating with members of the other sex who are at least thirty years older than himself—will be considered a desirable or good mode of sexual comportment. Although the act of sex, in its own right, can practically never be deemed bad or immoral, the manner in which the individual performs this act may well be, under almost any usual circumstances, self-defeating or antisocial and hence immoral.

5. Normally, it is better for an individual to follow the sex customs and laws of his social group if flaunting them will bring real and noxious penalties. Thus, if he is highly likely to be socially ostracized, fired from his job, or jailed for engaging in nonmarital sex relations or homosexuality he'd better give serious consideration to refraining from such activities, no matter how silly or unjust he may consider the laws of his community to be. He would be wise, of course, to work very hard, through speaking, writing, and political activity, to change the laws of his society; but while they still exist and are still actively being enforced, he may well have to obey them.

If, on the other hand, the individual is vigorously opposed to the sex rules and laws of his land and he objectively perceives that he can fairly easily get away with not fully heeding them, he may often be wise in discreetly or secretly flaunting them. Thus, although adultery and noncoital sex relations leading to orgasm (legally termed "unnatural sex practices" or "sodomy") have been banned in many of our states for the past century, there are virtually no indictments or convictions under such laws; and it is generally quite safe, though technically illegal, to unobtrusively ignore them. Again, although it has long been considered "wrong" or "illicit" for young people in our culture to have premarital intercourse, most males and many females actually achieve reputation and status by having them. Consequently, disobeying the sex rules of one's community is often sane and moral, especially when one is convinced that these rules themselves are essentially insane and immoral.

6. No sex act is holy, sacred, all-important, or god-impelled, except by arbitrary definition. Sexual intercourse is hardly holy, since abstinence, masturbation, and noncoital sex relations are legitimate practices which have distinct value to many people. Marriage is not a sacrament, unless a couple think it is; and when it is viewed in this manner it has enor-

mous limitations, problems, and anxieties attached to it. Even love between the sexes is never all-important, as many individuals live happy existences with minimal or no experience of it. Whenever, in fact, a sex, love, or marital act is deemed to be sanctified, this act or rite itself tends to become more important than the human individuals who are partaking (or not partaking) in it; and, from a humanistic standpoint, immorality or the needless sabotaging of human satisfaction then tends to occur.

On the other hand, many sex acts are more valuable for certain purposes than are other activities. Thus, sex with companionship or love may, at least in the long run, be more enjoyable than sex without affection; and an hour in bed with a new partner may be more exciting than an hour with one's usual partner. A rational individual will therefore try to maximize, without unduly attempting to deify, his sexual enjoyments; and he will similarly try to help his partner achieve the more important, rather than the all-important, satisfactions she would like to attain. Similarly, the rational individual will try to minimize sexual constraints and annoyances, without ridiculously amplifying them or damning those who are instrumental in sexually frustrating him.

7. Sex codes would better be applied undiscriminatingly to all competent adults in a given community, and applied under a single standard that pertains to both males and females. Women, for example, would not, under a rational code, be criticized and penalized more severely than men for unconventional sex behavior or for bearing illegitimate children. Nor would teenagers and younger children be arbitrarily and unduly held in check sexually, except for special reasons (such as their diminished ability to take proper contraceptive precautions). Sexual discrimination, however, may never be completely eradicable and may even have some advantages. Thus, in almost any conceivable society in the present and near future, females are more likely to select as sex partners males who are handsome, strong, sexually competent, bright, and self-accepting. A total sexual democracy, where there is truly equal justice for all, is therefore probably not going to exist.

8. In a well-ordered and reasonably fair society, the citizens would better resort to verbal protest, to the ballot box, and to peaceful demonstrations in order to try to effect desired sexual changes. Thus, feminist movements have during the

last fifty years helped win a good many rights for women that they had previously not had; and some powerful organizations are presently still working for greater equality of the sexes and are doing so in peaceful ways, using due processes of law. But it is conceivable that if sexual tyranny reigned—if males, for example, began physically subjugating and violating women —violent revolt against the oppressors might possibly at times be in ethical order.

9. Man would better base his sex morality on humanistic precepts: on the nature of people and their desires (rather than the assumed nature of supernatural gods and their supposed sexual rules) and on the fulfilling of these desires in the present, near-future, and more distant future. The fact that the lower animals have certain sexual proclivities—which the Kinsey reports made a little too much of—and the supposition that Jehovah and Jesus had certain hard-and-fast sex rules have nothing to do with humanistic sex ethics. Our sexual morality would better be based on human biology (including the primacy of the cerebral cortex over the lower brain centers) and social learning. If men and women frequently enjoy oral-genital relations they can hardly be deemed to be immoral on the grounds that such relations are "bestial" or "ungodly."

But man also has the power to significantly change some of his sexual "nature." He can train himself to be sexually constant in spite of his natural varietism. He can employ modern technology—such as electric vibrators, electronic music, and strobe lights—to affect his sexuality. He can use drugs, hormones, and other substances to make himself more or less sexual. There seems to be no good reason why he should not experiment in various ways to modify his sexual desires and potentialities, as long as he can increase his satisfactions in this manner without unduly surrendering or minimizing other advantages and benefits.

10. Humanistic ethics include the primacy of human over sub-human sex goals, desires, and satisfactions. If lower animals are employed, for example, for purposes of bestiality, for the obtaining of sex hormones or stimulants, or for other purposes, this is normally an ethical pursuit of man. But humans would better be duly humane and uncruel to animals in any sexual use they make of them, because otherwise intra-human values tend to suffer.

11. Rational ethics include provision for slight and serious modification of virtually all sex codes, especially as environmental conditions change and perhaps the biological nature of man changes too. If we discover, for example, an entirely harmless, perfect method of birth control, codes which now make it unethical or illegal for fourteen-year-olds to have sex relations with each other or for adults to have intercourse with young teenagers might well be liberalized; while if new forms of venereal disease break out and are rampant, more stringent rules regarding nonmarital relations might be in order. But the alteration of sex customs and laws would better be carefully approached, and made with considerable concomitant fact-finding and discussion.

12. Sexual immorality would better be defined not in terms of an individual's acting unfairly toward or harming another but in terms of his *needlessly* or *gratuitously* injuring this other. A boy may harm a girl if he accidentally gets her pregnant; but he may not be unethical unless he has adequate contraceptive means available and he gratuitously and foolishly decides not to employ them. However, since it is easy to interpret the terms "needlessly," "gratuitously," and "unfairly" sloppily, and since a sex-love partner can be exploited with little trouble, people would often do best to lean over backwards not to injure or to take advantage of each other sexually, even when at first blush it appears that they are legitimately and needfully doing so.

13. It is preferable for partners, in their sex-love affairs, to concentrate on their interpersonal relations and to have *I-Thou* relationships in some instances. But insistence on maintaining deep interpersonal, and especially *I-Thou,* relationships in all or most instances is unrealistic, impinges on the freedom of choice of the partner, and is likely to cause immense amounts of anxiety and rigid constraint. Sex or sex-love relations of an "exploitative" or *I-It* nature are perfectly ethical as long as they are entered honestly, with the full consent of the "exploited" mate.

14. Man is to some degree individually responsible for his sex actions and therefore would better accept the penalties of performing them. But he is also powerfully influenced by his inherited biological drives and the social environment in which he is reared; consequently, although he is partly responsible for, or causes, his own sex-love mistakes and misdeeds, he is

never entirely accountable for them. With considerable hard work and thinking, he can control many, but never all, of his sex ideas, desires, and acts.

15. When an individual commits a wrong, mistaken, inefficient, self-defeating, or antisocial sex deed, he may justifiably be termed a wrongdoer or a person who has acted irresponsibly. But to say that he is an evil or bad person, a rotter or a louse, is an unscientific overgeneralization. He is only a mistake-maker who will tend to make more sexual errors in the future if he is savagely condemned and cruelly punished. It would be far better if he were fully accepted as an imperfect creature, were not totally devaluated or damned, and were encouraged to become more problem-centered rather than self-centered, so that he could work at being a little less error-prone in the future.

Sexual morality, then, when seen in terms of rationality, essentially consists of the individual's following certain sane, sensible, and nondefeating values. He normally wants to live a good life, including a good sex-love life, himself; he also wants to live it, almost always, within the context of some social group; so he follows rational rules that will (a) prevent him from foolishly harming himself and (b) stop him from senselessly and needlessly harming others, and thereby in the short or long run damaging himself. Sexual morality is merely a sub-heading under general humanistic morality.

The fact seems to be, though we often deny it, that human beings are both biologically and sociologically prone to think, emote, and act in self-defeating and immoral ways—in their general and in their more specific sexual behavior. They believe, usually with great vigor and bigotry, several major irrational ideas. For example, they very frequently and insanely hold that they positively *must* be loved and approved by others; that they are no damned good as human beings when they perform imperfectly; that other people absolutely should and must act fairly and nicely toward them (and if they don't are complete blackguards who should be utterly damned for all time); and that they should live in a world of supreme certainty instead of the real world of probability and chance.

As a result of these highly irrational ideas, people in our own and other cultures tend to think crookedly about themselves, about others, and about the world. They spend considerable time and energy condemning themselves and others

—instead of observing that although a person's deeds or performances may indeed be wrong or inefficient, he as an ongoing process, he as a living human, cannot be legitimately given a report card and thereby deified or damned. And they keep railing at the universe for not being easier to live in than it is—instead of actively working to diagnose its ills and evils and to change them. Consequently, they make themselves inordinately anxious, guilty, depressed, hostile, self-pitying, defensive, and avoidant.

Sexually, people tend to be, if possible, even more irrational than they are nonsexually: for they not only condemn themselves and each other for various wrongdoings, but frequently they inaccurately define what is wrong. Thus, if we were to apply the standards of sexual morality listed above to our everyday behavior, we would probably discover that most of the sex acts which have been historically deemed to be sinful in our society—such as masturbation, premarital intercourse, noncoital sex relations leading to orgasm, and occasional homosexuality—are not really unethical, since they do not needlessly harm their participants nor anyone else. But many of the conventional and highly legal sex activities in our culture—such as a husband's insisting that his wife satisfy him without his taking any real pains to satisfy her, or a wife's refusing to divorce a husband for whom she has little desire or liking—are actually quite immoral.

A genuinely humanistic view of ethics would indicate that people are only wrong or immoral when they gratuitously harm themselves and/or injure others; and that this is true for sexual and nonsexual actions. A humanistic outlook would perhaps even more importantly hold that even when he is indubitably wrong, no person is to be damned or condemned for anything he thinks, says, or does; that his deeds may very well be foolish or immoral but he is never a louse for performing them; and that if he works very hard—against the biologically based and socially inculcated tendencies to be an arrant, overgeneralizing, bigoted, religious-minded blamer of himself and other humans—he can enable himself to lead a much more satisfying sex, love, marital, and general existence.

# PART III

# Understanding
# Human Sexuality

## 5. *Sex Research*

LEON SALZMAN

Scientific research in the area of human sexual behavior is a new phenomenon historically. The earliest research referred to by Dr. Kinsey[1] in his summarization of authentic sex research, was published in 1915. Since that time there has been a considerable proliferation of such research, and the results have a meaning for humanists who are reassessing the place of sex in the system of human values, morals, and behavior. A great deal of the research has contributed toward making sex a more integral part of human life. These findings have tended to strip away the mystery, ignorance, and fear which had helped make sex taboo as a topic of discussion. They have established that sex behavior in man is more intimately involved with his humanness than with his animal heritage. Thus while the biology of the sexual function is crucial to an understanding of its role, it is only a background for the infinite variety of manifestations which grow out of man's capacity for loving relationships and his need for intimacy, commitment, and sustained companionship. Only when we can fully comprehend the cultural, sociological, existential, and uniquely human aspects of the sexual function, will we be able to manage it responsibly and thereby enhance our capacities to enjoy it more fully. We no longer need feel that sex is an overpowering urge which cannot be guided through understanding and insights.

Sex research, now very extensive, embraces anthropology, sociology, psychology, biology, and psychiatry. To the extent that it has been valid and enlightening it has illuminated what heretofore was unknown and therefore feared. It has given us a degree of control and direction in our own living as well as providing guidance for generations yet to come.

The Judeo-Christian ethic has played a most significant and determining role in producing many sexual difficulties by viewing sex as sinful, immoral, and ungodly unless carried out within the limits prescribed by the church fathers as they interpreted the holy writings. Consequently, research into sex and other psychological matters has lagged far behind our investigation into man's physical world. It is astonishing, but nevertheless true, that in the decade of a landing on the moon and the use of miracle drugs in the treatment of hitherto resistant diseases we have only recently made basic discoveries about the physiology of the female reproductive system and the nature of the female orgasm. It was not too long ago that, while the stars could be observed with the newly discovered telescopes, the diseased female, because of modesty or prudery, forced the physician to examine her blindly with his hands under the sheets that covered her nude body. Inquiry into a patient's sex life was considered to be rude and insensitive, and was avoided. Usually any investigation (physiological or otherwise), discussion, conversation, or serious exploration of this area of human activity was discouraged, if not positively forbidden. This was true even though sex was a lusty activity in certain historical periods. At other times it was de-emphasized almost to the point of totally denying its existence. Christian morality, symbolized by the Victorian era in the West, relegated sex to the privacy of the bedroom and made any aspect of it unavailable to the scrutiny of the scientist or physician. As the time of liberation for the female as well as the male progressed, the swell of progress in the medical sciences in the 1900's made it inevitable that sex and sexual practices would become the subject of scientific study.

Little wonder, then, that physicians, moralists, and other students of human behavior moved into the twentieth century unbelievably ignorant and burdened by a catalogue of errors, distortions, prejudices, and superstitions about sex and sex behavior. Consequently Freud's views were met with severe criticism, condemnation and disbelief. While he took a revolu'tionary position for his day, it is now clear that he too was bound by the tradition and prejudices of his period. Nonetheless, his emphasis on sex did open new vistas for exploration of the role it played in the life of man. Some of his misconceptions, however, incorporated and sanctified in psychoanalytic theory, became impediments in our explorations of the psychology of the male and the female, homosexuality, and, in fact, the role of sex in the development of personality and mental disorder.

What was the effect of Freud's work, and how did it enhance and improve the quality of man's living in the direction of a more complete utilization of his skills and resources? Freud's work meant that human sex behavior became a focal point of concern of psychologists, physicians, and scientists in related disciplines. Psychoanalytic investigations took their initial impetus from the libido theory which presumed that the sexual instinct was the major directive force in human development. These investigations, however, tended to focus on sex primarily as an animal instinct rather than as an activity between two people involving a multitude of emotional reactions. Since sex activity in man generally takes place in an atmosphere of tenderness and mutual regard, it resembles animal activity only to the extent that it is an act of procreation. Its biological significance in man is only a small part of its total importance. So, although the Freudian revolution resulted in sexual enlightenment, it also caused much distress and mischief because it continued to support and encourage outmoded ideas of sex and sexual development. In recent years there has been a much greater emphasis on the interpersonal aspects of sex behavior, a development which takes into account the extraordinary capacity of sex to fulfill many of man's needs aside from the biological function of procreation.

The first significant study of sex behavior following Freud's epochal contribution was that of Alfred C. Kinsey and his colleagues who in 1948 published the first volume of an extensive statistical investigation of the sex habits of the American male. This study, which both sustained and dispelled many inaccurate beliefs regarding sex behavior, stirred up a storm of controversy. The study was based on intensive and extensive interviews by trained interviewers, and inevitably suffered the limitations inherent in this type of research.

One of the major difficulties in this study as well as in Freud's work was the problem of semantics. Inevitably some misconceptions would be reinforced, since by adopting existing notions and labels regarding sex behavior, the confirmation of these concepts tended to follow. In addition, the interviewers themselves, being students of the prevailing sexual theories, tended to reaffirm these theories.

For example the data revealed very high percentages of masturbation in the general population. While this might still be true, the tendency to label genital play prior to puberty as masturbation was a scientific error caused by the failure to distinguish between the common genital exploratory activity of children and sexual exploratory activity of the older person.

As another example, if the idea of a universal homosexual stage of sexual development was accepted, the questions asked concerning homophilic activity would likely support the concept. The distinction between non-sexual play exploration prior to adolescence, which may involve the genitals and truly sexual play, in which orgasm was the goal of such activity, would not be made. Therefore, Kinsey reported very high rates of homosexual interest and activity, tending to support the idea of a universal latent homosexual tendency. Yet, the notion of a universal latent homosexual tendency is presently in great dispute, and there is much evidence to suggest that it is a misleading and invalid concept with regard to human sexual development. Yet here again, further research has tended to refine the concepts and helped us understand and deal with homosexuality.

The Kinsey Reports on the male and the female added to our understanding of sex practices dimensions which had been only suspected, but neither finally validated nor openly discussed. It dissipated many confusions and misconceptions about the widespread prevalence of variations in positioning during coitus and encouraged a greater tolerance of variety. What heretofore had been considered perverse or unacceptable was recognized as being practiced widely in all segments of the population. What had been looked upon as the activities of unhealthy or sinful individuals, were seen more clearly as manifestations of healthy sex interest and activity.

The Reports also helped to clarify the issue of morality

in sex behavior by exposing the physiological and psychological nature of some sex activities which previously would have been viewed as immoral or bestial. Examples are oral-genital contacts or masturbation. The data showed not only the numbers of people who engaged in such behavior but helped build the concept that such behavior was human, reasonable, and responsible. When common, nonexploitive sexual behavior could be identified as being in the realm of acceptable human practice it could then be considered normal or appropriate and therefore not immoral. The widespread tendency towards secrecy in sexual matters had led many people to believe that they alone were engaging in activities which were unusual and degenerate. The effect of the Reports was to make sex more enjoyable, lifting the burden of guilt and self-depreciation from such activity. Sex could be allowed to play a more active role in people's lives without their feeling unworthy or obsessed by doubts and concerns about whether they were perverse or degenerate.

Kinsey's study was therefore, in almost every sense, a great advance in liberating man from the unreasonable confines of his rigid prejudices and the prevailing ignorance regarding human sexual behavior. It exposed many superstitions about masturbation and other aspects of sex behavior which, while still extant, allowed for more refined research which could later clarify and distinguish those which were pathological. It stirred a great interest in sex, and encouraged much discussion in scientific circles as well as in the population at large. The effect was to produce greater understanding and thereby decrease the sexual "hang-ups" of many people, increasing their capacities for enjoyment and fuller living. The Kinsey report was limited by the necessity of its being an interview procedure rather than an observational study. The conclusions about sexual physiology were through interpretation of the data. Some of the unfortunate myths about female orgasms, masturbation, homosexuality, and female sexuality tended to be perpetuated. But in the benefits which were directly derived from the study and the areas for further inquiry that were suggested, it was a humanistic achievement of great value.

The more recent Masters and Johnson study[2] has broadened our knowledge of the physiology of human sexual behavior. This has been true particularly with regard to the female, about whom knowledge has been surprisingly and shockingly inaccurate and inadequate. While the male sexual apparatus had been available for study for some time, the physiology of the female sexual function was clouded in ignorance and mystery and distorted by false scientific conceptions. The nature of the female orgasm, for example, was not clearly understood until Masters and Johnson described its physiology in detail. Freud postulated a "double" orgasm, clitoral and vaginal, the vaginal being a more mature experience. The tendency therefore was to view clitoral eroticism as immature. This was firmly negated by the Masters-Johnson study. They definitely stated that from a physiological point of view the clitoral and vaginal orgasms were not separate entities, and therefore the emphasis in therapy in attempting to change the locus of the orgasm was fruitless and pointless, leading to much mischief and distress. Masters and Johnson clearly showed that the clitoral glands and the lower third of the vagina are the active participants in the female orgasm. The tendency to reduce clitoral eroticism to a level of psychopathology of immaturity because of its supposed masculine origin is a travesty of the facts and a misleading psychological deduction.

Once this was demonstrated, then the different techniques and the various positions described or advocated to increase vaginal orgasm are superfluous, since regardless of the size or location of the penis in the vagina, it rarely comes into direct contact with the clitoris. However, the clitoris is continuously stimulated during coition, because the erection and engorgement of the clitoris causes it to retract into the swollen clitoral head, and the active thrusting of the penis provides stimulation and friction on the glans by moving the clitoral head over the clitoral glans. Thus, if any position is more effective for the female, it is when she is superior, or on top of the male. It is notable in this connection that, in terms of sexual adjustment, the discussions and explorations of variations in positioning had been discredited and avoided in the past either because they were considered vulgar or degenerate, or because of the notion that the female's passive role requires the male always to "be on top." Thus the possibility of discovering new approaches for producing orgasm in the female was prevented by prior conceptions and misinformation about the physiology of the female genitalia.

Masters and Johnson exploded other myths. They showed that the female is capable of multiple orgasms, while the male requires a refractory period before another erection is possible. They also found a need for continuous stimulation in the female until orgasm occurs, since the sexual tension in the female can fall instantaneously if such stimulation is discontinued. This capacity for multiple orgasm and readiness to respond to sexual stimulation requires regular and consistent sexual activity in the female for her to respond most adequately. It is likely that the most common cause of frigidity and difficulty in achieving orgasm in the female is due to infrequent sexual intercourse. Significant facts and physiological data with regard to the primacy of the male, penis envy, the importance of penile size, and other cherished traditional concepts were shown to be invalid.

These selected items from the Masters and Johnson study show how their research findings have served not only to clarify the facts about sex behavior, but how they have altered the capacity of human beings to cope with misconceptions and to enjoy sex as a part of a relationship. At the same time they have altered and will continue to alter our moral judgments about sexual matters.

This project stirred up much controversy. There were noisy objections from ministers and other self-styled moralists, as well as from social scientists. They described the study as inhuman and unethical because not only did it interview the respondent, but it observed the subject in the act of sexual intercourse with an ingeniously designed glass penis with an enclosed camera. This raised a cry of intrusion into the privacy of the sex act that combined serious scientific concern with overzealous and quasi-moralistic indignation. Their objections were belied by the clear benefits that could be derived in increasing our knowledge of human sexuality and thereby enabling us to relieve human distress. By disproving, for example, the notion of the "double" orgasm which had plagued and afflicted innumerable women since Freud's time, they relieved woman of the burden of trying to achieve the impossible in converting one type of orgasm into another, when only one type existed.

These critics tended to put sex in a privileged and exclusive position in human psychology that encouraged the supporters of the repressive, sin-oriented notions of sex activity.

Unwittingly they gave scientific support to the opponents of a liberalization of sex education and an extension of human knowledge. By viewing sex activity as distinctive and beyond the realm of human physiology they gave valuable support to the regressive attitudes in the church which continues to view sex both as an evil and as a "special" activity which it would much prefer to ignore rather than recognize. The progress towards humanizing sex came from the growing recognition that it had no special place in man's functioning except that it was a source of considerable pleasure and required closeness, intimacy, contact, and commitment. While it is valid and necessary to indicate that the observation of the sex or the absence of a real partner instead of an artificial one clearly alters the sexual performance in a psychological sense, it does not alter the physiology in any significant way. Yet, even if it does, it is necessary to overcome the prejudices and handicaps of past anti-scientific pseudo-moralizing and study man as a natural animal as well as a thinking, philosophical being. In the age of sputniks, satellites, and interplanetary travel, we really need to know just how the body functions in every system, including the sexual. This study has paved the way for a major change in sexual attitudes, with particular regard to the female and her role in the sex act. By exposing many false notions of the physiology of the female, it has enabled the psychological and psychiatric helper to be more useful in treating some of these difficulties.

Many significant studies have also been carried out by sociologists, anthropologists, psychologists, medical educators, and social workers. In addition to the taxonomic and physiological studies, they have greatly expanded our understanding of the patterns of sexual development and conduct as they unfold in the individual's socio-cultural and economic background. This has permitted us to view sex behavior as variable depending upon the culture. The research of Mead[3] and of Ford and Beach[4] are significant in this regard. They showed that extensive differences exist in patterns of sexual behavior contributing to the moral stability of a culture. This allows for all kinds of sexual arrangements which are learned through experience rather than being biologically innate.

Recent sexual research has begun to provide us with data about the relationship of sex behavior and other aspects of the individual's life. Considerable data has been forthcoming with regard to sexual conduct such as promiscuity and the individual's background.[5] These studies indicate a close relationship between broken homes (60%, Lion study) and promiscuity in girls. They say

Contrary to popular belief, no evidence was revealed to indicate that this problem is produced by above average sex drive. In fact, the majority of habitually promiscuous patients used promiscuity in an attempt to meet other problems rather than in an attempt to secure sexual satisfaction.

Likewise Safier[6] believes "Promiscuity . . . was revealed to be a problem in interpersonal relationships." This was also revealed in the Greenwald[7] study which concluded that the background and personality of call girls reveal a marked incapacity for satisfactory interpersonal relationships. Pollak and Friedman[8] conclude that ". . . for sexual delinquents acting out serves as a release valve for unstable, unendurable family tensions and may even function as a homeostatic stabilizing procedure for the family."

Christensen[9] and Kirkendall[10] showed in their research that marked differences in cultural attitudes and variations in degree of affectional involvement are significant in determining the impact on the emotional life of individuals involved in premarital intercourse and in illegitimate pregnancy. The stability of marriage is, of course, also affected.

Some studies of illegitimately pregnant girls show wide variations in their backgrounds and motivations. Young,[11] who felt that these girls were neurotic, unhappy, and with poor interpersonal relationships, regarded their pregnancy as "a battleground on which the struggle (with the dominating parents) was fought, and the baby was an integral part of that struggle." With Young's study the significance of culture again appears, for her subjects came from homes for unwed mothers.

The same kind of investigation has now been carried forward with unwed fathers. The unwed father has often been regarded as seductive and irresponsible. Pannor and others[12] who carried on a study suggest that unmarried fathers, as well as unmarried mothers, are many times afflicted with defective interpersonal relations.

Reiss[13] has shown how much more complex sex standards are than we usually think. In his study he distinguished four different standards. They were (1) abstinence (which is the socially approved standard); (2) the double standard (which is very common but is now weakening at various points); (3) permissiveness without affection; and (4) permissiveness with affection. Reiss feels that the last of these four standards is the one which is gaining ground while the first two are losing. He also anticipates that permissiveness without affection, which has never been a strong standard anyway, will not become one. These standards are practiced differently in different social classes in the population, and are often varied from time to time in the life of a single individual.

Some sex research has humanistic significance in making human beings out of persons who were formerly called perverts or deviants. We have already noted how the Kinsey Reports found mouth-genital contacts and masturbation a very common human experience. This helped to make these experiences a more normal human sexual association.

For example, in recent years we have had several studies of homosexuality which help us see persons who experience homosexual associations as persons with the same essential human problems as everyone else. Much has been written about different kinds of homosexuals ("passive," "active," "masculine," "feminine") and about the tell-tale signs of homosexuality. Also the notion has persisted that homosexuality was incurable and that all homosexuals are neurotic and unhappy. Two different investigations[14, 15] have studied homosexuality and have found wide differences in homosexuals as regards their patterns of sexual behavior, and their wide ranges in social adjustment—from some who are obviously neurotic and unhappily adjusted, to others who are efficient in their employment, satisfactorily adjusted to others, and fully able to take their place as functioning citizens. Homosexuals cannot be fitted into a particular mold.

Sexual research has thus not only broadened our understanding but increased our ability and willingness to deal with sex as an activity to be enjoyed and practiced in whatever manner is conducive to the greatest mutual enjoyment. Consequently the manner of stimulating the glans and clitoris, whether by means of the mouth, finger, or vaginal insertion, should not necessarily be viewed in terms of either normality or maturity. Although there is preferred posture to insure procreation and mutual orgasm, a more enlightened attitude toward sex should avoid assigning priorities to particular methods of achieving sexual satisfaction or patterns of sexual behavior. Despite the fact that laws regarding sex behavior in many parts of the world still cling to categories of "normal" and "deviant," modern psychological theory tries to avoid such labeling, particularly with regard to variations of sex behavior. This is particularly applicable to the prevailing notions of activity or passivity. The assumption that the male must be aggressive in sexual intercourse, and the female passive, no longer is valid. Each partner must be passive *and* aggressive, and must participate mutually and cooperatively in the interaction. The unfortunate persistence of labels attributable to one sex as opposed to another has led to untold misery in the form of feeling guilty, inferior, inadequate, or even "homosexual," when one's inclinations are somewhat different from prevailing notions concerning the role of each sex. The female has been the major victim in this hangover from Victorian morality and scientific infantilism. Since, under this notion, the mantle of being passive and submissive falls on her, she has been required to wait on the desires and demands of the male and to be subject to his particular program for sexual activity. To encourage or direct the male's sexual activity was to step outside of the "female" role; to suggest or recommend measures that might enhance her enjoyment would be aggressive, or too "masculine." Consequently, she has been expected to be patient and long-suffering and to depend on the man's good will and competence for her enjoyment. When she has refused to function in these prescribed ways, some psychoanalytic theorists have insisted on labeling her behavior as "penis envy," "masculine protest," "latent homosexuality," or "refusal to accept her proper biological role." Such labels are remnants of outmoded conceptions of female psychology.

Simultaneous orgasm likewise is an ideal outcome of the sex act, but in view of the recent findings with regard to the time necessary for sexual activation, it is now clear that it can hardly be a regularly expected outcome. To determine sexual adjustment on the basis of success in achieving simultaneous orgasm is therefore a mistaken romantic notion.

Since the rewards of the extensions of our knowledge are manifest and incontrovertible, one must acknowledge that sex research is not only moral but absolutely necessary. As long as we recognize the limitations of such research and do not overstep the boundaries of privacy we must extend our research into the still comparatively unknown area of homosexuality and the multitude of other sex perversions. Our knowledge is still rudimentary and horizons can be extended only by learning more about the valid role sex plays in personality development.

Such research can inform us in ways that can improve our teaching and learning in the area of sex behavior and thereby free us of prejudice and unnecessary grief and guilt. The far-reaching socio-cultural studies will enlighten us as to the variability of sex practices and the universality of much variational behavor. This can not only enlighten but add to our zest and enjoyment of this human activity. It will make clear that biology is only a small part of sex behavior and that our culture and its effect on our early development is vital and more relevant to our actual behavior.

Research into sex must continue in order to bring our information on this human activity into line with our knowledge of the rest of the human organism. The sex function has no greater or lesser validity as a moral problem than any other human physiological function. The reasons it was singled out for theological and moral concern lie in its significance beyond man's physiology. We must overcome this hangover from the past which derived from our ignorance and impotence and move towards greater enlightenment in order to make our living fuller and more constructive on every level.

In summary, sex research contributes in several ways to a humanistic outlook. The Freudian research brought sex into the open—it became an integral part of life rather than something submerged and denied. The Kinsey Reports made clear how pervasive sex and sexual adjustments are, while Masters and Johnson helped dispel misconceptions which had long contributed to human miseries and failures. Other research projects have shown us how sex is related to the total personality. Sexual patterns are learned, and their expression is conditioned by the individual's sense of self-respect, his emotional capacities for warmth and participation as well as a feeling of achievement. A number of research findings have dispelled stereotypes and have made human beings out of hackneyed, lifeless forms. Many misconceptions about men and women have been eliminated. Homosexuals, illegitimately pregnant girls and unwed fathers have become persons with needs, ambitions, and anxieties like their compeers'.

Research does not always simplify problems; it may well make them more complex. However, by increasing our understanding it makes better communication possible. Since humanists are concerned with man and his vicissitudes, the area of sex research is within his serious interest and concern.

## Notes to Chapter 5

1. Alfred C. Kinsey, *Sexual Behavior in the Human Male.* Philadelphia: W. B. Saunders, 1949.
2. William H. Masters and Virginia E. Johnson, *Human Sexual Response.* Boston: Little, Brown and Co., 1966.
3. Margaret Mead, *Male and Female.* New York: William Morrow, 1949.
4. C. S. Ford and Frank A. Beach, *Patterns of Sexual Behavior.* New York: Harper and Brothers, 1951.
5. Ernest G. Lion, *et al., An Experiment in the Psychiatric Treatment of Promiscuous Girls.* San Francisco: City and County of San Francisco Department of Public Health, 1945.
6. Benno Safier, M.D., *et al., A Psychiatric Approach to the Treatment of Promiscuity.* New York: American Social Hygiene Association, 1949.
7. Harold Greenwald, *The Call Girl.* New York: Ballantine Books, 1958.
8. Otto Pollak and Alfred S. Friedman, Editors, *Family Dynamics and Female Sexual Delinquency.* Palo Alto: Science and Behavior Books, Inc., 1969.
9. Harold T. Christensen, "The Impact of Culture and Values," *Individual, Sex and Society.* Ed. by C. Broderick and J. Bernard, Baltimore: The Johns Hopkins Press, 1969.
10. Lester Kirkendall, *Premarital Intercourse and Interpersonal Relationships.* New York: Julian Press, 1961.
11. L. R. Young, "Personality Patterns in Unmarried Mothers," *Understanding the Psychology of the Unmarried Mother.* New York: Family Service Association of America, 1947.
12. Reuben Pannor, *et al., The Unmarried Father.* New York: National Council on Illegitimacy, 1968.
13. Ira Reiss, *Premarital Sex Standards in America.* Glencoe, Illinois: The Free Press, 1960.
14. Martin Hoffman, *The Gay World.* New York: Basic Books, 1968.
15. Evelyn Hooker, "Male Homosexuals and Their 'Worlds,'" in Judd Marmor, ed., *Sexual Inversion.* New York: Basic Books, Inc., 1965.

# 6. *An Appraisal of Erotic Emotion and Autoerotic Behavior*

## WALTER R. STOKES

This discussion will relate to the perception of erotic emotion and feelings, associated fantasies, and autoerotic sex behavior; also something of the moral and cultural values assigned these factors and how they facilitate or hamper social maturation and adjustment. The author's orientation is that of scientifically founded humanism.

In support of effective communication it seems well to define at the outset what humanism means to the author. It is conceived as a very broad, rationally based concern for human welfare, derived and guided by applying the basic principles of science to the human life experience and resting its authority upon the worth of the scientific method. Specifically rejected as sources of irrefutable authority are the formulations of tradition, religion, and the law. This is not meant to imply that these guides to behavior should be disregarded or that they have no value; rather, it is simply a statement of refusal to be unalterably bound by their assumed authority and involves a belief that they should not be held sacrosanct or exempt from the challenges posed by the progress of behavioral and life sciences.

It is readily acknowledged that as yet there is no genuine science of human behavior. Nevertheless, it is felt that we have moved far enough in that direction to place tentative faith in the best of what we have if, at the same time, we are prepared to yield flexibly to innovations that offer reasonable promise of improving the quality of human existence. Actually this is simply a way of affirming faith in man's greatest evolutionary strength: his capacity for successful adaptation.

Historically and in present-day fact, our traditions, religions, and laws do not have a distinguished record as interpreters of erotic emotion or in guiding its expression. In a general way these sources of authority have been united in support of a deeply ingrained assumption that erotic feelings are sinful, harmful, or of dubious worth unless somehow associated with a heterosexual romantic relationship involving marriage and the reproductive process. Despite this view, the fact is that a considerable portion of all human erotic emotion and behavior is experienced in a solitary or autoerotic manner, with no interpersonal contact other than through the imagery of fantasies. Examples of this are seen in much of the erotic life of infants, children, and adolescents; also in the erotic fantasies and behavior of many widows and widowers, many singletons, and among numbers of persons in the late years of life.

In the absence of a sex partner erotic feelings have a strong tendency to culminate in self-applied genital stimulation (masturbation), usually to the point of achieving orgasm. According to Hebraic-Christian moral tradition, this constitutes inexcusable sin and degradation, at any age and under any circumstances. Even in our supposedly more enlightened and humanly liberal generation there remains much bias against autoerotic sex preoccupation and all overt expression of it. This is strikingly verified by the written questions submitted by young people when the author has invited anonymous written questions concerning sex. Always the question that leads in frequency is the expression of anxiety about the feared ill effects of masturbation. Thus none of us should allow ourselves the illusion that specious guilt regarding masturbation is today a dead issue. It is not. On the contrary, it should remain a matter of grave concern to the humanist who seeks to free mankind from bonds of guilt that are supported only by irrational mythologies of religious and cultural tradition.

Unquestionably the most serious problem created by our

traditional taboo against masturbation is the damaging effect it has upon infants and very young children. During the early months of life it is impossible to apply this taboo without conditioning a child to feel that erotic emotion is disgraceful: a shameful handicap in his striving to become a good and socially acceptable person. The long-range effect of such conditioning is severely injurious to personality growth. Our newly developing information and insights into "critical learning periods" of infancy and early childhood should cause us to be more concerned than ever with eliminating the masturbation taboo from child-training practices.

Within recent years qualified observers have agreed that from earliest infancy all children of both sexes have erotic feelings and, unless restrained or intimidated, will display genital interest and engage in some degree of overt genital self-stimulation. The only matter in doubt is that of adult attitude and policy when confronted with such infant behavior. Certainly some improvement in parental attitude has taken place as a result of professional counseling, as in the popular writings of Benjamin Spock and many others. However, a large segment of our population remains unaware of the new approach and many who attempt to use it are not successful because of the guilt and anxiety hanging over from their own childhood sex training. Full cultural readjustment in a matter of this sort seems likely to demand the sustained effort of several generations.

The importance and urgency of wise revision of our sex training of infants and children has been underlined by the findings of some quite recent research. For example, the studies of Money and the Hampsons have shown decisively that gender identification is indelibly imprinted by the age of approximately two and a half years. Other studies have brought out the importance of very early affectional relatedness as an element essential to adequate adult sex behavior. It is becoming increasingly clear that a human infant must experience what Ira Reiss has called "nurturant socialization" if he is to function well as an adult. It seems wholly unlikely that this critical need can be satisfactorily met if a child is caused to feel that his sexual emotions and behavior represent a severe barrier to social approval and the attainment of trusting, affectionate human relations. During the period of infancy when adult attitudes cannot be qualified or explained we have no rational choice but to accept infant sex responses uncritically and without show of hostility.

As an infant acquires the use of language and extends his social contacts, it is unavoidable that some guidelines about sex behavior be provided. This is no easy task, even if approached in the kindest manner. One reason for this is that each child is a special person, with uniquely individual characteristics. Another is that we have not yet had much rational experience in this area and have few well-tested rules to guide us. However, it is the author's observation that young children rather readily accept adult guidance when it is realistic and is accompanied by affectionate concern.

If, on the other hand, adult behavior is hostile and clearly reveals that the adult is far more concerned with his rigid notions than with the child as a person, there is likely to be a breakdown of effective communication, and the child's ability to socialize his sex needs will be damaged. Unfortunately many parents have difficulty grasping this and tend to attack any sexual behavior of their child from a compulsive sense of righteous anger generated by their personal repressions and fear of what others may say or do. It appears reasonable to predict that as sex comes more into the open in our society parents will increasingly abandon this traditional way of handling the sex behavior of their children. When they can do so the problems of sex guidance will be greatly eased, to the profit of everyone.

Parents who do not frighten their child about sex may assume that he will very likely do more or less masturbating. They have an obligation to advise him about the common taboo concerning this and may counsel him about avoiding social difficulties. No damaging guilt can result from this if it is done in a way which clearly indicates to the child that the parent has no harsh or unpleasant feelings about masturbation.

In our society a child will soon find himself in serious trouble if permitted to act out his every erotic impulse. Some controls and some degree of self-discipline are essential. But it should be recognized that emotions which cannot be acted out are likely to find expression in fantasy. In the construction of his fantasies the child should not be left at the mercy of what he can glean from the world about him: a world saturated with pornography, obscenity, sado-masochism, and the empty, false, romantic glamour versions of sex.

The wise parent should not only discard all traces of our negative traditions regarding masturbation but should in addition see that there is available in the home literature which provides a basis for the development of sound erotic fantasies that place sex in a setting of warmth, affection, and social responsibility. The most critical element respecting this is the personal example provided by the parents in their relationship with each other.

Our society still gives considerable support to the idea that there is something evil and degrading about the nocturnal seminal emissions (wet dreams) which are usual in males after the onset of puberty. Recent scientific investigation of this phenomenon has confirmed how utterly erroneous such thinking is. Careful observations, under experimental laboratory conditions, have shown that the average male has several full or partial erections during each night (averaging 3 to 5 times). These generally occur during periods of dreaming. Often the dreaming is erotically colored and sometimes culminates in a seminal discharge. This is, in fact, a normal autoerotic aspect of male sex life. There is reason to believe (clinical impression of many psychotherapists) that a counterpart exists in the sleeping state of the female, although this has not been subjected to scientific investigation.

Recent scientific studies on severe sensory deprivation have revealed the vast power of erotic emotion and fantasy formation under conditions of extreme solitude, and isolation from the distractions and inhibitions of our customary waking state. Many who have experienced such isolation are astonished and shaken by the nature and intensity of their erotic feelings and fantasies and have been understandably reluctant to give a full report of their experience for public examination.

Beginning at early adolescence, or for some much earlier, masturbation is usually associated with erotic fantasies. If these are of a kind that reasonably well anticipates heterosexual behavior which is affectionate and mutually desired there is no problem. However, there may be cause for concern if these fantasies involve bizarre or seriously deviant expectations, such as those consistently including sado-masochism or other types of behavior which are incompatible with achievement of a sound real-life sex relationship. Here the basic problem is not the mere character of the fantasy but the life experiences which have induced it. Strongly compulsive, bizarre fantasies are a symptom of defective personality development and mental illness. They should be approached through psychiatric evaluation and treatment rather than through an educational approach. If such aid is not available or acceptable it seems wiser that the subject person should have an outlet through masturbation rather than acting out his unacceptable or antisocial fantasies.

For virtually all persons who have a comfortable attitude toward it, masturbation is likely to prove a useful and harmless substitute for or supplement to other sex outlets all through life. This is strikingly so during adolescence because our present society places so many roadblocks in the way of intercourse. Except during infancy and early childhood, masturbation is, at best, an unsatisfactory substitute for the rich emotional quality of a truly mutual intercourse experience. But it does serve to release sex tension, provides harmless pleasure, and aids in avoiding serious social penalties. The author, like many other professionals, has observed that today mutual masturbation (a compromise with the desire for intercourse) is widely used as a temporary substitute for actual intercourse (which carries a much higher risk of undesired complications). Of course this is not masturbation in the usual sense since it involves a real-life interpersonal relationship. It may be foreseen that as reliable contraceptives become more available to young people, the incidence of mutual masturbation will decline and the frequency of intercourse will increase.

During the course of married life, masturbation may play a valuable role supplementary to intercourse. This may be in times of illness or separation from the spouse; during menstruation; during the late stage of pregnancy; or to smooth out unevenness in mutuality of sex desire. At times mutual masturbation may prove more satisfactory than the solitary kind under circumstances where intercourse is not possible or feasible. There is no valid reason why either marital partner should feel in the least guilty or disturbed because masturbation is utilized in this way, so long as the husband-wife relationship is basically a good one. Indeed, it should be mutually recognized as a natural and desirable outlet, under appropriate conditions.

The author has observed that among unmarried young

adults the ability to masturbate without feelings of guilt is correlated with a more dignified and discriminating way of relating to the opposite sex than is seen among many who fear and shun masturbation and are compulsively driven toward the opposite sex as their only permissible outlet. In this sense masturbation may be said to have a genuinely affirmative moral and social value. Nevertheless, it is surprising, in the course of clinical counseling, to note how many young people shy away from masturbation because of a deeply rooted conviction that it is degrading or harmful and inferior to any intercourse experience, even one of very poor quality. Such a view ill serves human dignity and tends to push those who hold it into stupidly judged, miserably unhappy liaisons.

Some men and women who have enjoyed an excellent marital relationship but who become single through loss of the spouse find masturbation helpful but a decidedly unsatisfactory substitute for the high-quality intercourse to which they have been accustomed. In the younger age brackets, however, these people usually do not long remain unmarried. It seems that if they possess the qualities essential to establishing a good marriage these same qualities continue to make them attractive as marriage partners, following the loss of a spouse. This is not because of superficial glamour characteristics but because of their maturely affectionate way of relating to the opposite sex. The author has noted that such mature persons generally remarry within a fairly short time, even when encumbered by responsibility for one or several children. For these mature and sexually experienced people, dissatisfaction with masturbation comes not from feelings of guilt but from absence of the affectionate erotic interchanges which occur in a good marital relationship. It is not meant to suggest that a mature intercourse relationship of high quality is possible only in marriage; merely that in our society it most often occurs when fostered by the closeness and security of marriage.

There are some persons who go through life with no overt sex outlet except that of masturbation. For many of them this is probably better so, since they are likely to be handicapped by grave defects in their capacity to achieve satisfactory personal relations with the opposite sex. Unless such defects could be corrected through psychotherapy their efforts to adjust to someone in a real sex relationship would fail and create unpleasant complications in their lives.

# 7.   The Homosexual Revolution
## —A Status Report

DONALD   J.   CANTOR

Obscured by the Negro revolution, the homosexual is, almost unnoticed, pursuing and advancing his own revolutionary cause. Like the Negro, and like every other group that has fought to establish its rights, the homosexual first had to discover that he deserved rights, that what he had been told about himself was not true, that his intrinsic merit equaled that of his detractor, that he need not feel guilt and inferiority by definition. The homosexual is achieving this sense of inner worth and is thus becoming able to withstand identification, in some instances even bear notoriety in service of his cause.

There was a time when homosexuality was thought to be a result of excessive debauchery, or a morbid predisposition activated by onanistic practices, or the placement of a male soul in a female body, or vice versa. Some postulated that homosexuality was a congenital abnormality, and others explained it in terms of hormonal composition of the body. Thus, early theory, when coupled with theological condemnation ("Thou shalt not lie with mankind, as with womankind: it is abomination." Leviticus 18:22; "for even their women did change the natural use into that which is against nature. . . . Men with men working that which is unseemly. . . ." Romans 1:26, 1:27) made the homosexual easy to despise, for not only were his acts sinful but his condition was either freakish or degenerate or both.

The movement for homosexual rights could not, therefore gain until at least one of those premises was challenged. Freud did just that. Freud maintained that all persons are born with a psychic sexual duality, the capacity to express both male and female characteristics. He traced the existence of homosexual tendencies to Oedipal trauma but did not identify such childhood difficulties as the exclusive cause. Today, the bulk of psychiatrists will point to the child's resolution of the Oedipus complex as crucial, but admit the existence of other childhood conflicts as possible causes. In short, most will concede that no one really knows what causes homosexuality.

It was the late Dr. Kinsey's study of the sexual habits of the white American male and female which provided the impetus for the homosexual movement. Kinsey and his researchers concluded that one's sexual direction is conditioned by the effects of initial sexual experiences and the subsequent failure of cultural pressures to alter this direction. Kinsey considered homosexuality to be a capacity inherent in humans, not in some only, and not due to a failure to resolve infantile trauma. He wrote: "The homosexual has been a significant part of human sexual activity ever since the dawn of history, primarily because it is an expression of capacities that are basic in the human animal."

When Dr. Kinsey and his associates set forth their finding that 37 percent of white American males have had at least one homosexual experience involving orgasm during their lives, they delivered a body blow to homosexual mythology from which it can never recover, for the stereotyped homosexual—the effeminate, mincing dandy—clearly was not one of every three males, and this meant that the great majority of persons who had expressed homosexual inclinations looked just like those who despised them. The inferior image, the crucial difference which had made the mythological homosexual ridiculous, and thus easily persecutable, was suddenly labeled false. Kinsey also attacked the old convenient notion of sexual categories, the idea that one was homosexual or heterosexual the way one was American or alien, and showed instead that sexual activity covered a broad spectrum, much of which was a mixture of homosexual and heterosexual, not clearly either. Thus was the purity of the heterosexual sullied.

Kinsey forced society to see that, instead of having just heterosexuals and homosexuals, it had many active bisexuals, and many more who were potentially so.

Ten years later, in 1958, the Wolfenden Report was issued in London, and the homosexual movement was blessed with a champion of unimpeachable qualification and respectability.

This report by an English parliamentary committee would have been important solely because it recommended that private, adult, consensual homosexual acts be made lawful, but it was infinitely more important because of the caliber of its membership and because of its depth of research. The Wolfenden Report considered the varied arguments against making such acts lawful—i.e., that homosexuality deprives society of children, that homosexuality creates nervous, undependable persons, that homosexuality menaces the health of society, that homosexual behavior threatens the family, and that homosexuals may turn eventually to minors—and rebutted them all. This Report concluded that overpopulation, not underpopulation, was the social danger, that nervous homosexuals are so because of the present law and not because of their homosexuality, that homosexuality is no threat to the social health, that homosexuality is no greater threat to the family than heterosexuality, and that, if anything, legalization of private, adult, consensual homosexual acts would decrease homosexual overtures to minors since only these would remain unlawful.

The Wolfenden Report, however, served a greater function than the arguments and conclusions it advanced. It occasioned a great parliamentary debate, one which became a national and then an international education. Homosexuality, once a totally unmentionable subject, a contamination even to contemplate, became a topic people actually discussed and thought about and argued over—all without apparent injury.

Since the Wolfenden Report, more has happened to focus on and alleviate the troubles of the homosexual in the United States than in all the years prior.

In 1961, Illinois amended her criminal statutes and now does not make adult, private, consensual homosexual acts a crime.

In 1966 the criminal law of New York state came close to being similarly revised when a bill was presented to the legis-

lature which would have made adult, private, consensual homosexual acts lawful, but this bill was amended on the floor of
the legislature and such acts remain misdemeanors in New
York state. But this last-minute failure is of far less import
than the fact that the attempt was made to liberalize New
York law and that it nearly succeeded. The same is true of an
unsuccessful try in Minnesota in 1963. A similar bill was
introduced in the 1969 Connecticut Legislature and it was
passed.

North Carolina amended its sodomy statute in 1965, eliminating a punishment of not less than five nor more than sixty
years, and substituting in its place a fine or imprisonment "in
the discretion of the court." The eradication of the five-year
minimum sentence constitutes definite progress. Since the
American Law Institute has drafted its Model Penal Code
with this recommendation in it, in light of the influence of
the Institute and the prestige of its members, there can be
little doubt that like amendments will be offered in other states
and probably again in New York.

But the true progress of the movement cannot be solely
or even primarily gauged by statutory changes, although these
changes are the primary goals. Much more crucial at this time
are developments within the churches and within the homophile organizations themselves. The churches are important
because homosexuality is mainly despised for reasons based
upon the religious concept that homosexual acts are sinful.
Thus, if the revolution of the homosexual is to succeed, it
must reach the churches. This it is doing.

The Methodist Conference and the Congregational Union
indicated support of the Wolfenden Report in 1958. In Philadelphia, during November of 1965, a special symposium met
to discuss the homosexuality question in its various aspects,
many different disciplines being represented. The reason, I
was told, for the symposium's being convened was that the
United Presbyterian Church had felt the need to speak to the
problem (churchmen, I have learned, never speak *of* or *about*
a problem, but only *to* it).

In Hartford, Connecticut, the Greater Hartford Council of
Churches has for four years had a committee to study homosexuality and devise means by which the church can assist
homosexuals, both as a group and as individuals. Great interest
in this work has been manifested by other councils of churches
throughout the United States. Denver's Council of Churches

has been particularly active in this area of concern; San Francisco, in 1964, formed the Council on Religion and the Homosexual, its purpose being "To promote a continuing dialogue between the religious community and homosexuals"; and since that time several similar councils have been formed in other large American cities. And, in New York, the George W. Henry Foundation has, since 1948, rendered assistance in many different forms to homosexuals in trouble, through the quiet but inspired efforts of its Executive Director, Alfred A. Gross. It has received backing from the Episcopal ministry, in particular, and now has a Connecticut branch which has broad Protestant support. In November, 1966, The National Council of Churches, Department of Ministry, meeting in White Plains, New York, discussed the relation of the church and the homosexual, and in August of 1966, The World Council of Churches, meeting in London, held a seminar on this question.

As to the homophile organizations themselves, they are not only existent and operative, but are becoming vocal and militant. There are presently over 40 such organizations. They are no longer content to provide social camaraderie and mutual reassurance; they are evolving into organs of protest, media for propaganda, and active lobbyists. The subject of homosexuality is becoming not only an accepted topic for discussion but one of the topics most often discussed. In 1968 Station WBAI in New York had a sixteen-program series which dealt with the subject of homosexuals. Homosexual leaders are also moving actively to counsel homosexuals on problems such as applying for jobs within the Federal Civil Service system from which they are presently so unjustly barred. The Washington Mattachine Society has published a widely distributed pamphlet entitled "How to Handle a Federal Interrogation" and has also provided counseling for homosexuals faced with interrogation and administrative hearings. Their leaders do not shrink from publicity or shun public identification. The Mattachine Society of New York in 1966 tested and protested local ordinances against serving liquor to homosexuals by staging "sip-ins," an effort which has improved the situation in New York immensely. In San Francisco an association of "gay bars" has been formed to protect its members against both legal and extralegal pressures. The Homosexual Law Reform Society of America in Philadelphia has organized public demonstrations and distributed leaflets protesting the exclusion of homosexuals from the armed services. Mr. Clark Polak, Executive Secretary of the Homosexual Law Reform Society, like other homosexual leaders, has appeared on radio and television, at symposia, before service organizations, and has spoken to a great variety of audiences to decry the injustice America inflicts on its homosexuals. When the Florida Legislature contemplated legislation deemed inimical to homosexuals, Richard Inman, President of Atheneum Society of America, Inc., now The Mattachine Society of Florida, Inc., not only propagandized and lobbied, but had articles sympathetic to his cause printed and distributed to all legislators. Homophile organizations have picketed the White House, Pentagon, State Department, U.S. Civil Service Commission in Washington, Philadelphia Navy Yard, The United Nations and Independence Hall in Philadelphia, among others. In fact picketing Independence Hall has become an annual affair. A survey taken by and of the Florida Mattachine Society indicated 82 percent of those questioned were in favor of public picketing by homosexuals, and sentiment in other homophile groups in the country appears similarly inclined. On the campuses of Columbia, Cornell, Stanford, and New York University accredited homophile organizations have been formed for students. A noteworthy first occurred in 1968 when the New School of Social Research inaugurated a full semester course entitled, "Understanding the Homosexual"; also the homosexual, his definition and problems, are being included in such diverse courses as criminal law and abnormal psychology in other institutions.

The personal involvement of homosexuals in public advocacy of their views often accomplishes infinitely more than the propagation of those views. It serves the function of exposing the stereotype for the ridiculous nonsense it is. Every time a homosexual leader appears publicly, walks to his seat without swaying, dressed without frills, talking without a lisp, forcing his audience to the realization that they would not realize he was homosexual if he didn't tell them, a great stride is made. These leaders know this and thus seek constantly to address groups of all kinds. Nothing induces a man to feel tolerance more than seeing similarity between himself and the ones previously scorned. Difference is the root of prejudice, and prejudice dies as differences dissipate.

Those who administer the law give further evidence of

this new feeling about homosexuality. Prosecutors, in deciding to prosecute and on what charges, and judges, in determining how to sentence, are good barometers of current social values. There is an unmistakable tendency today to allow homosexuals to plead guilty to lesser charges than those for which they were arrested and to sentence leniently, often with probation in place of incarceration. A study of the disposition of arrests for felonious homosexual acts in Los Angeles County showed that only six-tenths of one percent (3 defendants of 493) received ultimate felony dispositions. The remainder were all treated as misdemeanor offenders and the great majority received suspended sentences, probation, or fines. John Gerassi, in his book, *The Boys of Boise*, indicates that this trend is not restricted to the larger, supposedly more sophisticated metropolitan centers, but is a present fact of legal life in Boise, Idaho, as well. Some urban police departments now have representatives to maintain liaison with local homophile organizations.

There are other extremely important philosophical influences which are having and will continue to have their effect on the law and the relation of the law to the homosexual. One is the opinion that law should not legislate morality, but should rather confine its proscriptions to those areas where acts or omissions have demonstrably injurious social consequences. This is not, of course, a philosophical innovation; the same notion was quite eloquently advanced by John Stuart Mill in his essay *On Liberty,* and by others of note, but its adoption with specific reference to the question of homosexual acts by a Catholic body is of special importance.

When the Commission which produced the Wolfenden Report was created, it requested the view of many different committees representing churches, professions, and other organizations. The late Cardinal Griffin of Westminster commissioned The Roman Catholic Advisory Committee on Prostitution and Homosexual Offenses and the Existing Law, and the report of this body, while stating "all directly voluntary sexual pleasure outside of marriage is sinful," nonetheless also states:

It is not the business of the State to intervene in the purely private sphere but to act solely as the defender of the common good. Morally evil things so far as they do not affect the common good are not the concern of the human legislator.

This singularly statesmanlike report went further, adding the following particularity:

Attempts by the State to enlarge its authority and invade the individual conscience, however high-minded, always fail and frequently do positive harm. The Volstead Act in the U.S.A. affords the best recent illustration of this principle. It should accordingly be stated clearly that penal sanctions are not justified for the purpose of attempting to restrain sins against sexual morality committed in private by responsible adults. They are, as later appears, at present employed for this purpose in this country and should be discontinued because:
  a) They are ineffectual;
  b) they are inequitable in this incidence;
  c) they involve severities disproportionate to the offense committed;
  d) they undoubtedly give scope for blackmail and other forms of corruption.

The position advanced by this report gives a rationale for allowing private, adult, consensual homosexual acts to be lawful, to those who regard those acts as morally odious, and therein lies its special significance and value. Now the one with moral objections can be approached, and often persuaded, to favor law reform on the fundamental basis of the need to separate theological morality from state power; the cause of the homosexual thus becomes identified with, and understandable to, all those groups whose history contains instances of persecution resulting from the joinder of morality and criminal law.

The second new philosophical position is that sexual acts should not be condemned morally simply because of their nature, but rather that sexual acts, like any acts, are moral or not depending upon the intentions behind them and the effects of them. In an address before the Missionary Society of the Berkeley Divinity School, on November 23, 1964, Dr. Gross, of the George W. Henry Foundation, expounded this view as he has continued to do since. In the January, 1967, issue of *The Living Church,* a weekly magazine of the Episcopal Church, the Reverend R. W. Cromey, Vicar of St. Aidan's Church in San Francisco, calling for homosexual law reform as recommended by the Wolfenden Committee, stated:

I believe that the sex act is morally neutral. There is no sex act which in itself is sinful. . . . I also believe that two people of the same sex can express love and deepen that love by sexual intercourse.

Acceptance of this view would necessarily lead to the law reform sought by the homosexual in light of the absence of any valid utilitarian reasons for the present restrictive laws.

In his book *Time for Consent?* Dr. Norman Pittinger, one of Protestantism's most highly regarded theologians, said:

Homosexual acts between persons who intend a permanent union in love are not sinful nor should the Church consider them as such.

I am ready to say that in homosexual love of the kind I have been discussing God is present. He is present in the loving relationship and also present in the acts which express and cement that love.

The progress made by the homosexual toward equality has been assisted by a rash of plays (*The Toilet, A Taste of Honey, The Sign in Sidney Brustein's Window, Staircase, The Boys in the Band*), movies (*Victim, Darling, The Leather Boys, Therese and Isabelle*), non-fiction books (*The Homosexual Revolution, In Defense of Homosexuality, The Homosexual in America, Homosexual Behavior Among Males*) and fiction by such established authors as Jean Genêt, Gore Vidal, and James Baldwin. In the law of obscene communication, the United States Supreme Court has facilitated the creation and distribution of literature dealing with homosexuality, and matter designed especially for homosexuals, by ruling that homosexual materials, including male nudes, are not *ipso facto* obscene. As the result of *Mishkin v. New York* decided by the Supreme Court on March 21, 1966, material is obscene if the dominant theme of it taken as a whole appeals to the prurient interest in sex, not of the average man, but rather of the members of any special group—such as homosexuals— for which such material was designed and to which it was primarily disseminated.

The attitudes thus expressed should be contrasted, to be appreciated, with a 1922 Ohio case in which the judge referred to males who commit homosexual acts as "human degenerates" and "sexual perverts," or the 1938 Maine case in which the Maine Supreme Court had this to say:

The statute [sodomy] gives no definition of the crime but with due regard to the sentiments of decent humanity treats it as one not fit to be named, leaving the record undefiled by the details of different acts which may constitute the perversion.

Contrast it also with the older attitudes manifested in the sodomy statutes of the various states. In fourteen states the forbidden acts, which include acts between males and females as well as between persons of similar sex, are described as "abominable" or as both "abominable" and "detestable." (What does "detestable" add that "abominable" omits?) In seven states the acts are called "infamous." In ten states the phrases "crime against nature" or "against the order of nature" are used adjectively; in three states "unnatural," "abnormal," or "perverted" are used. The depth and degree of antipathy which once characterized the public view of homosexual acts can be best appreciated when one recalls that no other crimes, including premeditated rape and murder are so described.

It would be facile and utterly misleading to imply that the American homosexual is on the threshold of victory in his battle for equality. It is still painfully true that every state but Illinois condemns the private, adult, consensual acts of homosexuals as criminal, that in seven states life imprisonment is a possible sentence for such acts, and that in thirty-five other states the maximum penalty is at least ten years. When Sir Cyril Osborne, Conservative Member of Parliament, said during debate, "I am rather tired of democracy being made safe for the pimps, the prostitutes, the spivs, the pansies, and now, the queers," he may have spoken for a distinct minority in England (a 1967 Gallup Poll in England showed 60 percent of those polled favored homosexual law reform), but it is probable that he reflected the opinions of a larger percentage of Americans, though many would not be quite so intense about it. John Gerassi tells us that only a decade ago a great number of Boiseans thought that homosexuals were naturally communists.

But the trend is clear. The opposition to homosexual law reform is progressively diminishing. The large amount of extortion and blackmail which has victimized the homosexual has reached public consciousness and created sympathy, and forced upon the public the realization that these anti-homosexuality laws, even when not strictly enforced, set the stage by their very existence for this extortion and blackmail. People are aware that England has finally made adult private, consensual homosexual acts lawful, and wondering whether our oldest teacher has yet another lesson for us to learn.

There is a new sense of perspective alive in the land, born at Hiroshima, which has equipped men to appreciate the dimensions of real danger, and has made them less able to view alleged sexual dangers such as homosexuality quite as seriously as once was possible. There is a sense of reappraisal, an unwillingness in an age of incredible change to presume the rightness of doctrine simply because doctrine is and was. Fittingly, sexual mores are getting perhaps the most serious reappraisal, partially because of the pill and intrauterine device, but more, I think, because the sexual dogmas have had the greatest rigidity and least realism. Homosexuality therefore is benefitting, as part of the general field of sexuality, from this rising examination of the old rules governing intercourse out of marriage, abortion, censorship, and divorce.

There is also not a new, but an increased, sense of the dignity of man and of man's right to dignity. The goals of the Negro are now national goals to an extent never before even approximated, not because he is Negro but because he is human. The homosexual is being gradually recognized as one seeking similar goals and deserving to achieve them.

Where a sexual act is done publicly, it is a nuisance and an invasion of the public's right to public propriety. It deserves punishment. Where a sexual act is committed with a minor, it is an invasion of the minor's right to privacy until he reaches the age of consent. It deserves punishment. Where a sexual act is done through force, duress, or fraud, or under any circumstances where consent is absent, it is an assault and deserves punishment. But where the act is private, between two consenting adults, where there is no victim, where nothing occurs but the physical expression of affection, it should not be punished.

Equality for the homosexual is an ethical imperative and the American people are beginning to realize this.

# PART IV

# Cultural Influences

## 8. *A Neuter and Desexualized Society?*

CHARLES WINICK

The next few generations are likely to be involved in sexual choices and situations which are unprecedented, certainly in American history. These new developments reflect such contradictory factors as the culture's libidinization, depolarization of sex, the flourishing of voyeurism on an unprecedented scale, and the perfection of the technology of genetic engineering. They will pose and are already raising a number of ethical issues of great consequence.

### Decline in Libido

Our social and cultural climate is currently so libidinized that sexual energies, which are probably finite, are being drained to an extraordinary extent by the stimuli in our surroundings. As a result, there could be less and less libido available for traditional kinds of sexual activity involving relationships with people.

Paradoxically, our age of so much libidinization of mass media could be the beginning of an epoch of declining sexual behavior. Why? The few studies which have explored the relationships between sexual attitudes and behavior suggest that a society with liberal attitudes toward overt sexual expression is likely to have less sexual behavior than a culture which places sanctions on such expression. We may identify as the Godiva Principle the proposition that people will be attracted to sex in proportion to the extent to which it is prohibited. As our society accepts sex more casually, its members may engage in less sexual behavior.

One study compared the relationship between sexual behavior and attitudes in a group of college students among three matched groups in: (a) the intermountain region of the United States; (b) the Midwest; and (c) Denmark. One conclusion of the study was that the Danes had the most liberal attitudes but the least premarital activity.[1] The intermountain students disapproved most explicitly of premarital relations but engaged in such relations more frequently than either of the other groups. We can speculate that the Danes were under the least pressure and therefore engaged in the least sexual behavior.

Additional evidence on the inverse relationship between sexual attitudes and behavior comes from survey data.[2] Persons of lower socioeconomic status are much more likely than middle or upper classes to express disapproval of nonmarital intercourse. However, male Kinsey interviewees with a grade-school level of education engaged in 10.6 times as much nonmarital intercourse as college men.

It would seem that more liberal sexual attitudes are likely to be correlated with less expression of libido. As we develop more permissive attitudes, we shall probably be less interested in sexual pursuits.

Further clues to the decline in the amount of libido which is available for sexual relationships can be found in studies of the effect of contraceptive pills on the incidence of sexual intercourse. It would be logical to expect that the 9,000,000 women who currently use the pill would engage in substantially more sexual intercourse than they did before this new contraceptive technique became available. In fact, we find that there is no substantial increase in intercourse on the part of women using the pill.[3] This non-increase is occurring even though many women are able to remind themselves, each day, of their potential as sexual partners and of their freedom from fear of pregnancy, at the time they ingest the pill.

We can speculate that the pill will ultimately lead to a

decline in sex relations because it routinizes such relations, as so many other aspects of our culture have been routinized.

## Depolarization of Sex

Certainly, one of the most extraordinary aspects of American sex roles for the last 25 years has been the extent to which masculinity and feminity are becoming more blurred and a strange neutering is moving to the center of the stage of at least middle-class life.[4] As sex becomes increasingly depolarized, its ability to excite and incite is likely to decline.

Documentation is hardly needed to confirm that men and women increasingly are wearing each other's clothing. Their leisure activities tend not to be sex-linked. In the home, a husband is often a part-time wife, and vice versa. Furniture related to either sex is disappearing, e.g., the leather club chair or the boudoir chair. American men use three times as much fragrance-containing preparations as their wives. Men have been wearing more jewelry at the same time that women are sporting heavy chain belts.

The shoe is the one item of costume which reflects gender most sensitively, perhaps because the foot's position in the shoe is so analogous to the position of the sexual organs during intercourse. As men's shoes have been looking more tapered, higher, and delicate, women's shoes have become stubbier, heavier, and lower.[5]

The blandness of social-sex roles is reinforced by the neuter quality of much of the environment in our beige epoch. Scotches, beers, and blended whiskeys succeed to the extent that they are light or bland. The convenience foods which have revolutionized our eating habits are bland. Even the cigar, once an outpost of strong aroma, has become homogenized. In a society in which, as Mies van der Rohe said, "less is more," our new buildings tend to be neuter.

This blurring lessens the range of satisfactions available to people and leads to a decline in the quality and quantity of experience available to them. But an even more pressing source of concern for the humanist is the ability of our society to survive at all, if the current trend toward depolarization of sex continues. We can state this proposition paradigmatically: (1) A society's ability to sustain itself and to grow creatively is based on the ability of its members to adapt to new situations. (2) Such adaptability is intimately related to the strength of the feelings of personal identity of the people in the society. (3) At the core of any person's sense of identity is his or her awareness of gender. (4) To the extent that a man's sense of masculinity or a woman's feelings of femininity are blurred, such persons might potentially possess a less effective self concept and be less able to adapt to new situations.

If this paradigm is correct, the depolarization of sex which is now endemic in this country could be a prelude to considerable difficulty for us. It could bring about a situation in which the United States may have to choose between our laissez-faire sexual ethic, with its seeming potential for social disaster, and the kind of rigid sex-roles which are associated with authoritarianism. It is interesting to note that China and the Soviet Union have adopted a puritan ethic which, if our hypothesis is correct, may actually encourage sex expression *because* it is so anti-sexual.

The humanist philosophy is clearly opposed to authoritarianism and its attendant rigidity of roles and quashing of individual differences and personal style. Yet, studies of the mental health implications of various kinds of family structure have tended to conclude that almost any male-female role structure is viable, provided that there is clear division of labor and responsibilities.[6] It is disconcerting to consider the possibility that our open society's ambiguous sex roles may be almost as pathogenic as the rigidities of authoritarianism.

What can the humanist do about this situation? If he agrees that masculinity and femininity should be preserved, he can realize that a number of decisions available to him may contribute to this end. Certainly, we can control the costume and appearance which we present to the world. We can choose the shapes and colors with which we surround ourselves. The toys and dolls which we get for children can reflect gender differences.

The names which we give to children can communicate maleness or femaleness quite explicitly. We can select leisure activities which make possible an expression of masculinity and femininity. In many other ways, we may exercise options which permit us to avoid being locked into the traditions of the past while still expressing modern forms of masculinity and femininity.

## Voyeurism

Of the many pop-sociological descriptions of the period since the end of World War II, certainly one of the most apt is the Age of Voyeurism. We see and look and ingest with the eye to a degree that is perhaps unparalleled in human history.

If we hypothesize that an increase in one form of sexual expression is related complementarily to other outlets, we can speculate that the great increase in voyeurism is taking place at the expense of coitus and other interpersonal kinds of sex expression.

We know from several studies of readers of peep magazines like *Playboy* and *Confidential* that masturbation is a very popular, and perhaps the most frequent behavioral response, to the magazines. It is probable that movies which explicitly present some form of sexual intercourse (e.g., *I Am Curious, Blow-Up, I, A Woman*) will become ever more popular. Such movies and the plethora of print materials presenting sexual or erotic content may be expected to move people in the direction of masturbating activities rather than interpersonal relations involving sex.

Voyeurism not only is satisfying in itself, as can be inferred from the extraordinary success of *Confidential* and *Playboy,* but it can also inhibit socially constructive action. Thirty-seven New Yorkers heard Kitty Genovese being attacked and murdered and yet did not respond in any way. It may be that the satisfactions provided by fantasizing about Miss Genovese were sufficiently strong to block any impulses toward going or looking outside or phoning the police. Voyeurism is seemingly rewarding enough to inhibit more socially constructive action. There is every reason to expect that our culture will be doing more peeping and less of other kinds of sexual behavior.

## Genetic Engineering

Yet another sexual deterrent is the perfection of procedures for freezing sperm and storing it for extended periods. Many routinely successful impregnations with sperm which had been frozen for several years have occurred and the children show no defects traceable to the manner in which they were conceived.

Procedures are being perfected for removing an unfertilized egg cell from a woman's ovaries, fertilizing it by human sperm in a laboratory flask, and keeping the resulting embryo for an extended period. Such procedures will make it possible for a woman to have babies by proxy. The egg cell from $A$ could be fertilized in a test tube by sperm from $B$ and nurtured in the body of $C$. This is even now done in the breeding of sheep and rabbits.

Genetic engineering is an almost inevitable result of the availability of such procedures. What would the humanist position on such matters be? Let us assume that the application of principles of genetic engineering leads to a decision to minimize breeding by a specific ethnic group. How could a humanist deal with such a situation? There would be a clear conflict between the presumed needs of society and our unwillingness to label any group as intrinsically and permanently inferior.

Yet if we are to abide by principles of genetic engineering, we presumably shall have to make such evaluations. One of the reasons that the United States is the only civilized country without a system of financial allowances for children is the fear of some legislators that the major beneficiaries of such help would be members of some ethnic groups which are believed to be inferior.

Once the genetic counsellor begins to advise potential mates and combines his skills with computer capabilities, romantic love as we know it may be doomed. Life will not only be different but it will be considerably delibidinized.

### Why Sex?

The several trends noted above would seem to be working toward an overall decline in sexual expression. A key ethical issue, then, in the next several decades would seem to be why people should engage in the various kinds of sexual behavior which involves others. The strength of the sexual drive is not self-sustaining and, as the culture drains more and more libido, people will have less occasion for engaging in sexual relations. It certainly will not be necessary for purposes of procreation. Presumably other levels of personal satisfaction will become important.

The affirmation and expression represented by sexual relations with others are human values which are too fulfilling to abandon. A humanist view of the sexual scene could encourage its adherents to make every effort to counter the trends which threaten to make sexual expression, in terms of relations with others, a historical subject. The very ability of our society to survive is at stake.

## Notes to Chapter 8

1. H. T. Christiansen and C. R. Carpenter, "Value Discrepancies Regarding Premarital Coitus," *American Sociological Review*, 27, 1962, pp. 66-77.
2. Stanton Wheeler, "Sex Offenses," *Law and Contemporary Problems*, 25, 1960, pp. 267-268.
3. "Birth Curbs Affect Sex Relations," *Medical Tribune,* January 22, 1968, p. 3.
4. Charles Winick, *The New People: Desexualization in American Life*. New York: Pegasus, 1968.
5. Charles Winick, "Status, Shoes, and the Life Cycle," *Boot and Shoe Recorder*, 156, October 15, 1959, pp. 100-101.
6. Charles Winick, "Dear Sir or Madam as the Case May Be," *Antioch Review*, 23, 1963, pp. 35-79.

# 9. On Obscenity and Pornography

EDWARD SAGARIN

Unless it be to designate a note at the foot of the page, the asterisk might well be removed from modern typewriters and that valuable space be devoted to something more useful, like ♂ or ♀ —particularly if these symbols are to be condensed into a single symbol, when what Charles Winick has described as desexualization or neuterization proceeds to take us headlong on the path to H***.[1] For nothing is unprintable, at least in the area of sex, and nothing is left to the imagination, unless it be virginity and chastity. The only dirty word that remains in the American language—and a four-letter word at that—is spelled C-U-B-A.

It has been said, and repeated to the point of boredom if not of understanding, that what is improper at one time becomes quite proper at another, and that the obscene and the pornographic are not timeless absolutes (but what is?). As R. D. Laing has said about schizophrenia[2] and as the labeling school of sociologists is fond of repeating about deviance,[3] so it can be said of pornography: Pornography is whatever is called pornography, in a society and in a language community where certain things are called pornographic.

Thus, pornography changes with time and place. Noah Webster, that great lexicographer, purged the Bible of its dirty words, preferring *breast* to *teat* and even *smell* to *stink*.[4] Poor Noah! How the floodgates have opened since your time! What

105

would you say if you could know that two centuries after your birth, the dictionary that dares to bear your name had to apologize because, for commercial reasons, it omitted one obscenity, thus making its list of words under the letter "f" incomplete?[5] What would you say? I suggest that, like the editors of Webster's *Third New International Dictionary of the English Language,* you would have pointed with pride to the inclusion of all other obscene synonyms that denote the parts of the body and biological acts committed by human and animal.

But one does not have to dig deep into the early days of American life to discover how the pornographic and the obscene have changed in character and in flavor. In the 1920's, the censors were not content with banning *Ulysses* and *Lady Chatterly's Lover,* unquestionably serious works of art that were written without benefit of asterisks. Such a mild play as Edouard Bourdet's *The Captive,*[6] a French import about lesbianism, was closed by the police; today it would be closed by a bored audience that would wait in vain to see the central character, a married woman, resolve her difficulties by an *amour à trois* on the stage, while the curtain remains high (for nothing happens behind the curtains, only below them), and with a call to the audience to join in a manifestation of participatory democracy.

Nor need one go back to the inglorious twenties! In the 1940's, the courts in many jurisdictions banned Edmund Wilson's *Memoirs of Hecate County,* and today it is difficult to find the objectionable passages,[7] (unless prosecutors at the time were objecting to a few lines in which the narrator placed a kiss on an unmentionable part of his girl friend's body). When Wilson mentioned the unmentionable, he did so in language that Shakespeare would have considered prudish.

Perhaps one of the clearest indications of the rapidity of social change in the area of the obscene and the pornographic is the Ralph Ginzburg case. Some six years after his conviction, later upheld by the Supreme Court, for publishing—or was it for advertising?—pornographic literature, Ginzburg was still fighting the case; and a *New York Times* reporter commented that since that conviction, "a virtual revolution in sex and the arts has come about," making Ginzburg's condemned publications "look tame to many observers."[8] And this was apparent not only to legal observers, but to the public, to churchmen, and to students of human sexual expression.

Yet the numerous references to changing mores, and specifically to a society's acceptance in one era of what was banned in another, can be quite misleading. For pornography cannot be defined as the graphic presentation of sexuality (or of any other biological phenomenon); pornography is rather the presentation of such material in a manner outrageous to large sectors of people in that society, people who find such a presentation offensive and in bad taste.

I should prefer to modify the definition of pornography offered by Paul H. Gebhard and his colleagues at the Institute of Sex Research who state: "Pornography is material deliberately designed to produce strong sexual arousal rather than titillation and which usually achieves its primary goal."[9] They then proceed to point out that "the Hindu sculptor who with some religious symbolism in mind depicts coitus has not produced pornography, even though his work may inflame the imaginations of most Occidental viewers." This definition, by including the concept of "strong sexual arousal" and by omitting any reference to its being in a manner and of a type labeled outrageous in a given society, leads the researcher into a *cul-de-sac*. Thus David Sonenschein, basing his view entirely on research at the Institute, points out that "a number of other cultures [other than modern Western, presumably] have managed the overt expression of what we call 'pornography' (exposure of genitalia and sexual activity) without evidence of widespread individual and cultural damage."[10] All of this may demonstrate that cultures can survive "with different definitions and conceptions of the human body and sexual activity," but it disregards the effect on the individual of exposure to what is defined as pornographic in a given culture.

We are living in a time of pornographic revolution, if not of sexual revolution. Large amounts of material, defined by the "official culture" as immoral and outrageous, are today being legally rather than surreptitiously published and distributed. This in itself does not prove that there has been a revolution in sexual practices—a matter debated and debatable. Some contend that whatever is done today was in the repertoire of past generations, performed then more covertly but not less frequently; and others hold to the belief that mores have undergone deep changes with new attitudes being translated into practices. But whatever the answer, the public expression of sexual things is entirely unlike what it was a few years back, and it is challenging one's credulity to assert that this public expression is not the consequence of other changes in the social order and does not have consequences of its own for man—the doer and actor.

The public and semi-public dissemination and presentation of material still considered lewd and lascivious, and making an appeal exclusively because its erotic content is socially disapproved, is widespread. Both its defense and its condemnation are usually expressions of wishful ideology, little backed up by research. Some critics are fond of asserting that little or no harm can come of pornography, and perhaps even some good. "Pornography is far from being a strong determinant of sexual behavior," write John H. Gagnon and William Simon,[11] who suggest that it might be "a paper tiger" rather than a raging menace. "Pornography is only a minor symptom of sexuality and of very little prominence in people's minds most of the time. Even among those who might think about it most, it results in masturbation or in the 'collector' instinct."[12]

There remains little information on the effects of pornography. A number of problems are involved, and they should be separated from one another and studied on their own merits. They may lead us to contradictory and mutually exclusive conclusions, as far as public policy is concerned. But before one can locate the answers, one must pose the questions; among others, there might be these:

What harm is done, if any, to some individuals, perhaps because of their youth or impressionability, by dissemination of material, not only erotically arousing, but suggesting such deviant pathways as sadomasochism and homosexuality? What are the dangers to free interchange of expression when suppressive measures are taken against the dissemination of such literature? What of the rights of the public, or of such members of the public as do not wish to view or to be confronted with pictorial and other literature offensive to them, to be protected from the display of such material? Are there people who are assisted in meeting the problems of daily living in a socially acceptable way because they can find a fantasy outlet in pornography? And are there others who, by the exposure to such literature, are driven to acts of an antisocial nature; and who, there is good reason to suspect, would not have committed these acts without the exposure? What is the role of obscenities as part of the arsenal of oral violence against one's enemies? What will be left when the youth have charged their war-wongering enemies with being the illegitimate off-spring of female canines and of performing maternal incestu-ous copulation, and have made this charge so frequently that the words have lost their sting?

Both the harmfulness and harmlessness of obscenity have been argued with little substantiating evidence. To say that pornography can do no harm is to contend that books and the printed word, graphics and slogans, cannot move people and influence their thoughts and hence their actions. Pornogra-phy can indeed be one factor in bringing some people to seri-ous criminal acts, as a careful reading of the work of Gebhard and his collaborators (Gagnon among them) will indicate. These writers state that of those sex offenders whose offenses included violence or duress, "between one-eighth and one-fifth reported arousal from sadomasochistic noncontact stimuli." "While it is probable that in a few cases such stimuli triggered an offense, it seems reasonable to believe that they do not play an important role in the precipitation of sex offenses in general, and at most only a minor role in sex offenses involving violence."[13] Among those most responsive to pornography were the aggressors against minors, of whom the writers report: "They seem in general a group of uninhibited young men who respond unthinkingly and violently to various stimuli. Their reaction to pornography is merely a part of their exaggerated reaction to almost everything."[14]

What complicates this matter is not only the probability that for some youth pornography serves as a safety valve, but also that the most innocuous tracts may implant false or harm-ful ideas in the heads of the young and impressionable. Thus a youth may be led in a direction unpredictable for a single person, although perhaps not so for larger numbers. What could happen to a young man exposed to innocuous reading about sex? Most likely, he would masturbate, which he would have done anyway, but if aroused he might do it that day, or a little sooner, or more frequently. No harm done, and per-haps some good! Or perhaps he might be sufficiently excited to use more persuasion on the teenage girl friend than he had employed hitherto, resulting in nonmarital petting to the point of orgasm, or to intercourse by mutual consent and probably to mutual enjoyment. If he and the girl friend have been prop-

erly educated in birth control and in sexual behavior generally, then there should be no unpleasant consequences, either
in the form of pregnancy or guilt, and perhaps some pleasant
ones resulting from their actions.

But what if, frustrated, aroused, searching, pressed by
what he has seen, read, and heard, seeking to handle it within
the framework of a moral order to which he wishes to adhere
but increasingly cannot, beset by conflict, the youth has an
outburst of uncontrollable violence? He attacks a girl. No one
can dismiss the event as being harmless to either party, or as
being good. From every point of view, it is an evil, and it
should have been avoided. That it could have been triggered
by innocent literature as well as pornographic would not lead
anyone to advocate a return to mass illiteracy. That the pornographic might more frequently than the innocent literature
be a cause of such an event can be inferred by the very
meager and tentative research findings. And, in the end, one
inquires: What are the risks, and how big are they, in permitting the dissemination of the pornographic; and, to look
at the reverse, what are the risks in suppression? Are there
greater risks for society when hard-core pornography is disseminated than when the young (or others for that matter)
read *Playboy, Esquire,* Shakespeare, the Bible, or some other
material on sex distributed by a biology teacher or a church
group?

The wide use of pornography has brought sex to the
taken-for-granted spot on the American scene. Children today
know; they know early; and they know a good deal. They
have, or believe that they have, only small details to learn
from their parents, and most young people are confident that
they can teach a good deal to their grandparents about sex
(except that they think it is too late for the grandparents to
learn, which shows that the youths themselves have something
to learn).

Whether or not a generation that grows up with little
secrecy and mystique surrounding sex will be able to integrate
sexuality better into its life, and will be able to derive from
sex more enjoyment and less guilt, has not been demonstrated.
Will such a generation have more meaningful experiences, in
the sense both of experiences that are more meaningful and
more experiences that are meaningful? Man has suffered from
the guilt surrounding sexual desires and from the punishments

inflicted on himself and others for doing that which was most natural for him. Man has deliberately denied himself the pleasures of sex. Will the openness of sexual expression and depiction, of sex language and discussion, be liberating to man? These are unanswered questions, and those who rush with answers give the ones they hope to find.

We are in an era of revolt against censorship. There are all sorts of enemies who are called by every epithet in the arsenal of the articulate, but there are no more blankety-blanks. The publication of the works of Joyce, Lawrence, Cleland, and lesser figures, has not caused the graffiti-laden walls of civilization to come tumbling down. The fear that our world would collapse as did that of the Romans before us, while all our Neros fiddled around with one another, is not seriously promulgated today. Yes, the world may indeed collapse, but because mankind could not learn to control his technology, has allowed his environment to become lethal, did not know how to handle the energies he had unharnessed from within the atom, and could not prevent men of different nations, languages, colors, and religions from annihilating one another.

Whatever harm might be accomplished by pornography —and in individual cases it is hardly possible to deny such harm—there is some good to society by its dissemination; and some hurt to individuals, the social order, and to human freedom and aspirations by anti-pornography. Of the former, the social good of pornography, it acts as a force demanding greater self-reflection from within society, creating a counter-culture to the staid, puritanical, and taken-for-granted world. It is a call for sexual revaluation, and that means that it is a force against stagnation and conservativism. As for the hurt, the suppression of pornography results in the establishment of a great force of law-enforcement agents, self-appointed or government-appointed, as morals defenders, who are to state what reading and looking can be corrupting to others, although they are themselves immune from corruption by the same exposure. It is an unnecessary restraint upon freedom of expression, artistic and inartistic. It has potential for use against political and other opponents and it can be destructive of a democratic process, when there is no clear and present danger. Whatever danger there is in pornography is quite unclear, and certainly not imminent.

But there is a danger—and not that of backlash. It is that while taking sex for granted and accepting it, the new generation will also see it (as did its parents and grandparents, though for other reasons) as dirty rather than as casual. Other generations saw sex as filthy because they understood that it was being hidden, that it was being made pretty for them, and that behind closed doors something was taking place which, if it were not dirty, would not be surrounded by hush-hush. The asterisks left nothing to the imagination; they simply told the reader, who could fill in all the missing letters with much greater ease than in the simplest crossword puzzle, that the forbidden was just that because it was defined as dirty.

The figleaf has been taken away, and what do we have? The beautiful nude, *Venus de Milo,* Michelangelo's *David*? No, these have always been with us, except for a few moments when they were draped by latter-day barbarians. Instead, suggestive poses and orgiastic depictions, inartistic and inelegant, appeal to the prurient by demonstrating sex as prurient-appealing. Where once *The Kiss* by Rodin was a depiction of sexual arousal, today such a normal, affection-laden, sensitive expression of loving and lovemaking would be unnoticed; and the sculptor, artist, or poet would take these two young lovers and dehumanize them by making their approach to each other genital and impersonal.

And this is the way it must be, if we are to have pornography, for by definition pornography is the socially disapproved appeal to the libido. Those involved today with the public demonstration of sex and body, with public statement of sex as raw and crude, are as much antisexual as were former generations of Comstocks and decency legionnaires. The antisexuality of former days consists of the depiction of that same body as gross and ugly in order to shock and offend. The generation that tore away the figleaves was not content with that accomplishment but proceeded to replace the lovely organs of man and woman by crudely constructed distortions.

It is no wonder, then, that obscenity is a weapon against one's enemies. If one accepted sex, one would not vilify an opponent by referring to him in terms synonymous with sexual organs or acts, for these would be complimentary. Perhaps that is why the youth are calling their opponents in uniforms, "pigs."

## Notes to Chapter 9

1. Charles Winick, *The New People: Desexualization in American Life.* New York: Pegasus, 1968.
2. R. D. Laing, "The Study of Family and Social Contexts in Relation to the Origin of Schizophrenia," *Excerpta Medica, International Congress Series No. 151,* pp. 139-46. In this paper, Laing defines schizophrenia as "a condition that afflicts people diagnosed as schizophrenics," and again: "Schizophrenia is the name for a condition that most psychiatrists ascribe to patients they call schizophrenics."
3. Authoritative sociologists in this school of thought include Edwin Lemert, Howard S. Becker, Kai Erikson, and John Kitsuse, among others.
4. Allen Walker Read, "Noah Webster as a Euphemist," *Dialect Notes,* 6, 1934, 385-91. Webster's *Holy Bible* was published in 1833; there is a brief discussion of this episode in Peter Fryer's *Mrs. Grundy: Studies in English Prudery.* New York: London House & Maxwell, 1963.
5. Reference is made here to *Webster's Third New International Dictionary of the English Language.* Springfield, Mass.: G. & C. Merriam Co., 1965.
6. Edouard Bourdet, *The Captive.* New York: Brentano's, 1926.
7. In a book devoted to pointing out the "sexy parts" in literature, Robert George Reisner, *Show Me the Good Parts: The Reader's Guide to Sex in Literature.* New York: Citadel, 1964, the author is unable to cite any particularly arousing passages in Wilson's work, describing it rather blandly: "An intellectual of affairs carries on two. One is with a highbrow girl and the other is with a lowbrow." See Edmund Wilson, *Memoirs of Hecate County.* New York: Doubleday, 1946; paperback edition by Signet.
8. *New York Times,* April 10, 1969.
9. Paul H. Gebhard, John H. Gagnon, Wardell B. Pomeroy, and Cornelia V. Christenson, *Sex Offenders: An Analysis of Types.* New York: Harper & Row, 1965, p. 669.
10. David Sonenschein, "Pornography: A False Issue," *Psychiatric Opinion,* 6(1), February, 1969, 11-17.
11. John H. Gagnon and William Simon, "Pornography—Raging Menace or Paper Tiger?" Trans-Action, 4(3), July-August, 1967, 41-48.
12. *Ibid.*
13. Gebhard *et al.,* p. 669.
14. *Ibid.,* p. 671.

# PART V

# The Marital Ideal

## 10. *Sex, Society and the Single Woman*

LUTHER G. BAKER, JR.

In no society anywhere has there been a warm and accepting home for the unmarried. "Be fruitful and multiply and replenish the earth," has been a divine dictate so deeply intrenched in human cultures, of whatever religious stamp, that those who fail or refuse to obey the injunction are suspected of personal aberration and accused of social irresponsibility.

The situation has been especially serious for the single female. The "myth of the feminine mystique" has probably nowhere produced more psychic damage than among unmarried women. Set in a society which idolizes motherhood and views the purpose and function of the female sex as biological progeneration, these "unhappy misfits" are often considered by the community as a whole, and even by themselves, as a kind of vague neuter gender, pitied as somehow not quite making the grade as real women.

These attitudes are reflected in two nearly universal major preconceptions about women. The first is that woman is inferior to man, needs man to guide and support her, and therefore should remain subordinate to man. The practical implication of this theory for the never-married woman is plain: it is not proper for her to be unmarried! At best she is denied the assistance of a man who might lead her to personal fulfillment; at worst she is denying the very order of nature and laying herself open to psychological and even behavioral aberrations.

The second preconception is that women find fulfillment as human persons primarily through marriage and motherhood. If this be true, it is obvious that a woman never married and never bearing children is doomed to "half a loaf of life."

These theories stand out in bold relief in the literature and practices of the ages. Nearly all primitive cultures developed imaginative tales explaining the existence of the two sexes. Perhaps the most familiar is that found in the Sacred Scriptures of the Hebrews.

Then the Lord God formed man of the dust from the ground and breathed into his nostrils the breath of life and he became a living being. Then the Lord God said, "It is not good that man should be alone; I will make a helper fit for him." So the Lord God caused a deep sleep to fall upon the man, and while he slept took one of his ribs and closed up its place with flesh; and the rib which the Lord God took from the man he made into a woman and brought her to the man.[1]

An ancient Sanskrit story opens: "In the beginning, when Twashtri came to the creation of woman, he found that he had exhausted his materials in making man, and that no solid elements were left."[2]

All the ancient narratives clearly place man in the dominant position. He is described as created first, and of the best material, while woman was brought into being as a kind of afterthought and created out of obviously inferior material.

In the Hebrew account woman is the product of a minor and inconsequential part of man. His dominant position is further reinforced by the curses consequent to the Sin of Eden. "In sorrow shalt thou bring forth thy children," Yahweh said to the woman, "thy desire shall be to thy husband and he shall rule over thee."

Aristotle shared this view. "The female is a female by virtue of a certain lack of qualities," he writes, "and we should regard the female nature as afflicted with a natural defectiveness."[3] The "Compassionate Buddha," Cato the Elder, Augustine, and many other formulators of tradition all agreed. By the middle ages the attitudes toward women reached their lowest point. Two fifteenth-century German Dominican theologians assigned by the Pope to produce a "manual of witch-craft" zeroed in quickly on the central issue.

A woman is beautiful to look upon, [but] contaminating to the touch. She is a necessary evil, a natural temptation, a domestic danger, an evil of nature. She seethes with anger and impatience in her whole soul. There is no wrath above the wrath of a woman. Since women are feebler both in mind and body it is not surprising that they should come under the spell of witchcraft [more than men]. . . . A woman is more carnal than a man. All witchcraft comes from carnal lust, which in women is insatiable.[4]

The intensity of antipathy has moderated, but on the whole this view of woman has persisted into the modern era. The sentiment of that notable English poet, John Milton, aptly sums up the prevailing mood.

                    . . . though both
Not equal, as their sex not equal seemed;
For contemplation he and valour formed,
For softness she and sweet attractive grace,
He for God only, she for God in him.

To whom thus Eve, with perfect beauty adorned:
"My author and disposer, what thou bidst
Unargued I obey: so God ordains:
God is thy law, then mine: to know no more
Is woman's happiest knowledge, and her praise."[5]

The historic roots of these stereotypes lie in biologic soil, in "the nature of things." The life span of primitive woman was closely associated with her years of fertility. Possessing no sure knowledge of the reproductive process, and with a high premium placed on fecundity, females normally conceived as soon as they were physiologically able to do so, and with recurring regularity. Throughout most of human history most women have died before reaching the end of their reproductive capacity. Thus being "heavy with child" nearly all her adult life, and with several small children to tend, some still suckling, it was a practical necessity that she be supported and protected by a man, who being free and physically stronger could exact his "pound of flesh" for such aid. It is easy to recognize the influence of these facts of life on the development of the dominant-submissive pattern of male-female relationships.

Until comparatively recently in Western society, the life expectancy and "production expectancy" imposed on the female have combined to keep her in her historical "place" as keeper of the hearth and mender of men's socks. Since "what is" is so often taken for "what ought to be," this arrangement of masculine-feminine function was considered to be written into the nature of the sexes, divinely created that way from the beginning.

It might be supposed that changes in the basic character of human existence would produce changes in social attitudes. But such is not the case with respect to beliefs about women. In spite of the lengthening of her days far beyond reproductive capacity and the reduction in both the number of her children and the number of her child-bearing years, the long tradition of feminine inferiority still leads woman to seek and submit to the passive role. And there are numerous obliging voices to assure her that her purpose and capacity are limited to the role of man's helpmeet.

A 1959 study by Eugene Nadler and William Morrow illustrates the contemporary mood. They report that among a sample of 83 men in two mid-western colleges there was a strong "anti-woman authoritarianism." In spite of the gains made in equality between the sexes, a majority of these college men believed women are inferior and "should be kept subordinate."[6]

In connection with another study this writer found a strong bias against women in contemporary religious thought and practice. A national officer of a large Protestant body stated in a communication that, family democracy notwithstanding, "authority should be located in the Christian father who is head of the house and makes final decisions." In this same study another correspondent considered it an "unmitigated evil" for a woman to be employed outside the home. "It makes her too independent!"[7]

During the 1950s and early 60s several voices were raised against the traditional positions. Margaret Mead, Phyllis Rosenteur, Helen Gurley Brown, and Betty Friedan, among others, have protested mightily against the historic subjugation of the fairer sex, and have called for a revision of the assumption that woman's glory lies in motherhood. There was an immediate backlash among the traditionalists, both male and female. In an article titled "The Honor of Being a Woman," Phyllis McGinley cried out "Our bodies are shaped to bear children and our lives are a working out of the process of creation."[8]

Frances Pellegrini echoed this theme in rhapsodic prose which sings "I'm Lucky!" In "I'm so Glad to be a Woman," she described the joys of motherhood and waxes lyrical over "polished brass, fresh sheets, and draperies."[9]

How effectively these molders of public opinion have done their job may be indicated by the phenomenon known in college as "senior panic." Among most college females not only is spinsterhood viewed as a personal tragedy, but off-spring are considered essential to a full life. Betty Friedan reports a survey which revealed that a majority of Vassar students would willingly adopt children, if necessary, to create a family.

The general acceptance of the stereotypes is illustrated by a Gallup Poll survey conducted in 1962 for the *Saturday Evening Post*.[10] "The American female," the report states, "has a strongly rooted purpose. It's home and family—motherhood. Motherhood is her happiness if she has it, her despair if she does not." Included in the sample were 1,813 married women, nearly all of whom said their chief purpose in life was to be a good wife and mother. Typical of those who have accepted the popular image was one wife who declared, "Women who ask for equality with men are fighting nature. They wouldn't be happy if they had it. It's simply biological."

The grip of tradition is so tenacious that even the majority of the "voices crying in the wilderness" previously mentioned still succumb to its hold. While plaintively urging modern women to be persons, too, Margaret Mead finds it necessary to sell this achievement as a vicarious motherhood. "Full acceptance of responsible life in society," she writes,[11] "is having children." In *The Single Women* Phyllis Rosenteur[12] offers fine practical advice to the single girl. But it is clear that this condition is to be tolerated only so long as necessary. A fitting sub-title to the book would be "What's Wrong With Marriage, and How to Get in on It!" Helen Gurley Brown appears at first to see women as human, but in fact hers is the same old libidinal law in a different cover (or bed jacket!) In *Sex and the Single Girl*[13] she openly accepts the notion that women exist mainly for male sexual pleasure (except that she insists on enjoying it, too) and that the "rich, full life" is really marriage.

Of the now "older" feminists, perhaps Friedan comes closest to a truly liberating view of womanhood. Radically rejecting the "myth of the feminine mystique," she urges every person, irrespective of sex, to creative human endeavor, and says that women owe it to themselves and to society to develop all their human powers. It is only after a woman has "actualized" all her potential as a person, physical, spiritual, intellectual, that she can enter into a sharing relationship with a man in which both may continue to develop creative lives. In this she is closely allied with Erich Fromm, who believes that a truly creative marriage can be made only between a man and woman who have already made strides in becoming "whole selves."

Unfortunately, the work of Mrs. Friedan, helpful and potentially fruitful as it is, fails to come to solid grips with the situation of the never-to-be-married woman. The final fruit of woman's emancipation is not only that she "find her true self," but also that this achievement be reached in concord with "children, home and garden."

New hope seemed to dawn with the decade of the 70s. The current, sometimes militant "women's liberation movement," while as yet spawning no new charismatic spokesman, exploits the general revolutionist mood to renew the call, often stridently, for "women's rights." The anti-male stance of a few viragos is nothing new; Fanny Wright preceded them by several generations.

The present thrust of the movement, however, appears to be toward occupational equality, insisting on equal employment opportunity with equal pay. Concern touches upon marriage and family mainly by asserting the right of a wife-mother to establish and develop non-domestic pursuits. Now, as before, no prominent authority is suggesting that a woman might find human fulfillment entirely apart from marriage and motherhood. Most reinforce the ancient belief that her primary purpose and function are domestic, and advocacy of a larger area of creative endeavor is essentially in the interest of additional fulfillment. Thus now, as in every age of human history, the never-to-be-married woman is left just outside the pale of full human acceptance.

Opinions about the nature and potential of womanhood abound aplenty, but facts are scarce indeed. In a previous investigation the writer was unable to find any record of research testing the validity of the stereotypes under discussion. Several studies sought to explain why some women remain unmarried, but none attempted to measure the psychological results when they do. Accordingly, an investigative procedure was developed in an attempt to discover certain objective facts about the nature and degree of human fulfillment for never-married women.[14] Do such women in fact experience a lower level of human satisfaction than married women do? Is a woman who remains single less "fulfilled" than one who experiences motherhood?

Matched samples of thirty-eight never-married women and thirty-eight married mothers were compared, utilizing the California Test of Personality and certain other measurements of personal and social adjustment. The samples were matched in every important respect except for the variable of marriage and motherhood. *No significant difference was found on any item of the test.* The averages of the scores for both groups were significantly higher than the average for the female population as a whole, using scales provided for this test by the California Test Bureau. But on each of the twelve separate items on the test, both groups showed essentially the same pattern.

It is clear that the samples are biased groups. Members for both were drawn from Business and Professional Women's clubs, women who are sucessfully engaged in a profession or occupation which provides them with a large measure of satisfaction and contributes to high self-esteem. It is important to point out, however, that the satisfaction and self-esteem are shared equally by both groups, married and unmarried. On the basis of such measures as are presently available there is no scientific support for the contention that a woman not married or experiencing motherhood must inevitably suffer some retardation in personality development or a loss of satisfaction with life. Both the objective measurements and the subjective data from interviews clearly demonstrate that some never-married women do possess well-developed and psychologically integrated personalities and are able to enjoy rich and satisfying lives. Some, in fact, exhibit a higher degree of these elements than is true for the majority of women in the country.

The factor which appears to contribute significantly to this high level of performance, for both married and unmarried in this study, is significant employment from which the individual derives a sense of important contribution to her world. It is this which the women in both groups share, but which sets them apart from the majority of women. The implications of this theory will be discussed shortly.

Popular opinion notwithstanding, the study briefly described demonstrates that personal fulfillment, insofar as it can realistically be measured, does not depend upon marriage and parenthood. The never-married subjects in that investigation expressed no feelings of frustration, no sense of not being a "whole person" as a consequence of remaining unmarried. Their sense of personal worth comes not from their biological function as a female, but from their social function as a human being, from what they perceive as a creative contribution to their significant society.

The procreative function of woman should not, of course, be minimized. Obviously, the race cannot continue without it, and undoubtedly marriage and motherhood have brought deep satisfaction and human fulfillment to many women. This, however, may also be said of men. Depending upon his view of himself, a man, too, may derive intense emotional satisfaction through marriage and parenthood. But this is not necessarily his primary avenue to personal identity. If he perceives himself to be "bread-winner," an indispensable source of his family's well-being, and if his family constitutes his "significant society," then it may be through contribution to them that he derives identity as a person of worth. He may also, or even instead, perceive his occupation or some worthwhile volunteer community service as a means of creative endeavor and a source of personal fulfillment. It does not occur to anyone that his fulfillment as a human being lies in the biological process of fathering a child. Fulfillment in relation to being a father comes from the subsequent contribution he makes to those who are significant to him.

Just as insemination is what a man does with his biology, so fetal development is what a woman does with her biology. It is obviously true that the physiological involvement is considerably greater for woman than it is for man, but it remains nonetheless a function of the body, not of the "person." Personal fulfillment as a mother comes not from giving birth to a child (not all women who bear children are "fulfilled"), but from the subsequent contribution she makes to the developmental needs of the child. Furthermore, just as a man is able to make a creative contribution to some significant society and hence achieve a high sense of personal worth without ever impregnating a woman, so a woman may accomplish a similar sense of personal fulfillment without ever having been impregnated by a man.

The theory that a woman achieves personhood—"humanity"—by creative contribution to her significant society helps to explain the plethora of literature lamenting the frustrated dissatisfaction so frequently expressed by young mothers. For several years the writer was in a position which afforded considerable opportunity for meeting with small groups of mothers, most of them young and with two or three preschool children. A sense of frustration and futility was readily apparent among these groups. It was common to hear such phrases as "boxed in," "rat race," and "dead end."

These young wives and mothers feel defeated and disillusioned. They married, most of them, on the conviction that this defined their humanity, that home and family comprised their goal and meaning in life. That they are disappointed is putting it mildly. Many view with regret their unfinished education; exciting adventure seems to beckon from outside the home, but they have neither the time nor the energy to respond.

Why is this so? Why have husband and children not fulfilled them? Why do they not feel satisfied in their contribution to this "significant group?"

The answer lies in changing life-styles and in technology. Historically, the responsibilities of homemaking undoubtedly have challenged the ingenuity of wives and mothers and demanded their complete dedication to its accomplishment. Mother has been indispensable to the well-being, even the survival, of her family. It is not difficult to understand the origin of the assumption that "the nature of things" ordained feminine fulfillment through domestic channels.

It is doubtful that the average modern wife-mother is able to achieve a similar sense of indispensability in contemporary role-diffused social patterns. Modern technology has largely robbed the traditional housekeeping chores of their soul-satisfying craftsmanship. Today's housewife is no longer satisfied in this role. In addition to the possible "joys of gardening, fresh sheets and draperies," she must seek elsewhere for creative outlets. This is not to denigrate homemaking and child rearing. These are important functions, for both men and women. It is to point out that homemaking alone does not satisfy, and that a frustrated and dissatisfied woman makes a poor mother. It is also to insist that since human fulfillment apparently is not achievable through domestic channels alone, the never-married woman may very well be able to achieve it through other channels entirely.

In his systematic formulation of human development, Erik Erikson raises an issue which directly impinges on this consideration. In his scheme each of the "eight ages of man" has its unique and distinctive developmental tasks and is characterized by continual change in personality structure and fulfillment.

The major task of the sixth stage (young adulthood), he says, is to achieve a "sense of intimacy," to share with others or another in a deep affectional relationship that "identity" which was accomplished in the previous stage, to fuse self-identity with that of others. This task is accomplished, Erikson writes,

. . . in the solidarity of close affiliations, in sexual unions and orgasms, in close friendships and in physical combat, in experiences of inspiration by teachers and of intuition from the recesses of the self. The avoidance of such experiences because of a fear of ego loss may lead to a deep sense of isolation and consequent self-absorption.[15]

Many people, past and present, believe that the loss of sexual intimacy inevitably dooms the never-married to some degree of psychic frustration. The biologic elements in Erikson's list of fusing opportunities, the "sexual unions and orgasms," it is claimed, are eliminated only at the expense of complete fulfillment. On the other hand, the majority of single women in the writer's study previously discussed have apparently passed through this stage successfully, most of them without the benefit of sexual union.

There is wisdom in the old maxim, "to live is to love, not to love is not to live." Commonly love is defined as heterosexual involvement, the "solidarity of close affiliation" between a man and a woman. But the women in the study have not had a man. Have they therefore failed to love?

This question was put to the never-married women, who were interviewed privately. If to live is to love, and these bear every mark of living, with what or whom is their loving? It became apparent that love may have many partners. Family, friends, work with people, all have provided reciprocal relationships of intimacy. Close affiliation with persons, inspiration in connection with work or some soul-satisfying endeavor, and the sense of belonging which comes from participating with others in some significant and meaningful enterprise, these have provided opportunity for self-abandonment and a fusion of identity with others which has produced Erikson's "intimacy" without the "sexual union" popularly considered essential.

This point of view is supported by the analysis of love provided by Erich Fromm.[16] "Love is not primarily a relationship to a specific person," he writes, "it is an attitude or orientation of character which determines the relatedness of a person to the world as a whole, not toward an 'object' of love." Love is giving, not getting, a dedication to the well-being of another, or others, and as such may have many outlets, many objects. In fact, according to Fromm's view, unless and until one has learned to love, has become a loving person, has found numerous "objects" for his love, he remains incapable of entering into a loving relationship with one person. "Unless erotic love is also brotherly love, it never leads to union in more than an orgiastic, transitory sense."

Far from being essential to love, to "intimacy," sexual union may be a hindrance to its accomplishment if it be mistaken for the "real thing." "Sexual attraction creates for the moment the illusion of union, yet without love this 'union' leaves strangers as far apart as they were before."

It cannot be denied that sexual union between two persons who have established a truly loving relationship may indeed strengthen their fusion and deepen their sense of intimacy. For some persons this is one of the most satisfying forms of intimacy. It must also be recognized that some people, denied this common experience of humanity, may nevertheless find other satisfying forms of intimacy which will enable them to live happy and productive lives. It is gratuitous indeed to insist that the spinster, because she can never experience the normal conjugal function, is destined to remain a frustrated and unfulfilled "old maid."

Erikson's discussion of the "seventh age of man" seems to challenge an assertion previously made. The basic task of this age is "generativity," and refers to the process of establishing and guiding the next generation. Children, he claims, are required for one's complete fulfillment as a human being. Dorothy Fisher once remarked that the majority of human beings would be unbearable if they had no children to bring them up! As Erikson expresses it, "Mature man needs to be needed, and maturity needs guidance as well as encouragement from what has been produced and must be taken care of." He is referring here not to the fruit of man's spiritual labor, but of his biological seed, which is, for a woman, the "fruit of the womb." "The concept of generativity is meant to include such more popular synonyms as productivity and creativity, which however, *cannot replace it.*"[17] (Author's emphasis.)

This would seem to preclude the unmarried woman from passing through this stage of development. But our investigation has produced women whose "womb has been barren and whose paps have never given suck," who yet exhibit all those characteristics of personality by which we judge a "whole person." Moreover, one can think of people, married and with children to bring them up, who yet remain unbearable! If generativity is biological, why is it not accomplished automatically by those who exercise this function? "The mere fact of having or wanting children," Erikson admits, "does not achieve generativity. In fact, some young parents suffer, it seems, from retardation of the ability to develop this stage."[18]

What, then, makes the difference? Careful consideration suggests that in order for children to facilitate the parent's continuing development as a mature human being, the parent must bring to that situation a personality capable of accepting the responsibilities that go with creativity, the care and concern, often anxiety, that accompany parenthood, and the willingness to "lose one's self" in the creation and development of a small part of on-going humanity.

It is not having children that makes the difference, but the quality of personality which is brought to the task of parenthood. We must now ask if this quality of personality might not find other objects of responsibility and concern than children. As "intimacy" for a woman may be accomplished in other relationships than sexual, so generativity may surely be experienced in giving one's self in creativity and productivity which is not necessarily biological.

The traditional opinion that women can find satisfaction and fulfillment only through marriage and motherhood is supported neither in theory nor in fact. The persisting stereotypes are perpetuated partly by observation of single women who seem to fit them, who are driven by neurotic needs stemming from some early lack in personal development. There are, of course, neurotic women among the unmarried. And the same may be said equally of the married. There is ample evidence that personality adjustment and marital status are not related.

Clearly, current popular attitudes about the single woman need to be revised. Contrary to common opinion, some women remain unmarried not because of a "peculiar personality," but out of choice or lack of adequate opportunity. Nor does the continuing single condition necessarily deny a woman adequate satisfaction and fulfillment in life. Granted full acceptance by her society and provided with opportunities of creative social service, a never-married woman may be just as "whole" and "wholesome" as anyone else.

The majority of women do marry, and most probably will continue to do so. For many women marriage surely provides the most meaningful and significant relationship, and education for creative marriage and family living must continue. However, it must also be recognized that some persons are destined to remain unmarried and that this fate need not be considered "doom."

There is no way of knowing how many great persons have "died aborning" and how much creative contribution society has lost by its subtle insistence that everyone must marry. A clue to such loss may be seen in the dearth of truly accomplished women in any of the arts or sciences. Few great composers, orchestra conductors, or painters are female; no woman is in the upper echelons of the space program. Even the traditionally female occupations list men in the top spots, at the creative level. The chefs, the creative clothes designers, even the outstanding hair stylists are usually male.

Surely this state of affairs is not the consequence of an innate lack of ability in women. In spite of those who would like to believe it, enough evidence is available to show it isn't so. The explanation lies in a lack of incentive, opportunity, and the fact that the most productive years of a woman's life are confined to a limited and uncreative sphere of activity. Agnes De Mille points to an inconsistency between the overt and the covert expectations confronting young women.

> It matters not a whit how you educate a girl, what techniques or attitudes you teach her. If she knows that her man will not welcome her talents she is going to proceed timidly. Put any gifted child at the keyboard, train her, exhort her six hours a day, but let it be borne in upon her that in recorded music there never has been a first-rate woman composer and that no man will consider her work without condescension, and worst of all, that within herself she may provide conflicts that she cannot hope to surmount, and you may get results, but they won't be Beethoven.[19]

It is true that a few women have risen to creative heights, but these are the exceptions. They have somehow escaped the pressures of personal limitation and proceeded to develop and use all their creative powers as though it were perfectly legitimate to do so. The majority, however, have not escaped. Whether married or not, they have been trapped in the domestic box society sets for the female, and she sees herself as unfit for the world's real work and incapable of significant creativity.

There need be no fear of a decline in the population upon establishing the position that it is acceptable for a woman not to marry and bear children. Enough will marry to insure the survival of the race, and it is proper that they should. Marriage and motherhood can be most rewarding, and those performing these roles should do so joyously and with devotion. But a joyous devotion should also characterize the spirit of those few who by choice or by chance remain unmarried and who dedicate themselves to some other form of creative endeavor. This is often impossible, however, because of the social stigma attached to the unmarried and because without a man women are limited in social acceptance.

In 1961 there were 12,764,000 single women fourteen years of age and older in the United States. Statistical trends suggest that one in seven of today's girls will never marry, and while this obviously constitutes a minority, it is the kind and size of minority which cannot be overlooked, and which for the sake of society as a whole and the individuals who comprise it, must be integrated in creative ways into the fabric of social life.

The never-married woman, because of her greater personal freedom, possesses the possibility of making a significant contribution to her society and can add strength and stability to the whole. The opportunity of performing such a function must be based on a far greater acknowledgment of the acceptability of remaining unmarried, and on the ready inclusion of the single woman into social life as an individual in her own right. Marian Sheldon, Dean of Women at the University of Illinois and herself a single woman, recently lamented, "Must society always balance the numbers, and hostesses invite guests in the manner of Noah's Ark, 'and the animals came in two by two, the elephant and the kangaroo'?"

When once we lay to rest the absurd notion that only in pairs are people persons, then the unmarried woman, having achieved such personhood without marriage, will be freed from the restraints that inhibit her productive efforts on behalf of all mankind.

## Notes to Chapter 10

1. Genesis 2:7, 18, 21-22 (RSV).
2. Queen, Stuart, et al. The Family in Various Cultures. Chicago: Lippincott, 1961, p. 1.
3. Beard, Mary. Woman as a Force in History. New York: Macmillan, 1946, p. 143.
4. Hunt, Morton. The Natural History of Love. New York: Knopf, 1959, p. 177.
5. Milton, John. Paradise Lost. New York: Columbia University Press, 1931, Book IV, 295-299, 634-638.
6. Nadler, Eugene B. and William R. Morrow. "Authoritarian Attitudes Toward Women and Their Correlates." Journal of Social Psychology. 49:113-123. 1959.
7. Baker, Luther G., Jr. "Changing Religious Norms and Family Values." Journal of Marriage and the Family. 27:6-12. 1965.
8. McGinley, Phyllis. "The Honor of Being a Woman." Readers Digest. 75:63-66. December, 1959.
9. Pellegrini, Frances. "I'm so Glad to be a Woman." Ladies Home Journal. 77:63. February, 1960.
10. Gallup, George and Evan Hill. "The American Woman." Saturday Evening Post. 235:15-32. December 22, 1962.
11. Mead, Margaret. "The Secret of Completeness." Good Housekeeping. 150:72. May, 1960.
12. Rosenteur, Phyllis. The Single Women. New York: Popular Library, 1961.

# 11. *Is Monogamy Outdated?*

## RUSTUM AND DELLA ROY

### *Monogamy: Where We Stand Today*

The total institution of marriage in American society is gravely ill. This statement does not apply to the millions of sound marriages where two people have found companionship, love, concern, and have brought up children in love. But it is necessary in 1970 to point to the need for *institutional* reforms, even when the personal or immediate environment may not (appear to) need it. Yet many refuse to think about the area as a whole because of personal involvement—either their marriage is so successful that they think the claims of disease exaggerated, or theirs is so shaky that all advice is a threat. Is the institution then so sick? For example:

Year after year in the United States, marriage has been discussed in public and private session with undiminished confusion and increasing pessimism. Calamity always attracts attention, and in the United States the state of marriage is a calamity.

These are the words with which W. H. Lederer and D. Jackson open their new book *The Mirages of Marriage.* Vance Packard in *The Sexual Wilderness* summarizes the most recent major survey thus: "In other words, a marriage made in the United States in the late 1960's has about a 50:50 chance of remaining even nominally intact."

131

Clifford Adams concludes from an Identity Research Institute study of 600 couples that while numerically at 40 per cent in this nation, and in some West Coast highly-populated counties the *real* divorce rate is running at 70 per cent, that in fact "75 per cent of marriages are a 'bust.'" And Lederer and Jackson report that 80 per cent of those interviewed had at some time seriously considered divorce. So much for the statistics. Qualitatively the picture painted by these and 100 others is even bleaker but needs no repeating here.

There is no doubt then about the diagnosis of the sickness of marriage taken as a whole. Yet no person, group, magazine, or newspaper creates an awareness of the problems; no activist band takes up the cause to *do* something about it. Some years ago, we participated in a three-year-long group study and development of a sex ethic for contemporary Americans, and we found this same phenomenon: that serious group study and group work for change in the area of sex behavior is remarkably difficult and threatening, and hence rare. Thus, we find an institution such as monogamous marriage enveloped by deterioration and decay, and unbelievably little is being done about it on either a theoretical basis or detailed pragmatic basis.

For this there is a second major reason: marriage as an institution is partly governed by warring churches, a society without a soul, a legal system designed for lawyers, and a helping system for psychiatrists who almost by their very mode of operation in the marriage field guarantee its failure. Consequently, marriage is rapidly losing its schizophrenic mind, oscillating between tyrannical repression and equally tyrannical expression.

By the term "traditional monogamy," we refer to the public's association with the word, i.e., marriage to one person at a time, the centrality of the nuclear family and the restriction of all overt sexual acts, nearly all sexually-tinged relationships and heterosexual relations of any depth to this one person before and after marriage, expectation of a lifetime contract and a vivid sense of failure if termination is necessary. John Cuber and Peggy Harroff in *The Significant Americans* have called this "the monolithic code," and it is based on precepts from the Judaic and Christian traditions. All working societies are structured around such codes or ideals, no matter how far individuals may depart from the norms and whether or not they accept the source of such "ideals."

How does change in a code or ideal come about? When the proportion of the populace living in conflict with their own interpretation of the monolithic code, and "getting away with it," reaches nearly a majority, then *new* ideals must evolve for the social system to remain in equilibrium. We are convinced that although no *discontinuous* change in the ideals of a culture is possible, "traditional monogamy" as an ideal may be altered *in a continuous fashion* in order to respond to the needs of men and women today.

Traditional monogamy was *one* interpretation of the Judaeo-Christian tradition. We are convinced that for widespread acceptability any *new* ideals must be interpretable in terms of Judaeo-Christian humanism, the basic framework of mainstream "Americanism," and the most explicit humanism so far developed. Such an interpretation is neither difficult nor likely to encounter much resistance from the many other contemporary American humanisms which have not swung far from the parent Protestant humanism. But the importance of such an interpretation for "continental" middle-class America is crucial, as the tenor and very existence of the Nixon administration bring home to those who live in the more rarified climes of East or West Coast. If a new monogamous ideal is to evolve, it must be acceptable to middle America, liberated, affluent, but waspish at heart.

## Causes of the Crisis

Social institutions are the products of particular social environments, and there must be a finite time lag when an institution appropriate for one situation survives into a new era in which the situation has changed drastically. It is clear that "traditional monogamy" is caught precisely in this "overlap" of two radically different situations. It is important to identify precisely the particular problem-causing elements of change in the environment.

The sexual revolution has made it infinitely more difficult to retain monogamy's monopoly on sex.

We live in an eroticized environment which is profoundly

affecting many institutions. The change towards greater permissiveness and its effect on the sexual climate can be summed up in the aphorism, "What was a temptation for the last generation is an opportunity for this." Underneath it all are the measurable, real physical changes: the advent of prosperity, mobility, and completely controlled conception.

Parallel to physical changes are vast social changes. The eroticization of our culture oozes from its every pore, so much so that it becomes essentially absurd to expect that all physical sexual expression for a 50-year period will be confined to the marriage partner. Moreover, this eroticization escalator shows no sign of slowing down, and its effect on various institutions will be even more drastic in the future. Following are some illustrations.

The influence of the literature, the arts, the media, and the press on the climate for any institution is profound, and marriage is no exception. Caught between the jaws of consumer economics in a free-enterprise system and the allegedly objective purveyors of accurate information (or culturally representative entertainment), human sexuality has become the most salable commodity of all. Perform, if you will, the following simple tests: examine the magazine fare available to tens of millions of Americans; spend a few hours browsing through *Look,* and *Life,* and try *Playboy,* work up to something like *Cosmopolitan.* If you are serious, visit a typical downtown book shop in a big city and count the number of pictorial publications whose sole purpose is sexual titillation. Next try the paperbacks available to at least 100,000,000 Americans—in every drugstore: *Candy,* Henry Miller, *Fanny Hill,* the complaining Portnoy, valleys of dolls, and menchild in promised lands, carpetbaggers at airports, couples and groups. Does *one* speak of the beauty and wonder of uniting sex to marriage? Go see 10 movies at random. Will *The Graduate, I Am Curious,* or *La Ronde* rail against sexual license? Thus the mass media have had a profound effect on the American people's marriage ideals. They especially confuse those to whom their "traditions" speaking through emasculated school, bewildered Church, and confused home still try to affirm a traditionally monogamous system. Yet some have mistakenly denied that there is a causal relation between the media and our rapidly changing value systems. Worst of all, very few of those who urge the freedom of access to more and more sexual stimuli work to legitimize, socially and ethically, a scheme for increased sexual outlets.

There is a vast increase in the number and variety of men-women contacts after marriage, and no guidelines are available for behavior in these new situations.

Of the sexual dilemmas which our present-day culture forces upon the "ailing" institution of traditional monogamy, premarital sexual questions now appear very minor. For all intents and purposes premarital sexual play (including the *possibility* of intercourse) has been absorbed into the social canon. We foresee in the immediate future a much more serious psychological quandary with respect to extra- or co-marital sexual relations of all levels of intensity. The conflict here is so basic and so little is being done to alleviate it, that it is only surprising that it has not loomed larger already. Traditional monogamy as practiced has meant not only one spouse and sex partner at a time but essentially only one heterosexual *relationship,* of any depth at all, at a time. We have shown above that our environment suggests through various media the desirability of nonmarital sex. Further, our culture is now abundant in opportunity: time, travel, meetings, committees, causes, and group encounters of every stripe bringing men and women together in all kinds of relationship-producing situations. Our age is characterized by not only the opportunity but by the necessity for simultaneous multiple-relationships. One of the most widely experienced examples is that chosen by Cuber and Harroff in their study of the sex lives of some "leaders" of our society. They noted the obviously close relationship of such men with their secretaries with whom they work for several hours a day. But the same opportunity now occurs to millions of middle-class housewives returning to work after children are grown. They too are establishing new heterosexual friendships and being treated as separate individuals (not to mention as sex-objects) after 10 or 15 years.

Traditional monogamy is in trouble because it has not adjusted itself to find a less hurtful way to terminate a marriage.

From the viewpoint of any philosophy that puts a high value on response to human need and the alleviation of human suffering the mechanisms available for terminating marriage are utterly unacceptable. Traditional monogamy involves a lifetime commitment. Anything that would necessitate termination short of this must, therefore, be a major failure. "Divorce, American Style" demands so much hurt and pain and devastation of personalities that it is imperative that we attempt to temper the hurt caused to human beings. We must take as inescapable fact that about half of all the marriages now existing will, and probably should, be terminated. The question is how best this can be done to minimize total human suffering, while avoiding the pitfall that the relief of immediate pain of one or two persons is the greatest and single good. Full consideration must always be given to all the "significant others"—children, parents, friends—and to the long-range effects on society. The institution of traditionl monogamy will increasingly come under attack while it is unable to provide a better means to terminate a contract than those now in use.

Traditional monogamy does not deal humanely with its have-nots —the adult singles, the widowed, the divorced.

Statistically speaking we in America have more involuntarily single persons above age 25 or 30 than those who had no choice about a disadvantageous color for their skin. The latter have had to bear enormous legal and social affronts and suffered the subtler and possibly more debilitating psychological climate of being unacceptable in much of their natural surroundings. But this disability they share with voiceless single persons in a marriage-oriented society. Our society proclaims monogamy's virtue at every point of law and custom and practice, as much as it says white is right. Biases, from income tax to adoption requirements, subtle advertisements, and Emily Post etiquette all point to the "traditional monogamist" as the acceptable form of society. Unbelievably, this barrage goes on unopposed in the face of some tens of millions of persons outside the blessed estate. Monogamy decrees that the price of admission into the complex network of supportive relationships of society is a wedding band. Yet it turns a blind eye to the inexorable statistical fact that of those women who are single at 35 only 1/3, at 45 only 1/10, AND at 50 only 1/20 will *ever* find that price. In access to regular physical sexual satisfaction a basic human right on a plane with freedom or shelter or right to worship? For effective living in our world every human being needs individuals as close friends and a community of which he or she is a part. Traditionally, monogamous society has ruled, *ipso facto,* that tens of millions of its members shall have no societally approved way of obtaining sexual satisfaction. Much worse, because sexual intimacy is potentially associated with all heterosexual relationships of any depth, they must also be denied such relationships.

Here, surely, every humanist must protest. For it is *his* social ideal—that the greatest good of human existence is deep interpersonal relationships and as many of these as is compatible with depth—that is contravened by traditional monogamy's practice. Moreover, there is less provision today for single women to develop fulfilling relationships than there was a generation or two ago. The "larger-family" then incorporated these losers in the marital stakes into at least a minimal framework of acceptance and responsibility.

## A Theory for Change

Any vision of a better future for society presupposes, consciously or unconsciously, a value system and basic assumptions about the nature of man. A theory of man and life must precede a theory of monogamy. Our view of the nature of man is the Judaeo-Christian one. Man was meant to live *in community.* The normative ideal for every man is that he live fully known, accepted, and loved by a community of significant others. In this environment his individual creativity and his creative individuality will be realized to the maximum extent, and he can serve society best.

### MAN—COMMUNITY—SOCIETY

In this spectrum we have, as yet, not even mentioned marriage and intentionally so. There is a crucially important hierarchy of values, in which the individual's needs and the community's good are vastly more important than the "laws" or preferred patterns of marital behavior. Indeed, these "laws" must be tested empirically by the criterion of how well they have been found to meet the individual-community-society needs most effectively. It is important to see that the humanist is not committed, prima facie, to *any* particular pattern of men-women relationships.

Marriage, monogamous or polygamous, fits somewhere between the individual and community levels of social organization. Unfortunately, in many cultures the institution of marriage and the stress on the family has generally militated against, and sometimes destroyed, the community level of relationship.

This has not always been so—not even in America. The "larger family" of maiden aunts and uncles and grandparents, and occasional waifs and strays, has been a part of many cultures including that of the rigidly structured joint-family system in India and the plantation system of the American South. Tribal cultures abound. In the Swiss canton or settled New England town the sinews of community are strong enough to make them fall in between the extremes represented above and lying, perhaps, closer to the former. There is an inverse correlation between the complexity of a highly-developed society and the strength of community channels and bonds. It is in the technology-ruled society where we find men and women turning to the intimacy of marriage to shield them from further impersonalization when the second level of defense—the community level—has disintegrated through neglect. But monogamous marriage is altogether too frail an institution to carry that load also. A typical marriage is built frequently of brittle and weak members held together by a glue of tradition rapidly deteriorating under the onslaught of a half-dozen corroding acids—mobility, prosperity, permissiveness, completely controlled conception, and continuously escalating eroticization.

There is no question that the first and essential step in the evolution of monogamy is the recovery of the role of community in our lives. It appears to us, however strange a conclusion it seems, that precisely because our world has become so complex, depersonalization is an essential, ineradicable fact of our lives in the many public spheres. This requires then a radical restructuring of the private sphere to provide the supports we have found missing in the "traditional-monogamy" pattern. To know and accept ourselves deeply we need to be known and accepted. And most of us are many-sided polyhedra needing several people to reflect back to ourselves the different portions of our personality. With changing years and training and jobs this need grows instead of diminishing. Thus, it comes about that the humanist has a great deal to contribute to his fellows.

Our proposed modification of monogamy, then, has the re-emphasis of community as one of its primary goals. This is hardly novel, but it has been the conclusion of every group of radical Christian humanists trying to reform society for hundreds of years. And it was the New World which provided for them a unique opportunity to attempt the radical solutions. Hence, we have dotted across America the record and/or the remnants of hundreds of experiments in radical community living.

Today we believe that society's hope lies in working at both ends of the game—the basic research and the development. We need to become much more active in optimizing or improving present marriage in an imperfect society: changing laws, improving training, providing better recovery systems, etc. But alongside of that, we need to continue genuine research in radically new patterns of marriage. This can only be carried out by groups or communities. Further, we need not only those groups that seek solutions withdrawn from the day-to-day world, but those that are willing to devise potential solutions which can serve as models, for its eventual reform within the bourgeois urban culture.

### Basic Research in Marriage Patterns

We cannot here do justice to a discussion of possible models for radical new patterns of marriage-in-community. Instead, we wish only to emphasize the importance of such experimentation and its neglect, in our supposedly research-oriented culture, by serious groups concerned for society. It is hardly a coincidence that the yearning for community should figure so prominently in all utopian schemes for remaking society. The contemporary resurgence is described in B. F. Skinner's *Walden Two* or Erich Fromm's *Revolution of Hope* and Robert Rimmer's *Harrad Experiment*. It is being attempted in groping unformed ways in the "hippie" or other city-living communes, and is being lived out in amazingly fruitful (yet unpublicized) models in the Bruderhof communities in the United States and Europe, and the Ecumenical Institute in Chicago. And in rereading the details of the organization of the hundreds of religious communities we find that they have an enormous amount to teach us, on many subjects from psychotherapy to patterns for sexual intercourse.

Probably the most important lesson for contemporary America, however, is that communities survive and thrive and provide a creative framework for realizing the human potential if their central purpose is outside themselves and their own existence. The second lesson is one taught by the complex technology: wherever many persons are involved, *some* discipline and order are absolutely essential.

Were it not for the sheer prejudice introduced by a misreading of Judeao-Christian tradition, and its bolstering by the unholy alliance of state-and-church Establishment, we may well have learned to separate potential from pitfall in various patterns of communal living. The Mormon experience with polygamy is not without its value for us, and Bettelheim has helped shake the prejudice against nonparent child rearing drawing on data from the kibbutzim. Rimmer, perhaps, through his novels *The Rebellion of Yale Marratt* and *Proposition 31,* has reached the widest audience in his crusade for a variety of new marital patterns. He has dealt sensitively, and in depth, with the subtle questions of ongoing sexual relations with more than one partner—the threat of which is perhaps the most difficult taboo against communal life for most educated Americans. From some dozens of histories in personal and "marathon" encounter situations, we believe that Rimmer's portrayal of typical reactions is remarkably accurate. Most middle-class, educated Americans above 35 have been so schooled into both exclusivity and possessiveness that no more than perhaps 10 per cent could make the transition into any kind of structured nonexclusivity in marriage. But for the younger group, especially those now in college, the potential for attempting the highly demanding, idealistic, disciplined group living of some sort is both great, and a great challenge. It is here perhaps by setting up contemporary-style communities of concern and responsibility that young humanists can make one of their greatest contributions to society at large.

### Modifying Traditional Monogamy

No company survives on its fundamental research laboratory alone, although many cannot survive long without one. Each needs also a development group that keeps making the minor changes to its existing products in order to eliminate defects in design and to meet the competition or the change in customer needs. So too with marriage. While "far-out" re-search *must* proceed on new patterns, we must simultaneously be concerned with the changes that can modify traditional monogamy to meet its present customer-needs much more effectively—that is to say humanely.

Our society is pluralist in many of its ideals. The first and most important change in society's view of marriage must also be the acceptance of the validity of a range of patterns of behavior. The education of our children and of society must point to ways and points at which, *depending on the situation,* it is right and proper to make this or that change. Indeed, we can doubtless describe the era we are entering as one of "situa-tional monogamy"—that is traditional monogamy can still be upheld as the ideal in many circumstances, but, in specific situations, modifications are not only permitted but required.

### INSTITUTIONALIZING PREMARITAL SEX

Premarital sexual experience is now rather widely ac-cepted, covertly if not overtly, throughout our society. Espe-cially when we use the word "experience" instead of "inter-course," the studies from Kinsey to Packard support a very substantial increase in necking and petting including petting to orgasm. The new rise in "keeping-house-together" arrange-ments in college and beyond is spreading like wildfire. We see an opportunity here for a simple evolution of the monogamous ideal within relatively easy reach. Almost all analysts believe that postponing marriage by two or three years and making it more difficult—with some required period of waiting or even waiting and instruction—would be very beneficial. Tra-ditional marriage in its classical form enjoined a "decent" (six months to two years) engagement period partly for the same reason. One of the main drives toward early marriage is that there is no other way to obtain regular sexual gratification in a publicly acceptable manner. By one simple swish of tradi-tion, we can incorporate all the recent suggestions for trial marriages, "baby" marriages, etc., and cover them all under the decent rug of the "engagement." Engagements with a minor difference: that in today's society they entitle a couple to live together if they desire, and sleep together—*but not to have children*. Thus, engagement would become the first step that entitles one to legal sex—publicly known sex with contraceptive devices. By no means need this become the universal norm. Pluralism of marital patterns should start here, however. Many parents and various social groups may still urge their members to restrict engagements to a noncoital or nonsexual level of intimacy; but even here they would do well to legitimize some advanced level of sexual activity and by so doing they would probably protect their marriage-institution more effectively. Our very spotty feedback from student groups would suggest that "everything-but-coitus"—which is a lot more sex than the last generation's "little-but-coitus"—has some value as a premarital maxim. The humanist must also affirm that quintessential humanness is choice against one's immediate desires. He must point to the loss by this generation of perhaps the most exquisite sexual pleasures when it comes as the culmination of long-deferred desire of the loved one. We mourn the loss of Eros in a day when Venus comes so quickly, for it is Eros, who is human, while Venus reminds us that we are *human* animals. Well may we paraphrase the Frenchman and say: "In America we tend to eat the fruit of coital sex, green."

Along with the engagement-including-sex concept could be introduced the idea of "training" for marriage. Everyone falls for the training gimmick. Driver education, often taken after three years of driving, is still useful, and is induced by the lowered insurance rates. Similarly if society required a "marriage-education" course before granting a license, another important step in improving the quality of marriage would have been achieved.

### EXPANDING THE EROTIC COMMUNITY IN THE POST-MARITAL YEARS.

With the engagement-including-sex, we have broken the premarital half of monogamy's monopoly on sex. It is our judgment that for the health of the institution it will become necessary in America in the next decade to break the second half also—post marital sexual expression. (Recall that our theory demands that we seek to maximize the number of deep relationships and to develop marriages to fit in with a framework of community.) To do this we are certain that the monopolistic tendencies of relationships must be broken, and hence the question of sexual relations cannot be bypassed. We believe that in the coming generation a spectrum of sexual expression with persons other than the spouse are certain to occur for at least the large majority, and possibly most persons. If monogamy is tied inextricably with post-marital restriction of all sexual expression to the spouse, it will ultimately be monogamy which suffers. Instead, monogamy should be tied to the much more basic concepts of fidelity, honesty, and openness, which are concomitants of love of the spouse, but which do not necessarily exclude deep relationships and possibly including various degrees of sexual intimacy with others. In the studies and counseling experience of many, including ourselves, there is no evidence that all extra-marital sexual experience is destructive of the marriage. Indeed, more and more persons testify that creative co-marital relationships and sexual experience can and do exist. But most persons need guidelines to help steer them from the dangerous to the potentially creative *relationships*, and to provide help on the appropriateness of various sexual expressions for various relationships. A few practices are crucial:

*Openness:* Contrary to folklore, frank and honest discussions at *every stage* of a developing relationship between all parties is the best guarantee against trouble. We know of husbands who have discussed with their wives possible coitus with a third person, some to conclude it would be wrong, others, unwise; others to drop earlier objections, and still others to say it was necessary and beautiful. We know of wives to say it was necessary and beautiful. We know of wives who have said a reasoned "no" to such possibilities for their husbands and kept their love and respect; and many who have said "yes" in uncertainty and have found the pain subside. Openness is not impossible.
*Other-centeredness:* Concern for *all* the others—the other woman or man, the other husband or wife, the children—must be front and center in reaching decisions on any such matters.
*Proportionality:* Sexual expressions should be proportional to the depth of a relationship. This leads, of course, to the conclusion that most coitus and other intimate expressions should only occur with very close friends: a conclusion questioned by many, but essential for our theory.
*Gradualism:* Only a stepwise escalation of intimacy allows for the open discussion referred to above. Otherwise such openness becomes only a series of confessions.

It is important to discover the value of self-denial and restraint. It is incumbent on them to demonstrate, while accepting other patterns, their ability to maintain loving, warm relationships with both single and married persons of the opposite sex and of limiting the sexual expression therein in order, for example, to conserve psychic energy for other causes.

### PROVIDING A RELATIONSHIP NETWORK FOR THE SINGLE.

It is principally because of the fear of sexual involvement that the single are excluded from married-society. In the new dispensation, a much more active and aggressive policy should be encouraged to incorporate single persons within the total life of a family and a community. She or he should be a part of the family, always invited—but not always coming—to dinner, theaters, and vacations. The single person should feel free enough to make demands and accept responsibility as an additional family member would. The single woman, thus loved and accepted by two or three families, may find herself perhaps not sleeping with any of the husbands but vastly more fulfilled as a woman. No couple should enter such relationships unless the marriage is secure and the sexual monopoly not crucially important: yet all concerned couples should be caused to wonder about their values if their fear of sexual involvement keeps them from ministering to such obvious need. The guidelines for decisions, of course, are the same as those above. We know of several such relationships, many but not all involving complete sexual intimacy that have been most important in the lives of the single persons. Recently, we have observed that our present society makes it very difficult for even the best of these relationships to continue for a lifetime. And we see the need for developing acceptable patterns for altering such relationships creatively after the two-to-five-year period which often brings about sufficient changes to suggest reappraisal in any case. The dependent woman often becomes confident and no longer needs the same kind of support: the independent one becomes too attached and becomes possessive enough to want exclusivity. The mechanisms we discuss under divorce should no doubt operate here as well.

### LEGALIZING BIGAMY

It may appear as a paradox, but in keeping with the theory above and the pluralist trend of society, it is almost certainly true that contemporary-style monogamy would be greatly strengthened if bigamy (perhaps polygamy-polyandry) were legalized. This would provide a *partial* solution to the problems dealt with in the last two sections; moreover, it would do it in a way that is least disturbing to the monogamous tenor of society. The entire style—contract and living arrangements of most persons—would be unaffected if one woman in 20 had two husbands in the house; or one man in 10 had two wives— sometimes in different cities and frequently in different houses. There is a substantial unthinking emotional resistance to legalizing bigamy based partly on a supposed, but incorrect, backing from Christian doctrine. There is, however, no Biblical injunction sanctifying monogamy: the Christian humanist is not only free to, but may be required to, call for other patterns. Indeed, after World War II the Finnish Church is reported to have been on the verge of legalizing bigamy, when the great disparity in women:men ratio, which stimulated the inquiry, was found to have improved beyond their expectations.

In the next decade, this ratio is expected to get as high as 7:5 in this country, and it is higher in the highest age brackets. Various gerontologists have suggested the legalization of bigamy for the aged, and the capacity for social change in our society is so weak that perhaps bigamy will have to be legalized first under Medicare! It is indeed difficult to see why bigamy should not be legalized, once the doctrinal smokescreen were to be exposed for what it is.

MAKING DIFFICULTIES AND DIVORCE LESS
DESTRUCTIVE OF PERSONALITIES.

A reform of the total system of marriage *must* provide for a much less destructive method for terminating one. The first change required in our present ideal is to recognize that a good divorce can be better than a poor marriage. We can continue to affirm the importance of the intention of the lifelong commitment, but we must begin to stress the quality of the commitment and the actual relationship as a higher good than mere longevity. Early detection of trouble makes repair easier and surgery less likely. If we take our automobiles to be inspected twice a year to be safe on the highways, is it too much to expect that the complex machinery of a marriage could be sympathetically "inspected" periodically to keep it in the best working condition? Here the church and the university can help by showing the need for, and providing such "inspections." Conceivably a biennial or triennial marriage-marathon or weeklong retreat utilizing the newest insights of encounter groups could be made normative for all marriages. Such check-ups would in some cases catch the cancer early enough, and in others indicate the need for surgery. In any case, a failing marriage needs to be treated by a person or persons who are neutral on the value of divorce itself, committed to the goal of maximizing human potential, and not determined to preserve marriage for its own sake. We believe that a team of a marriage counselor and, where appropriate, younger clergymen or another couple who are close friends can, over a period of several months, help the husband and wife arrive at a wise decision most effectively. The use of a fixed-length trial period for either separation or continuance, after specific changes, with an agreed-upon evaluation at the end of the period has proved its real value in all the cases where we have seen it used. Our own experience has been that many of the worst situations are avoided if the couple can keep channels open to their closest friends—always working with them together. Two helpful changes need to occur here. First, it should be made much more acceptable to talk openly and seriously about marital tensions with close friends; and second, we should all learn the principle of never giving any personal information about absent *third* parties except when we think it can specifically do some positive good.

For ordinary divorce, it is difficult to see what the professional psychiatrist or lawyer-as-adviser can contribute; indeed it appears axiomatic that with traditional Freudian psychiatry there can be no compromise—it is simply incompatible with the rational approaches to helping even irrational persons. In most instances, its result is the introduction of wholly unnecessary polarization (instead of a reconciling attitude, even while separating) between two persons who were the most important in the world to each other. This we find tends to undercut the faith that such persons can ever have in any other person or cause. The price of so-called self-understanding is the mild cynicism which extinguishes the fire of the unlimited liability of love and drains the warmth and color from two the tragedy in the kind of situation when John married to Mary has become deeply attached to Alice. But this tragedy need not be compounded by bitterness, anger, and self-justification in the name of helping. We do know of couples lives. Neither paid psychiatrist nor loving friend can avoid divorcing and parting as friends: persons who *love* each other to the best of their ability and yet, after sober agonizing months of consideration, decide to separate. We know that that is the way it must happen in the future.

CONSERVING IDEALS: CHANGING THE MARRIAGE SERVICE.

Because our psychological conditioning is affected, even by every minor input, we can help preserve the monogamous *ideal* by bringing in honesty at the high points in its symbol-life. This would mean, for instance, minor alteration of the traditional-marriage service, and not necessarily to "water-down" its commitments. Thus, everyone recognizes the value of a lifelong commitment. But to what should that commitment be? To preserving a marriage when we know that half will fail and make all involved guilty over it? Why not, rather, a lifelong commitment to loving and speaking the truth in love? One can be true to this even if separation occurs. Why should not the marriage service make the closest friends— best man, maid of honor, etc., who have essentially trivial roles in the ceremony—take on a real commitment to become the loving community for the couple, covenanting to communicate regularly, stand by them always, but also to speak admonition in love whenever they see it needed. Even such a small beginning would symbolize the fact that each couple enters not only into a marriage but also into a much-needed community.

### Disease Diagnosed, Prognosis: Poor

The rebellion of the young reflects only intuitively their alienation from a science-technology dominated world which they have not the discipline to understand. The need for new and revitalized institutions that would provide every kind of support to individuals could not be greater. Inexorable logic points to the centrality of community in any such attempts. Yet no American, indeed Western, sociologist or psychologist of any stature (always excepting Skinner) has paid any serious attention to their structuring. We attribute this largely to their ignorance of the primitive Christian roots of their own heritage, and see in it the great loss to contemporary humanism of the insight and *experimental data* from these bold humanist experimenters of the last century. However, it is unlikely that in the permissive society it will be possible to demand the minimum discipline required for a community to cohere. What changes can we really hope for on the basis of present observations? On the basis of emotional reactions and capacity for change in attitudes to men-women relationships, sexual patterns, or marriage, which we have observed even in the most secure and highly motivated persons, we can only be discouraged and pessimistic. Always here and there the exception stands out: concerned persons acting out love in new ways demanded by new situations. We agree with Victor Ferkiss when he says in *Technological Man:*

There is no new man emerging to replace the economic man of industrial society or the liberal democratic man of the bourgeois political order. The new Technology has not produced a new human type provided with a technological world view adequate to give cultural meaning to the existential revolution. Bourgeois man continues dominant just as his social order persists while his political and cultural orders disintegrate.

Bourgeois man will persist and along with him, traditional monogamy. But for humanists, there is no release from the mandate to try to alter traditional monogamy to make it better serve human needs for "we are called upon to be faithful, not to succeed."

# PART VI

# Sex Education

## 12. *Developing Human Sexuality**

### LESTER A. KIRKENDALL

Sex education in the sense that it has been used in a formal situation reflects the divorcement of sex from the rest of life. Conceived predominantly for children and youth, it has been concerned mainly with reproduction, preventing "excessive" masturbation, and—with older youth—stressing the idyllic aspects of sex experienced for the first time in marriage and engaged in for the purpose of reproduction. Sex has been considered "a very delicate" subject, and in the prevailing atmosphere books were written which listed the precise words and phrases to be used in sex instruction of children. About the only reason for adult sex education seemed to be hopefully to prepare adults (if possible, parents) to transmit to their children the sexual knowledge supplied by experts. Had they not been required for this, adults could have dropped from the educational picture completely.

Education about human sexuality in a humanistic society

---

*An adaptation of the author's article "Sex Education: A Reappraisal" appearing in the Spring 1965 issue of the *Humanist*. Several paragraphs are also adapted from an article published in *Pastoral Psychology,* November 1970.

Sex education was the term originally used to describe the movement. Developing human sexuality is a broader term, and needs to come into wider and wider use.

and in a world which is changing as aggressively as ours must be looked at entirely anew. It must be harmonized with what we now know of man and his needs, and with the character of the reality we face. I wish to suggest seven ways in which the nature of sex education must be altered profoundly.

1. *Education for human sexuality must be deeply concerned with values.*

The prime purpose of education for human sexuality is to enable people to relate more profoundly, intimately, and lovingly. This is better accomplished the more we know of the nature of man. No value system or practice of morality long exists which runs counter to the needs of man, and what he basically seeks in life. This stipulation, of course, throws open the doors to controversy, for our knowledge of the nature of man leaves a lot to be determined.

Viewpoints in the professional literature range from a concept of man as an aggressive, self-centered animal, to the views of those who regard him as a complex animal, but essentially an organism whose basic needs are satisfied as he becomes a civilized social being. We cannot take the time to pursue this controversy, but one should know that a range of views exists. Two current and well known writers who hold that man is selfish and highly ego-centered, a creature of inherent aggressiveness, are Dr. Robert Ardrey in his books, *African Genesis* and *The Territorial Imperative,* and Dr. Konrad Lorenz in his book, *On Aggression.* The opposite view has its adherents. The studies of child growth and development by Rene Spitz and John Bowlby show that the absence of love and a sense of belonging hinders and dwarfs the growth and development of infants and small children. If the absence of love and affection are too pronounced, the child may not survive physically. The various anthropological writings of Ashley Montagu stress the need for love for mankind as a whole if he is to continue to exist as a species.

In his book, *Man Observed,*[1] Montague writes that,

the whole course of human evolution has led to [the fact] that human beings shall relate to each other as a loving mother relates to her dependent child. Such relatedness has had the highest selective value for the human species in all societies and in all times, and if men fail to recognize this or once having learned this truth ever forget it they will from that moment on be in imminent danger of destroying themselves. . . . The evidence for this statement is now, I believe, bombproof and it is available to anyone who cares to take the trouble to verify it for himself.

My own feeling is that scientists in divergent fields of learning have amassed evidence which indicates that while man has conflicting impulses to deal with, the cooperative, outreaching, altruistic impulses predominate and will triumph when given an opportunity. The evidence for this view of human nature is to me more convincing than evidence for the view that man is essentially hostile and unsocial, or that he is by nature goodness in all its purity. We do live in a neurotic world, one made so by human mistakes and errors. These occur not because of man's lack of desire or need for love, but from his inability to comprehend the complexity of his world and to communicate effectively with his fellows.

If man is by nature a social animal, then his moral code needs to be directed toward helping him develop his social capacities to the maximum. As I have noted, a moral code which stresses a pattern of conduct contrary to basic human nature will prove extremely difficult to enforce, even to maintain at all.

Since, however, man's need is essentially to give and receive love, to find satisfaction through his capacity to achieve and relate to others, and to realize his potentialities, rather than to satisfy a deity or a supernatural being, I would like at this point to suggest a change in terminology. I would like to drop the word "morality," certainly in the traditional sense. As we ordinarily speak of morals and moral behavior, particularly in the area of sex, our phraseology is judgmental, punitive, and endowed with the view that "you have no one to blame but yourself" for your difficulties. Interaction between persons, or interpersonal involvement of individuals with one another in the moral situation, is disregarded.

Our need is to help people become loving, responsible, fulfilled human beings with consideration and concern for others in their relationships. Behavior-science students are already familiar with this approach; they are concerned with understanding the character of people. The scholar wants to know how people have come to be what they are, what they may become, and how they may change. Basically the behavioral scientist is interested in the development of persons with whom others could live securely and with satisfaction. The people these leaders envision are the kind needed in a humane, responsible, compassionate society. In various of my writings, I have mentioned some of these scientists, and at the expense of omitting some will do so again. We have Eric Fromm talking about the productive man; Carl Rogers, the fully functioning person—the person open to all his experiences; Maslow, the self-actualizing person; Jourard, the authentic being who is able to disclose himself; Horney, the real self; Huxley, the fulfilled person; Glasser, the responsible person; Saul and Jahoda, the mature person; and Szasz, the autonomous person. Mowrer is concerned with the person of integrity. Nelson Foote and William Schultz discuss how individuals may develop in their interpersonal relationships. Montagu emphasizes the importance of love and the role of the cooperative person in human relations. In the field of theology, Fletcher, Cox, and Robinson talk about the caring, loving person. The scholars seem concerned with people whom we would like to live near, to have as neighbors and as friends; they are concerned with compassionate, responsible human beings.

This point of view is apparently what Girvetz[2] had in mind when he wrote,

Whether it be "self-actualization," "positive freedom," "relief from tension and anxiety," "dynamism," "creative interchange," "human dignity," "total personality," or something else (all of them inadequately and almost caricaturishly denoted in a bare list like this and even by the naked labels themselves), the source of values appears to lie in an integrated experience where problems do not fester but are resolved. . . . When a Karl Menninger, among others, demonstrates in detail the relation of mental health to the outgoing activities of what he does not hesitate to call "love," and the contrary pathological tendencies involved in withdrawal and cruelty, it can be argued that experimental and verifiable knowldege about man and his relationships to others is helping in some cases to justify, and elsewhere even to establish, norms of conduct.

If this view of man and man's striving for fulfillment were to be accepted and implemented it would require pronounced changes in ways of thinking. It would mark the end of traditional and conventional discussions about morals and morality. They would seem as outdated as a doctor bleeding a sick person to bring him to health. Much more meaning can be derived and help given by discussing how we can move positively toward the realization of that which is best in our human potential.

2. *With the diminishing need to use sex always in the service of procreation, a broader, pluralistic basis for the use of human sexuality is being developed.* This changing concept of sex must become a central concern in sex education.

The major function of sex historically has been procreation of the species and in the past, with mankind facing famine, pestilence, and high mortality rates, the maximum use of sex for reproduction was necessary to keep mankind extant. Those practices such as contraception, masturbation, and homosexuality, which encouraged the use of sex without providing the opportunity for reproduction, were forbidden and tabooed. But now a world population crisis is upon us. Instead of being underpopulated we are faced with such a growth in population as to make living upon the globe extremely difficult—perhaps impossible. If in the light of our basic population needs sex were always to be used only for procreative purposes, sex life would be scant and unrewarding, which is not within the will—or the need of people to accept.

Jetse Sprey,[3] writing to this point, sees our sexual attitudes and morality as now including functions and purposes quite apart from simple reproduction, more as ends within themselves. Procreation will still play a part, but for most individuals this will not represent its major emphasis or purpose. His comment is that sex is becoming institutionalized autonomously "in its own right, rather than primarily within the institutional contexts of reproduction and child-rearing. . . . The accent (given by people to sex) lies on its cultural dimension; the extent to which a given kind of social interaction is defined and legitimated as an end in itself."

The writers of *The Future of the Family*,[4] speculating on the future of sexuality in family life, think there is not much doubt about it—sex life in the future will be better. "But it will be different because it will center less and less on the sex act as we have come to know it, what we call sexual intercourse. There will be a much broader range of sexuality in the family—and it will probably not be limited to the family or the home."

Marshall McLuhan and George Leonard[5] write

Sex as we now think of it may soon be dead. Sexual concepts, ideals and practices already are being altered almost beyond recognition. Marriage and the family are shifting into new dimensions. What it will mean to be boy or girl, man or woman, husband or wife, male or female may come as one of the great surprises the future holds for us.

I hold the view that sex in its most satisfying form is more a matter of interpersonal relationships than of simple physical experience. Sex seems to me not an entity in itself, but an integral part of a relationship in which people are experiencing care and love for one another. It is one part of a total relationship. Emphasis on sex and its contribution is subordinated to a greater concern for building trust, sincerity, integrity, and a capacity for communication between partners. In one sense then sex may seem to mean less, yet in still another sense it comes to mean even more. Less as a sheer physical act; more because it has been built into the whole relationship. When sexuality has a real contribution to make, it becomes associated integrally with other parts of the total relationship.

I have worked too long in counseling not to see how quickly the concept of sex wholly as a sensory relationship can become superficial and meaningless. No relationship, no marriage can be held together by sexual experience alone. Satisfying experiences in sexual intercourse are not achieved simply by wishing. They are attained by couples who have given time to building emotionally and physically together. Furthermore, the understanding of how these associations are reached comes through concern for communication, integrity, genuineness, and sincerity.[6]

There are many kinds of associations to be considered. In the male-female relationships there may be associations of either long or short duration. The meaning of sex must be judged in terms of the total relationship which exists between the couple. Sex in which the possibility of procreation is ruled out may become play or joyous experimentation. It can easily have a different meaning from one relationship to another, and for a couple from time to time. Then too, there will be relationships in which there is no sex at all, or in a self-centered one, sex may be an overriding ego concern in which the major element is the physical experience with no concern for the protection, interest, or personality of the partner.

There is an increasing emphasis on sex as a source of play and pleasure. To many this may seem reprehensible, especially outside of marriage. Yet the thought of sex as play has been discussed from time to time. For example, Nelson Foote,[7] writing on "Sex as Play," made some significant points. He noted, for example, that play is often regarded as irresponsible and self-centered. For many people sex as play would have no meaning beyond seeking individual satisfaction. He speculated on whether it was the puritan tendency to frown upon play, or the puritan tendency to regard sex as intrinsically sinful, or both in combination, which caused the dislike which still confuses us. He noted that

play—any kind of play—generates its own morality and values. And the enforcement of the rules of play becomes the concern of every player, because without their observance, the play cannot continue; the spoilsport is sternly rejected.

He also noted that a play relationship called for "the dynamics of obligation and commitment," for without these characteristics the play arrangements themselves would break down.

Foote believes that sex play and activity have a contribution to make as a development sequence in the maturational process. Dr. Harlow, of the University of Wisconsin, in his study of baby rhesus monkeys, deprived them of various ordinary interpersonal relationships with their peers, and later found them generally unable to copulate, or if they were able, the females were inadequate and unsuccessful mothers. So at the subhuman level, as seen by Dr. Harlow, the meaning of sex as play seems to be a significant feature in development toward adulthood.

Still other aspects of pluralistic sexual behavior can be noted. Without question some couples will continue to live within the traditional arrangements. However, we are now finding couples living together without marriage for long or short periods of time, unmarried couples spending weekends or making trips together (as has been customary in Europe for some time), married couples deciding to have no children, coeducational college dormitory living, communal family living, and evidences of increasing interest and activity in homosexual experiences. In *The Future of the Family,* the writers comment on the future, "Too, we shall probably see a good deal more of homosexuality" as a result of the need to control population and of a freer acceptance of sex. In an earlier chapter Donald J. Cantor has already noted legal changes relating to homosexuality which point toward an acceptance of this philosophy.

Actually, if we could alleviate these restrictive features which prevent us from accepting and enjoying physical nearness and closeness many of our desires would seem less like homosexuality and become instead expressions of caring in day-by-day living. Our male-male culture in particular has been much less accepting of touch experiences among men than has been the case in other cultures. Hoffman[8] does an excellent job of analyzing how these rigid barriers affect men, and of placing male-male affectional practices versus sexual relations in a new perspective.

There seems a growing acceptance of close touch and affectional experiences for both male-male and female-female relationships. This all seems a part of a broadening, more encompassing basis in the use of sex.

3. *The distinction between what was and is personal in human sexuality and what has social significance has changed greatly within this century.*

Formerly, the chief social concern as it related to sexual expression was the repression of all aspects of sexuality from public consideration. Even accepted aspects of sex, such as intercourse in marriage, were barely discussable. The sexual conduct of persons who were following conventional patterns of chastity and non-exploitiveness was never mentioned nor openly recognized. Such individuals received neither approval nor support. This is even yet the case.

Such practices as masturbation, homosexuality between consenting adults, mouth-genital contacts, or similar variations from straight genital heterosexuality were considered of social concern because of their offensive, repellent nature. They violated moral sensitivities, and outraged feelings were brought to bear upon the violators either through the exercise of public opinion or through legal channels.

Today, the lessened sense of repugnance and the enhanced capacity among educated people to look at sexuality objectively suggest that some things which were formerly of social concern because they were offensive to some people should be either private, personal concerns, or of social concern for a very different reason.

We have already mentioned homosexuality, heavily interdicted by law because of its moral offensiveness. There is now a movement to make sexual practices between consenting adults of the same sex simply a matter for personal decision. The purpose would be to create an acceptance of homosexuals or bisexuals as individuals with the same rights to be respected and safeguarded as other citizens, or, negatively, to regard them as legal offenders only when they impose themselves upon or disregard the rights of others.

Another illustration of ways in which adequate or inadequate knowledge of sex becomes a matter of social concern is found in the field of population control. Lee Rainwater and Karol Weinstein[9] posited their study, *and the poor get children*, on the hypothesis that family-planning and conception-control practices are ineffective in lower-class families because of a basic inadequacy in sexual knowledge and communication. They asserted that, generally, in lower-class families the direct association between knowledge of the sexual relationship, and effectiveness in the application of contraceptive methods, is not understood. They found, for example, that women were seriously lacking in knowledge concerning their own physiology and the processes of fertilization and conception, and as a consequence were not at all clear what bearing the contraceptive methods they were attempting to use had upon the processes of conception.

Neither could some husbands and wives discuss their sexual relationship openly. Thus, the application of contraceptive methods was rendered ineffective and futile. Finally, the attitudes of some males toward achieving their own masculinity through reproduction prevented them from accepting the intervention of any contraceptive device in the intercourse-conception process.

In short, Rainwater and Weinstein demonstrated that effective contraceptive methods, and in the long run population control, were linked closely with physiological knowledge about sex, a capacity for free discussion, and attitudes toward sex roles and toward sex itself. Sex education is thus clearly tied in a socially significant way to family planning and population limitation policy.

What has produced this shifting emphasis about what is

personal and private, and what is of social concern in sex? Several factors which should be of particular interest to humanists can be cited.

First, we are living in a pluralistic society, where an infinite number of possible patterns of sexual behavior are being followed. Similarly, divergent views about sexual ethics and morals exist. Second, though pluralism in itself is enough to create a ferment, an even more powerful development has taken place. The power of imposed authority, especially religious authority, has vastly weakened. This authority is being replaced by rational thought resting upon data derived by scientific inquiry and logical analysis. Truth is that which can be demonstrated and validated, and an increasing reliance on scientific processes has considerably changed attitudes toward sex, and has given new meanings to many of its manifestations.

Attitudes toward masturbation provide an illustration. At the turn of the century, masturbation was regarded with abhorrence, and so its repression was a moral issue. Serious consequences which were said to arise from its practice were cited to support the taboos. Research, however, has failed to support these consequences, and has revealed them as rationalizations trumped up to support preconceived moralistic views.

Thus, in the face of scientific inquiry, it has become impossible to maintain these views. Though still found in some theologically-oriented discussions, the strictures against masturbation in professional books have almost disappeared. Some professional opinion now holds that rather than being a handicap, masturbation performs a certain developmental function at the time of sexual maturation.

Be that as it may, it is clear that the former social concern about masturbation in terms of its negative consequences has been completely undermined by scientific inquiry, and that its practice is increasingly regarded as a matter of personal choice.

Scientific developments have been largely responsible for the changing attitudes toward premarital chastity. Formerly, the standard of sexual abstinence in the premarital period was supported by the possible consequences of breaking conventional patterns. Pregnancy or venereal infection were real enough threats to motivate the sexual behavior of most dating couples. However, as science has developed methods and techniques for coping with these threats they have lost their power to motivate. The consequence is the rising challenge to the conventional standard; the problem is the lack of prior thinking which would help our society in developing the basis for a realistic and responsible standard.

All of this points to the need for a much expanded and sharply redirected program of education about human sexuality. Understanding of the shifts from personal to social, from social to personal, analysis of new social-sex issues which have been developing and of their scope and meaning must all be at the core of a modern sex-education program. Sex neither can nor should be repressed and denied simply because it is sex. It has a new and enhanced social significance and this needs to be understood.

The current uproar over sex education suggests that we really never did get to what was significant in sex. The deep, subconscious aspects of sex were never touched, and understanding in depth was never achieved. Most previous education dealt with facts—chiefly the obvious ones. The student did not learn the relation of his own sexuality to his personality and his pattern of development. The relationship between sex and love, between sex and the life cycle of human development, and ways in which sex becomes a motivating factor are not—have never been—included in sex education. If there had been any effective education in regard to such matters we might have escaped the sex-education imbroglio in which we have been caught up in the past several years.

4. *Adults should be the main target group of a sex-education program which would fit modern needs.*

Children and youth have typically been the target groups of sex-education programs, and they will continue to need help. But it cannot be said too often or too forcefully that it is adults who really stand in need. Since a view of sex in keeping with scientific knowledge and its relation both to individual and social living is so important, the necessary education cannot all be crammed into childhood and adolescence. It can be begun then but not completed.

Adults need education in their own right for several reasons: (*a*) it would make their own lives more satisfying, (*b*) adults must provide the climate of public opinion needed to support desirable changes in attitudes, customs, and laws related to sex, and (c) this education would help make intergenerational conversations possible.

One of the blocks to an adequate and effective sex-education program at any level is the overweening fear so many adults have of sex. They regard it as an impulse of such overpowering strength that any reference or discussion is likely to open the floodgates to an engulfing tide. Our sexual terror has come to be obsessive and neurotic (as note the present John Birch–Christian Crusade dissidence) and has, in fact, become a self-fulfilling prophecy in that it has enhanced the fears which already existed.

This fear has a long history, but I am convinced it has been built up out of all proportion to reality. When I began my professional work I felt as threatened as anyone else, but over the years I have become more and more aware that while powerful, the sex drive, like other impulses and drives, can be directed.

If this fear is to be dispelled, it must be understood in relation to the nature of man; only then will it disappear. Human nature, I believe, makes the need for relatedness and relationships so important that appetite satisfactions are generally subordinate. If this assumption is sound, we are here pointing to an important principle, namely, that any really meaningful education about sex must take place in a context of concern for human relationships. Rather than sex education, what is needed is more human-relations education. A genuine program of human-relations education would deal with all aspects of human living and interaction. It would be concerned with both the aggressive and the sexual impulses, their relation to one another, and their integration into a pattern of balanced, effective living.

Few parents go much beyond providing biological-reproduction facts. They are hampered not only by a fear of sex; they are lost in a morass of ignorance and contradictions about what human beings are really like. The correction of these deficiencies must be the central objective of the modern sex-education program.

Ordinarily, we consider the participation of parents in the sex-socialization processes of their children as having a stabilizing effect upon the family and the society. Such an outcome surely seems desirable, but it is clearly too much, under present conditions, to expect more than a few extraordinary parents to do this. They are too deeply enmeshed in the fears and inhibitions which surround sex in our society, and they are so emotionally involved with their children that they are rendered both blind and mute when it comes to dealing with them on sexual-relationship matters.

An effective human-relations—sex-education program for all adults would facilitate intergenerational discussions concerning sex matters. As it is, very few adults any longer participate in any realistic or effective way in the sex-socialization processes of youth. More extensive cross-generational discussions concerning sexual matters are badly needed. Few adults—except teachers—ever discuss or engage in direct personal dialogue with youth, or consider their problems on the basis of merit rather than their own particular biases. An understanding of sex in relationships, its use as play, as a method of communication, or as a unifying experience, if it comes to youth at all, must now come through literature or by the way of peers.

In my opinion we seldom take the time necessary with young people to develop and change sexual attitudes. Through my years in education I have spent hours with some individuals in discussions which seem to me and to them to have resulted in new concepts for them of self and sex. A learning pattern emerges repeatedly which illustrates the need for prolonged and spaced conversations. First is the period when the youth sizes up the adult. What can they say to one another, and what must they avoid saying? With increasing assurance, important, though very common, issues come to the surface. Then probing begins about one's own self and sexual attitudes. One becomes used to hearing himself raising serious issues about his own sexuality with his own voice. If the adult's attitude remains open and accepting the youth may now do one or more of several things. He may express his own sexual doubts and anxieties, and try to relate his own experiences to the role concepts he holds for himself. He may seek an evaluation which will provide him greater personal insights. He may seek to ascertain what place sex can and should play in his life. Obviously these are not things which can be simply explained in a one-way interchange. They must be mulled over and over again. Nor are they accomplished in one short talk.

This is the reason for urging much more and much freer interchange between the generations.

5. *We are living in an open, free choice society, which must alter the approach to the educational process.*

Forty or fifty years ago, sex education was rarely couched in terms of choosing among alternative patterns of sexual behavior. Only one course of action was considered—renunciation of all sexual expression in non-marital situations. In the face of such monolithic unanimity, the thought of consciously weighing and choosing a course of sexual behavior occurred only to the brash and highly emancipated. The flouting of conventional standards did occur, but it was surreptitious and regarded as a violation rather than as a matter of choice.

Quite a different situation exists in the 1970's. A very real freedom now exists for adolescent couples and for youth in mixed groups to speak openly and frankly about sexual matters. This freedom exists most clearly within the adolescent group itself. In discussing their high school dating relationships, many young people have mentioned talking with dating partners about whether or not they should engage in intercourse. Discussions about sex apparently now occur very early in many dating relationships. The more sophisticated youth talk about their sexual feelings and reactions, e.g., how boys feel about having erections, whether they have previously engaged in petting or intercourse, how girls react to menstruation, what an orgasm is like, what kind of standards should be held, what each finds sexually stimulating. Whether these conversations are intentionally (or inadvertently) an aspect of a seduction process is hard to determine. The one thing I am sure about is that they occur, and that this adolescent freedom to discuss and act is greatly aided and abetted by the freedom with which sex is portrayed and discussed in the movies and the mass media.

This openness in dating conversations is undoubtedly strong medicine for most adults to take. I have found many shocked and repelled by it, but we should remember that these are the children whom we have taught to be curious and exploratory, to be unashamed of their bodies, and to be proud of these attitudes. I have no unassailable proof of a cause-effect relationship, but I do think it is all a part of a general pattern of openness which has been developing.

Neither do I mention it to deplore it or to suggest that we beat a retreat. It is in fact in this kind of openness and honesty that I find our greatest hope for coping with the situation.

Because of this openness, young people of high school age and above are faced frequently with situations which require them to decide for or against participation in some kind of sexual relationship. This holds true not only for premarital intercourse in dating relationships, but for other possible sexual involvements as well.

One of the common decisions which many boys, and fewer girls, have to make is whether to accept or reject homosexual approaches or what seem to them to be homosexual advances. Many of these youths are so uninformed that they actually are not certain they are being approached. I know from experience in working with boys, that if they think a homosexual approach is occurring, they are likely to react in an exaggerated manner. They may either experience a paralyzing fear or exhibit an irrational and violent anger. These reactions are typically much conditioned by the cultural attitudes which instill a frightened, recoiling, antagonistic attitude toward homosexuals.

Many boys are likewise ill-prepared for the choices and decisions they have to make when they enter military service. Whether they should engage in homosexual activities, have intercourse with prostitutes and pick-ups, how to deal with the pressures which associates may exert on them, and how to evaluate the stories and opinions they hear are never discussed by adults who could and should help them.

Decisions as to whether or not to have premarital intercourse face the majority of young people, and many face the issue frequently. For example, in a study of first-year university women, Kanin[10] found that 62% reported "offensive and displeasing" experiences in dating with partners who attempted to gain some level of erotic-sexual intimacy unsatisfactory to the girls. The attempts had all occurred in the year prior to the girls' entry into the university—that is, during their senior year in high school. In a companion study involving university women, Kirkpatrick and Kanin[11] found about 56% reporting offensively aggressive episodes. There is no indication as to how many of the girls found erotic-sexual advances acceptable.

I conducted a pilot study involving 131 young college men.

This study was designed to find how many and what kind of sexual decisions these young men had made. It was based upon the assumptions that youth are now living in an open, free-choice society, and that practically all of them do meet situations in which they have to and do make choices concerning whether or not they will participate in premarital intercourse. Decisions about other kinds of sexual behavior were not investigated.

I found that 114 (87%) of the subjects reported 558 situations in which they had made decisions about possible heterosexual intercourse, an average of 4.9 decisions for each person. In a breakdown of this datum I found that 55 subjects reported 90 decisions in which they had rejected intercourse; 59 subjects reported 147 situations in which they had sought intercourse but had been rejected by the potential partner; 59 subjects reported that they had engaged in intercourse with 210 partners; 73 subjects reported 111 situations in which they had mutually decided with a partner to avoid intercourse. Only 17 subjects said they had never been in a situation in which a choice was necessary.[12] Clearly, the bulk of these individuals have lived in situations in which choices were necessary, and they made them. Did their education prepare them for decision-making? I think not.

6. *The chief determinant of sexual conduct is not factual information but the general feeling of personal satisfaction and fulfillment which the individual has been able to develop about himself.* One's pattern of sexual behavior is a reflection of his total life pattern. The Kinsey studies, because of the data derived concerning masculine sexual performance at adolescence, pinpointed this as the period of life in which males feel the greatest sex urgency. While this generalization is subject to some qualification it enables me to comment on the major determinant of sexual conduct, for it is with adolescent males that I have done most of my work.

I have found few adolescents who could be considered adequately or well informed concerning sex, yet I have found wide variations in their sexual behavior. This convinces me that sexual behavior is motivated by social and psychological factors which escape the notice of the casual observer. An adolescent boy does not experience overwhelming sexual desires simply because he is a physically normal adolescent boy. He will benefit from a clear knowledge of his sexual nature and a feeling that sex is a normal, legitimate part of him; this can be the contribution of a good sex education. But beyond that, whether he feels pushed by sex depends on factors quite independent of his physiology or his knowledge of facts about sex and reproduction. The urgency with which he feels sexual desire, and he will feel sexual desires, depends upon the degree of acceptance and pride he has developed toward himself, his feeling of achievement and worth in the things he is doing, and the extent to which he has felt love and acceptance in his home and among his friends.

An individual who feels he is accomplishing something with his life, that he is reasonably successful and is going places will generally find the management of sex no great problem. He will likely have some sexual experiences of one kind or another which I suspect he may enjoy more than the average person, since he is not blocked by inhibiting fears or guilt. He is not, however, driven to engage in sex with little regard for what this means to other persons, or to total situations. In other words, he is in a position to direct his sexuality. He can take it if it appears to offer fulfillment; he can put it aside when it does not. This is essentially the same point of view arrived at by Abraham Maslow[13] in his study of self-actualizing persons.

What does this mean for education about human sexuality? It means that problems of sexual misconduct need to be understood not in terms of a weak will, or an overpowering physical drive, but in terms of personal adjustment and effective or defective interpersonal relationships. The formation of patterns of fulfilling and responsible sexual behavior will be facilitated not by inveighing against sex as evil, or by the use of scare tactics, but by providing knowledge and, most of all, experiences which will enable individuals to establish meaningful and satisfying interpersonal relationships, and develop a sense of self-worth and achievement. As the individual finds increased satisfactions in his emotional relations with himself, his family, and friends, he will find decreased need for casual, irresponsible and self-centered experimentation with sex.

7. *The core of the educational structure needed for the kind of sex education envisioned here demands far more than can be provided by the public schools.*

This does not minimize or depreciate the role the schools

have played in the past, nor does it assume they will play any lesser role in the future. I am adding facets to the structure. While some important ones may without doubt be omitted, the following are certainly important, and will be instrumental in the success or failure of a program.

*a. Mass media.* The mass media are a very important educational force now, but too often their thrust seems to be in the wrong direction. Motivated by the possibility of commercial gain, the media tend to emphasize the sensational, to play up "slants," to ignore the really educational. This is not universally true; there have been some outstanding TV and radio programs, a number of good magazine articles, and some good books.

Nor is it fair to make the mass media fully responsible for what appears there. A circular effect certainly exists. The media help create a demand for and a certain frame of mind concerning sex. These in turn help stimulate more of the slanted, the sensational, and the irresponsible materials which appear. We can only hope that the media will develop a greater sense of their educational responsibility, and that public opinion and support will also develop for those producers who try to exercise that responsibility through better films, magazines, stage, and television performances.

*b. Professional preparation programs.* The sex-education approach we are suggesting means that various professional schools need to give much more attention than they have to educating their professional trainees about sex. Dr. Harold Lief of the University of Pennsylvania School of Medicine has made this point repeatedly with reference to doctors, and the same point could be made for lawyers, theologians, journalists, and law enforcement officers.

Teachers and counselors are professional groups particularly in point. In a few instances, teachers are given insights concerning sexual behavior, but for the most part this aspect of their education is ignored. Even though they deal with children, youth, and parents in situations which make a knowledge of psychosexual development important, this aspect of their education is still neglected.

Schools of medicine and law, and teacher-education programs—these and others—need to incorporate sex education in their preparatory and in-service training programs, and in the programs of their professional conferences.

*c. Adult education programs.* Churches, public schools, service clubs, and similar groups typically develop programs of interest to adults. They provide an avenue for reaching many persons out of school or past school age and can be very effective in sex education.

*d. Higher education.* Colleges and universities can make a highly significant contribution at this level. They have in their student bodies many future community leaders and those who will play an important part in molding public opinion. A sex-education program which will not only give help and insight for the present, but will also point the recipients to future leadership roles would be valuable and appropriate.

All of these education programs need to rest upon an ever-expanding knowledge of the nature of sex and how it fits into human living. This calls for research and for an increasing openness and willingness to analyze experience. Only in this way will we be able to separate fact from fiction, reality from myth.

Without doubt some will object that this is "too much sex" —it is sex everywhere. I do not mean to argue that sex must be harped about and dwelt upon incessantly. There are other things in life to be considered and experienced—this I know. The objectives I have in mind are openness and balance; I do not seek an out-of-balance emphasis on sex.

On the other hand, I expect there will have to be more talking about sex before there is less. The fact that it has been so tabooed and avoided makes almost any discussion of it seem out of proportion. The same feeling is expressed concerning race relations—"we would get along better with less talk about race." Yet any realistic person will recognize that before we arrive at an accommodation satisfactory to the various racial groups, much more discussion, rather than less, will be needed.

Not only the amount of talking, but its quality and purpose as well are important. We have had much discussion at certain levels concerning certain aspects of sex. The problem is that this has not been matched by discussion in other directions, and concerning other aspects of sex. It is only out of such interchange that the concepts needed to support modern sex education can be derived. Our problem is to get that interchange.

## Notes to Chapter 12

1. Montagu, Ashley. *Man Observed.* New York: G. P. Putnam's Sons, 1968.
2. Girvetz, Harry, *et al. Science, Folklore and Philosophy.* New York: Harper and Row, 1966.
3. Sprey, Jetse. "On the Institutionalization of Sexuality." *Journal of Marriage and the Family*, 31:432-440, August, 1969.
4. Farson, Richard D., *et al. The Future of the Family.* New York: Family Service Association of America, 1969.
5. McLuhan, Marshall and Leonard, George. "The Future of Sex." *Look*, 31:15, 56-63, July 25, 1967.
6. Kirkendall, Lester A. *Premarital Intercourse and Interpersonal Relationships.* New York: Gramercy Publishing Company, 1961.
7. Foote, Nelson. "Sex as Play." *Social Problems.* 1:159-163, April, 1954.
8. Hoffman, Martin. *The Gay World.* New York: Basic Books, 1968.
9. Rainwater, L., and Weinstein, K. *and the poor get children.* Chicago: Quadrangle Books, 1960.
10. Kanin, E. "Male Aggression in Dating-Courtship Relations." *American Journal of Sociology*, 63:197-204, Sept., 1957.
11. Kirkpatrick, Clifford, and Kanin. "Male Sex Aggression on a University Campus." *American Sociological Review*, 20: 52-58, Feb., 1957.
12. Kirkendall, Lester A. "Characteristics of Sexual Decision-Making." *Journal of Sex Research*, 3:201-211, August, 1967.
13. Maslow, A. H. *Motivation and Personality.* New York: Harper and Bros., 1954.

# 13. *Youth and the Search for Intimacy*

WINFIELD W. SALISBURY
AND FRANCES F. SALISBURY

## *Humanist Youth*

The young people who are creating a revolution in American sexual values and attitudes reflect a wide variety of youth and of youth subcultures. They vary from quiet, conservative couples trying out "the arrangement" to wild-haired guerrilla theatre groups, and Ken Kesey's Merry Pranksters (T. Wolfe, 1968). Their interests range through an incredible spectrum—politics, sensory awareness, encounter groups, meditation, mysticism, dreams, drugs, and ecology.

And, while these scattered threads have not yet been woven into a coherent subculture, these young people are significant for a number of reasons. First of all, they are not dissident have-nots, but our most pampered youth—white, urban, upper-middle class, college-bound or college-educated. Yet with their hippie communalism, sensuality, draft evasion, guerrilla theatre, and demonstrations, they are questioning the most fundamental assumptions—the very cultural-linguistic grid—of the industrial, technological, bureaucratic society that made them rich. The contrast with their peers, the still unquestioning "technocratic youth" who still make up the majority of our young people, is striking. Instead of running with Sammy, they are engaged in an iconoclastic process which Theodore Roszak has described as *The Making of a Counter Culture* (1969).

Secondly, from their location (West and East Coasts) and their class position, it appears they are what Fortune's *Youth in Turmoil* (1969) has described as "forerunners"; they hold the values and opinions that seem to be the wave of the future. The children of the counter culture, the forerunners, the searchers, the rebels, we have chosen here to call "humanist youth." This is to emphasize the contrast with "technocratic youth" who still accept and perpetuate the mechanistic assumptions, goals, and values of industrial society (see Watts, 1966, for a description of these mechanistic assumptions). The new rebels have become aware that technocracy's motto, "progress for the sake of progress," is the philosophy of the cancer cell and a paean to alienation and ennui. They are seeking a whole new radical order based on an identification with humanity, a naive but vital compassion, a growing ecological consciousness and a sensual awareness of self and nature.

It is our intention to discuss this new awareness in its sensual aspect, for "sensuality" is the word that has come to stand for the integration of intimacy and sexuality. The search of youth for new sexual experience has been widely chronicled by the mass media, but the sensationalist approach has often failed to recognize that the search for intimacy is just as intense and critical. The Institute of Human Abilities in Oakland, a commune-oriented counter culture institution, gives a "Basic Sensuality Course" designed to increase awareness of the profound connection between the capacities for sensuality and for intimacy. This program has proven immensely popular with the young, and groups have sprung up all over the Bay Area.

### The New Sexual Revolution

How do youth become emotionally and physically involved with one another? In addition to the blocks to direct relating created by our culture, most young people today receive no explicit education in the psychological and physical aspects of sexual relations. Instead, they learn about love and sex through fumbling approach-withdrawal episodes of slowly escalating dating experiences. This has been true of American adolescence for some time. But for youth who have come to value human relationships above the codes of a work-oriented society, something more is happening. They have become conscious of the conflicts inherent in relating and the deep human need for intimacy, and they are exploring a variety of solutions to the problem. The flower children were one of the manifestations of this change in point of view. Today, their ideas are accepted by many young people who refuse to adopt their extremes of dress, and who do not feel the intense need to rebel. This is exemplified by their tremendously favorable response to *The Harrad Experiment*. Robert H. Rimmer, the author, takes the view that sex is essential to the fulfillment of identity and the need for love. At Harrad College, intimacy is not merely a supplementary diversion in school life, it is life's most essential lesson. The entire design of the college contributes to creating experiences which increase the pupils' understanding of intimacy and the difficulty it involves.

Although this novel is extremely popular among college students, this is not to say that we are in the midst of an orgiastic revolution on campus. The scene is mostly one of talk. The recent Katz study (1967) of Stanford and University of California (Berkeley) students found that 60% of the males and 62% (Stanford) to 72% (Berkeley) of the females had not had sexual intercourse by the middle of their junior year. In addition, about 33% of the men and 25% of the girls still did little or no dating at the end of the senior year. The crucial emotional problem during the college years is loneliness, not excessive sexuality. Therefore it is important to understand that the new sexual revolution played up by the media is not one of deed; the revolution is one of ideas, sexual values, and attitudes.

What are the assumptions about interpersonal relating that humanist youth hold in general? Much of their philosophy is borrowed from the encounter group movement. Emphasizing emotional and sensual experience, they strive to act spontaneously on their "gut feelings." The prime ethic, summed up in the hippie motto, "Do your own thing," has been accepted as a dominant value by countless young people. We have been struck by the increasing impact of the hippie movement on students over the past three years. Reflecting this humanist rebellion against reason (read here "scientific technology") and efficiency, they stress self-realization and the priority of feelings. Any behavior is okay as long as it does not hurt oneself or others, a morality revealing sensitivity to interpersonal injury. The device of sumptuary laws, the Victorian bag of legislating morals, has been rejected.

What happens to sex in this environment of tolerance and searching for self-fulfillment? Most often, intercourse is defined as an act of relating, a process of mutual concern for feelings, not a means of self-gratification through exploitation. Taking their cues (rather carelessly) from Zen and the tantric tradition of Hinduism, these young people believe that sex should be a spontaneous pleasure and that it is, somehow and rather vaguely, inherently holy. However, this view has not led to rampant promiscuity. Most often, spontaneous sexuality occurs in the context of an established relationship. Old-fashioned chastity is no longer important, but, strangely enough, fidelity is, albeit overhauled to fit the contemporary scene. It may not matter how fast one relationship follows another, but one should remain faithful to whomever he is sleeping with at the time. Learning to trust oneself and the other is the problem they seem to be exploring.

In the transition from values to actual behavior, what patterns of sexuality emerge? In place of traditional courtship, we find many young people involved in short- and long-term relationships, as well as some experimentation in sex without love. In the context of these three patterns we can begin to raise questions about the meaning of self-realization, love, liberation, and spontaneity in the lives of young people who are seeking a way out of a technological nightmare on a polluted planet.

### Short-Term Affairs

There is little in the survey literature to indicate a vast increase, if any, in short-term affairs. Moreover, as registered statistically, it would be indistinguishable from the back-seat-of-a-car syndrome, more common in adolescence in present as well as past generations. However, our *impression* of youth shows several significant differences from the more typical "conquest" sexuality. They express a desire to know the other person completely and immediately. Their intense excitement does not come completely from sexual titillation (this is a projection of their elders). The excitement arises primarily from their effort to expose themselves before the other in their attempt to reveal the real feelings behind the mask of the persona. These young people energetically explore who they are while their identity is in transition. And they are often aware that their inability to sustain love reflects their personal uncertainty and fear of premature commitment. Their rationalization for short-term affairs hinges on their awareness of this problem. Several relationships offer the opportunity to experience a variety of individuals without binding commitment. They reason that in their confusion these experiences help them to understand their needs, capacities, and preferences, and render them better able to select a life-long mate. The admission of uncertainty, the need for self-exploration, and the desire for a truly meaningful marriage reveal their strong commitment to self-awareness and emotional growth.

Their behavior reflects certain areas of self-assurance. No longer ashamed about their sexual affairs as middle-class youth have usually been, they talk openly to their trusted friends and teachers. However, they rarely communicate in the same vein with their parents, and often go to some lengths to conceal their behavior. This is one area where the generation gap is very real.

The negative aspect of searching for selfhood in short-term affairs is found in the insecurity and damage to self-esteem born out of repeated failures at sustaining relationships. The problem, however, is not in anticipating the end of a love affair, but rather lack of awareness at the beginning of the unconscious influences that lead to the selection of the "lover." Youth place great value on selecting a new partner through the experience of "flashing" on someone. Their tendency is to celebrate their mutual positive behavior with the new partner and remain unaware of the negative.

One productive way of looking at the process of "falling in love" is in terms of Jung's discussion of the projection of the anima and the animus. Jung believed that socialization tends to overemphasize sex characteristics so that a *persona* (a "mask," an unconscious "front") develops that is a stereotype of the sex role. The characteristics that the culture considers to be associated with the opposite sex are then repressed and form a complex of unrealized needs and impulses in the unconscious. For example, the "anima" in a man may embody the tenderness, nurturance, fear, grief, capacity to cry, spontaneous joy, and artistic creativity that this man has repressed in order to appear cool, tough, and practical. The "animus" in a woman tends to embody discipline, creative intellectuality, *independent* rational opinions, self- and world-awareness, and whatever "sweet young things" are supposed to leave in the hands of men. By projecting onto the lover the animus or anima, people try to experience those qualities which they deny in themselves. "Flashing," then, has to do with the intensity of the search for our own self-denied characteristics and the creation of an arena in which the projected aspects of the self may be experienced. Frequently, in spite of the tremendous energy spent in trying to talk through common problems in relating and identity, young people have a hard time dealing together with their mutual projections in the context of the relationship.

However, in teaching Jung's anima-animus theory and its relevance to problems in relating, we have discovered that by the time students are college juniors and seniors, a number find these insights a valuable revelation about their own behavior. Once they grasp what projection means and see it operate, the process of their own projections seem to fascinate them. The younger the student, however, the less likely he is to understand the influence of his projections on his relating, and the more likely he will reject such symbolic analysis of his behavior.

Supporting that resistance is the code which prohibits putting another person down or "bum-tripping" him in any way. This "hippie philosophy" is compatible with the dominant culture's ban on face-to-face criticism, and itself arises out of the American cultural pattern which institutionalizes the evasion of intimacy. By giving a new label to this pattern, youth are able to claim the restriction as their own while still appearing loyal to a new counter-culture. And, while a great deal of verbal value is placed on love, youth tend to break off relationships when strain arises; neither the youth nor the adult culture encourages them to work through the emotional turmoil of interpersonal crises. It is an important step forward when lovers realize that the exposure of mutual discontent does not have to be a put-down, but can be an opening up of one's needs and feelings. What differentiates this process from a put-down is the mutuality of self-disclosure; but this seems a hard idea to grasp.

One of the prime values held by youth is the development of sensitivity to another's suffering, and, equally important, the expectation, in a healthy sense of affirmation, that others will also respect and remain sensitive to one's own vulnerability. The desire to keep open the capacity to feel pain as well as joy is a beautiful characteristic. However, sensitivity to pain is one thing and dealing with it is another. To children of American culture, the encountering of blunt negative emotion—anger, distress, fear, and pain—does not come easy. The fear of rejection is so deeply rooted that they make a virtue of denying hostility instead of recognizing the denial as a weakness. Instead of moving on to intimacy, they become trapped in a cycle of short-term relationships—projection, hopeful expectation, denial of internal negativity, disappointment in the partner or self, and withdrawal of feelings.

### Extended Affairs

Trial marriage, or simply living together, arises from the need not only for deep personal involvement but also for the comfort of a stable relationship and environment. Those who are able to sustain a sexual relationship are creating an emerging pattern of the extended affair through cohabitation. Though unmarried, they are usually not swingers, but tend to model their relationship after their ideal of a stable marriage. Like long-wedded couples, they refer to their partners as "my old man" or "my old lady." These affectionate terms invoke a compound fantasy-image of parent and spouse. The pretense of such roles structures the relationship as one of constant companionship and protection. They evoke the child's image of security in the parental home, rather than the excitement and adventure of being a resourceful man or woman. While these young people feel liberated from the stigma of extramarital sex taboos and the imposition of the marriage contract, and while they speak of the value they find in intimacy, their identity is still confused and they show signs of regression to childish overdependency. On the positive side, those who set up house together benefit by learning how to become (or not become) a compatible mate as they adjust to each other in glamourless day-to-day life. But when the relationship is no longer viable, and the fantasy of "playing house" is shattered, the anguish may be as severe as the pain of actual divorce.

### Sex Without Love

Sex merely for fun and experimentation does occur, albeit not as extensively as the media would have us believe. It is characteristic of only a small minority of humanist youth. In order to understand how it takes place, we must break through our culturally determined projection and moralizing. The reaction to promiscuity should be sympathetic and compassionate, not indignant. In Chinese Taoism, where nonjudgmentalism was understood as the key to salvation, all forms of sexual relations ultimately reflect the desire of man and woman (yang and yin) to unite and are, therefore, equally holy. Promiscuity, as we see it, is not itself the problem; instead, it is the fears and hostilities which lie beneath what appears to be an unhesitant relating. Once these blocks are dealt with, the fact that promiscuous behavior has occurred will become irrelevant. The idea of sin is important only if we believe our behavior is sinful; the past is not an albatross around our necks unless we make it so.

The ideal of sex as unpremeditated play was frequently expressed by various leaders of the hippie communities in Haight-Ashbury and elsewhere. This philosophy is also well documented in the hippie papers, the best of which were the original *San Francisco Oracle,* the *Los Angeles Free Press,* and the *East Village Other.* However, the Boston *Avatar* was one of the most openly sexual publications. The ideal stresses the importance of spontaneity and experimentation based on curiosity and natural impulse. This contributes to the self-image whereby an individual sees himself as liberated, uninhibited, an innocent child of the universe. Like the puritanism it is trying to replace, this ideal is not immune to criticism. It has its own dubious assumptions and tends to promote a lack of awareness in its followers in certain crucial areas. Promiscuity is the outward symptom indicating an obsessive need for acceptance. The fear of rejection renders one unable to discriminate among love partners and risk retaliation (withdrawal) by others. Unable to say no, one says yes with a vengeance.

Essential to the maintenance of this ideal is the belief that one is childlike and innocent, simply returning to a prior state of open delight in sensual joy. If we are pure and gentle in physical and verbal contact, how can we hurt each other? If we are innocent, we are not conscious of our own negativity. And if we are childlike, we do not have to assume adult responsibility for our sexual relations. Our sex becomes the spontaneous creativity of the universe expressing itself. In a general sense, perhaps, the most vulnerable aspect of this belief system is the premise that liberation means being naive, unrestricted, and unresponsible. The celebration of spontaneity arises in rebellion against our schedule-bound culture in which life is geared to the watch and the calendar. The trouble with a zealous dedication to spontaneity in quest of freedom is that it rejects the need for disciplined, conscious awareness in relating. It denies the intent or capacity to injure self and others, and it impedes the understanding of the process of projection which so profoundly interferes with a real awareness of another person.

For example, in the Haight-Ashbury (with which we are most familiar), there was an incredibly naive blindness to the capacity to hurt another, to hostility, and to the manipulation of others that was so obvious to outsiders. Attempts to discuss sanitation, venereal disease, hepatitis, drug problems, and the exploitation of teeny-boppers were likely to elicit a vehement rebuke to the older observer for bum-tripping others or being a hung-up square. The romantic myth of childish innocence was a sacred cow whose value was neither questioned nor examined. Only a few intellectual members of the community were able to understand the popularized Buddhism of leaders like Ginsberg and Gary Snyder and grasp the difference between liberation and license. In our view, liberation means awareness, not only of the web of life, but of one's own unconscious judgmentalism, tendency to manipulate, fear of one's own unconscious, and all the other monsters of the mind. We must see ourselves in our uglier aspects before we are truly liberated—and the vision must not be forgotten. Once this happens, we recognize that inherent in loving another is a struggle to reveal the self and to learn to be responsible to the self and the other person.

### The Difficulty of Loving

The vanguard of today's youth, like the rest of us, have a difficult time sustaining love. But unlike many of us, they are willing to explore outside the bounds of conventional relationship patterns and morality. They often see their parents' marriages as lifeless, empty forms lacking warmth, affection, joy, and the sense of fun in sharing, or "grooving together." The drinking, the killing of time and tenderness, the hostile put-downs, the voracious appetite for things, never saying what is truly meant from the heart—all these are part of the self-defeating games youth disparage in their parents. But striving for something more genuine in love is not easy, and the young are impatient. In spite of their sense of superiority, they find it hard to recognize their own game-playing and hang-ups. This fact has its roots in the nature of the culture's means of socialization through childbearing; we do not train our young to recognize and work through negative feelings to deeper levels of communication. As parents, we hide our failures in communication and our mistrust of those we love, which in turn prevents the open expression of feeling. The sturdy, fearless American is afraid of love.

Since they have been shaped by the older generation, youth also reveal mistrust in their relationships. Some mistrust the potential lover, feeling trapped (prematurely committed) or rejected. Others mistrust their own capacity to love, and anticipate a failure to come through the genuine understanding and acceptance of the other. In this regard, a theory has been developed by Professor Sinclair Kerby-Miller, at San Francisco State College, in his course, "Theory of Communication." It is based on the proposition that unconditional love is a rarely achieved ideal. Most frequently, love is tangled with mistrust. The problem in achieving love centers on our mistrust of the loved one and our fear of our deliberate, though perhaps unconscious, intent to injure him (her). When the latter is projected outward, our fear of rejection is compounded by our fear of retaliation for our hostile impulses. A vicious circle may develop which can be broken only by an awareness of willingness to deal with our game-playing—that is, an admission of our fear of being injured and our desire to injure. Only then are we free to relate openly, honestly, and intimately.

The forms that mistrust takes among vanguard and hippie youth have intrigued us over the past couple of years. We might call them defenses against intimacy or ways of holding out. We have seen familiar forms, of course, such as (1) *possessiveness,* a pattern that is practically *the* Western hang-up. And, they also (2) *belittle and demean* their partners to prop up weak egos. But mistrust is expressed in a number of forms which are fairly unique. For example, (3) the *dogma of spontaneity* is used to excuse irresponsibility. If a relationship is not spontaneous, if it has to be worked at, then it's a drag. When responsibility is asked for, the partner is accused of being possessive and "bum-tripping" the offended one.

The request for responsibility involves another problem. It seems to impose on one's "individuality," which is really to say, his independence from the partner. Thus, (4) *Doing your own thing* is ostensibly a commitment to self-actualization also a means of holding out from fully participating in a love relationship. In addition, the subcultural model of being (5) casual ("loose"), *playing it cool* and not getting "uptight" about problems discourages youth from examining their fears, defenses, and lack of trust.

Another syndrome characterizing the way youth avoid intimacy is shared love, or what we call (6) *spreading it thin*. The best example is the girl, commonly a member of hip communities or a commune, who takes on the role of Earth Mother. She loves and cares for everyone; and because she does not refuse anyone, she is responsible to no one in particular. A boy may see himself as a romantic, a revolutionary leader, or a guru, a spiritual guide, and thereby find a truly beautiful (it is, in his head) rationale for "screwing all the young chicks." The most exaggerated form of spreading love thin, found particularly in communes (or the more unstable crashpads that tried to pass as communes), was the demand to be totally accepted and loved constantly by all. The permissiveness of American Indian cultures or Buddhist mysticism might be the rationale, but on the emotional level it can be quickly recognized as a form of overdependency.

We have surmised that these difficulties arise from negative or insecure self-images. For humanist youth particularly, since they have rejected the dominant culture and its roles, insecurity results from their very search for other life-styles. They have refused closure; their social and sexual identity is in flux. Questioning the dominant social values, they become uncertain about their own personal value. Their appearance and behavior, outside of their function as protest, reveal unconsciously the low self-esteem that often develops out of identity confusion. Of course, one's sense of unworthiness (unlovableness) negatively affects one's ability to love, but fortunately, most youth have a strong drive for growth that makes this condition temporary. Next, we shall consider the elements that must enter into their awareness if their desire to become loving human beings is to succeed.

In tackling the crucial problem, his own self-image, the humanist youth is caught in a bind. The predominant ethic condemns both hostile feelings and aggressive actions. Consequently, he tends to repress, deny, and project his destructive impulses. The nonviolent ethic makes it very hard for him to acknowledge and manage negative feelings nonjudgmentally. However, because of the overriding value of self-exploration and inner growth he often responds with remarkable enthusiasm to the insights an instructor or counselor can offer him. While it is difficult to tell how much behavior change occurs, at least we have felt that the enthusiasm of humanist-oriented students over discussions of intimacy indicates that ideas have been planted in fertile ground. Perhaps we can briefly discuss some of the conditions for achieving intimacy in sexual relations which we have advanced in our classes and discussion groups.

First, and most crucially, we stress (1) *awareness,* meaning being aware of the self in the environment, learning to conceive oneself as a strand in the web of life in the biosphere. Alan Watts' *The Book* has proved to be a good introduction to this idea. From this view develops a sense of interdependence of the self with other human beings and the importance of intimate "no holding out" love relationships. As a resource at this point we use Watts' *Nature, Man and Woman.* Students respond to this work enthusiastically, for it seems to verbalize for them their ill-formed feelings of their deep need for affection and its inextricable connection with sensuality. Finally attention is drawn to the negative complexes revealed in their behavior—their mistrust, fear of injury, hostility and projection At this point Kerby-Miller's formula of love as the process of overcoming mistrust, and Carl Jung's ideas on the projection of the archetypes of the unconscious—the shadow (negative) self, the anima and animus—have proved to be valuable tools.

Once this groundwork is laid, other elements are brought in fairly easily. Once there is some insight, the student can see that he must have a fundamental (2) *trust* of himself in order to trust and love others. Basic trust opens the door to (3) *honesty* and (4) *acceptance* which facilitate the management of negative feelings. Trust in the ability to love permits one to become nonjudgmental. The process of loving communication is thereby characterized by the (5) *capacity to listen,* to perceive and respond to the other as he actually is, without the desire to manipulate him into idealized projection.

As work on the relationship progresses, one learns (6)

*how to expose oneself* before the other, to reveal real feelings and face conflicts openly. Sidney Jourard discusses self-revelation in *The Transparent Self,* and Mowrer's *The New Group Therapy* helps to illustrate the value of encountering. But one cannot gain much from self-revelation and encountering unless there is an (7) *openness to change,* indeed unless there is strong value placed on the process of growth we often label (8) *self-realization.* Next we have the need for (9) *patience,* which is difficult for young people. As mentioned earlier, ours is a future-oriented culture; we tend to live in anxious anticipation. This creates an impatience which makes it difficult for the young (or any of us) to enjoy the process of becoming. Once they have conceived what the end may be, young people want to be there *right now!*

Finally, there is the element of (10) *tenderness.* While many boys have difficulty expressing tenderness because it is associated with weakness and femininity, one of the striking aspects of the humanist movement is the cultivation by young males of "soft" forms of behavior, or so-called femininity. This is often symbolized by long hair, colorful dress, and gentle demeanor. Many young men are developing the realization that it takes strength and awareness to be tender and to express vulnerability openly. One encouraging sign for a young man comes at the time when he begins to allow himself to cry.

## Communes and Encounter Groups

Of course, intellectual insight into these aspects of relating is never sufficient. They must be experienced. For youth this means a process of testing themselves and applying insights to their actual lives. But many young people are not yet ready for a long-term heterosexual relationship, or not yet ready to expose themselves in their present relationship. As a consequence they seek out or create other "safer" arenas in which to practice their capacities to relate fully.

Many youth have found it "safer" and more enriching to share love than to engage in some mimicry of adult monogamy. This is why, at least on the West Coast, there have developed a startling number of communes, found in Seattle, Eugene, Mendacino and Marin Counties, California, San Francisco, the Santa Cruz mountains and Santa Cruz area, the Big Sur, and Los Angeles, to name several areas. The communes provide intense experience in learning to live with others openly and lovingly, and an enormous number of opportunities for direct intimate encountering over the issues most crucial to youth. There is often a fairly free sexuality with amazingly little possessiveness and guilt. Sometimes, there is a norm that sexual rights are open and to be shared by all. Most often, there are partnerships within the super-family structure which break up and re-form, providing a variety of experience.

However, the communes appeal to relatively few, and the encounter group experience seems to be growing into *the* educational vehicle for the growing category we have dubbed humanist youth. The experimental colleges (run by the associated student bodies) and the independent "free universities" on the West Coast now offer a large variety of encounter and sensory-awareness groups. The opportunity for self-disclosure and self-evaluation with candid feedback from a small group has a growing appeal to humanist youth. To experience oneself as a vital person in intense emotional relation to others allows young people to test and live out what they believe. As in any movement which has its faddist elements, some students have become encounter aficionados, mistaking hostility for being truly oneself. Most students find, however, that the encounter-group experience makes them better able to reveal deep feelings and face conflicts that heretofore they have avoided. Such accomplishments are essential to the success of long-term intimate relationships.

feeling that conception is largely decided by fate or God, rather than being an act for which parents must often (in the light of contraceptive powers) take responsibility. Having a definitely unwanted child in or out of wedlock is often a serious moral offense against oneself, the other parent, the child, other siblings, and society. Unwanted conceptions probably have many undesirable effects for parents and children, even though adequately controlled systematic research to test this hypothesis is hard to find.

After unwanted conceptions, many women have abortions. We believe expert abortions should be available to all, but under the existing legal and social framework abortion often produces medical, psychological and social problems, including severe guilt feelings. Good black-market abortion is virtually unavailable to the poor. An unsuccessful attempt can damage the fetus for life and/or upset psychological mother-child balances. Thus undesirable effects of abortion and attempted abortion are one cost of failure to control conception responsibly.

Many women who do not attempt abortion are tempted to do so, or are furious or depressed on discovering pregnancy. Many women shift from rejecting pregnancy to accepting the baby by the time it is born. But the best explanation in most cases seems to be that they have repressed their rejecting feelings. Repressing angry feelings does not keep them from showing through in disguised but havoc-producing ways. Often this involves the "overprotective mother" pattern, where excessive care and apparent solicitude mask death wishes and anger.

Such maternal or paternal hostility and rejection can make for tragic parent-child relationships, and for maladjusted, stunted children. Older siblings are sometimes neglected to make way for the unwanted arrival. Mothers and fathers often hamper and frustrate their own lives and marriage relationships. Even if only "wanted" babies were born, population would grow far too rapidly; unwanted babies not only may have sad personal and family effects, but sorely aggravate the population cancer. It is ethical for parents to avoid unwanted pregnancies, and for society to promote methods and circumstances which do the same; failure to do so is immoral.

To see whether unwanted conception was perceived as unethical, we gave college students nine cards listing "sins" including murder, theft, premarital intercourse with and without contraceptives, and having a definitely unwanted baby within marriage. This last item received the most variation in rankings of relative "sinfulness," suggesting that the morality of preventing unwanted babies is not a crystallized value, even among the new generation. Students from a conservative Protestant background did not rank this so "sinful" as more liberal Protestants. A number of Catholics thought it was more sinful for a married couple to use contraceptives than to have a definitely unwanted child.

### POPULATION CATASTROPHE

Helping stop population growth is not often thought of as a specifically moral and ethical matter. This is perhaps because traditional commandments, codes of conduct, and authority systems have no pronouncement on this very new problem in human experience. Yet that which promotes human well-being is ethical. There are few things which will have such far-reaching effects on humanity in coming decades as population control; any sane and balanced humanistic consideration of ethical urgencies must therefore rank birth control high. Sins of omission can be as grave as those of commission; failure to act in view of the population crisis, neglect or default which dooms the earth to become a swarming anthill in a generation or two, is grossly unethical. And at certain points, despite attempted politeness, these humanistic ethical concerns for population control run head on and with drawn swords into the present official Roman Catholic position on contraception and into some other ethical systems of traditional groups.

Despite feeble and sometimes frenzied efforts to apply brakes, we are hurtling at a growing speed into population calamity. After fourteen years in India, I am keenly aware of the grimy poverty and the tragically poor nutrition, education, medical care, and intellectual stimulation which go with it in developing countries—conditions traceable in part to population pressures which prevent economic advancement. In "rich" nations, many of the same influences operate among the poor, and riots and delinquency and tendencies to war may be aggravated by population growth. Man is stripping the earth of forests and topsoil, spreading concrete over everything, polluting air and water and landscape, and upsetting natural balances that have taken aeons to develop. The world of a century hence, with its projected population of six to

eight times the present one, will have few "natural" places
left, and will face problems resulting from almost unbelievable
congestion. A century in the eyes of history is but "as a watch
in the night," and responsible humans looking beyond their
own lifetimes must feel a grave burden to do something now,
for even action immediately is almost too late.

In our view the possible harm to humanity done by adultery, homosexuality, incest, theft, and murder is trivial compared
to that done by continuing the cataract of new and often unwanted babies we are pouring onto the planet—a cataract that
can be reduced by birth control. When the house is burning
down, it is not the time to worry about a broken windowpane.

### CONFLICT BETWEEN HUMANISTIC
### AND TRADITIONAL ETHICAL SYSTEMS

Humanism is not an organized bureaucracy, exerts no
concentrated social or political pressure, and tends to be very
tolerant of the behavior of those of more traditional per-
suasions. Traditional ethical systems often provide a sharp
contrast on each of these points. Yet in our view the humanist
who thinks matters through and acts on the logical conclusions
must condemn the present official stance of the Roman Catholic
Church on contraception. If Catholics have the right to look
through the spectacles of their beliefs and unswervingly decide
when others are doing wrong, those of a humanistic persuasion
have a right to use the ethical standards they believe in (with
equal conviction) and judge the official Catholic stance as
unethical, though sincere. Many Catholic laymen and religious
leaders are equally critical of the official Church position.

Perhaps it is time for non-Catholics to start swallowing
some of the same medicine they have been spooning out for
Catholics. They have been saying that Catholics should get over
their "petty" ethical quibbles over contraception; the same is
true about non-Catholic views on abortion, sterilization, and
freedom of choice to have as many children as desired. Abortion
and sterilization are highly effective population-control methods, medically safe when properly done, yet opposed by some
as immoral. As we have elsewhere emphasized, individual freedom of choice and action is often sacrificed for the good of
the group. If it is necessary to force people to have small
families, this seems strange because it has not hitherto been

necessary, but involves absolutely nothing new in principle. The most effective way to force family size down is through massive economic rewards and penalties, so massive that they could not be ignored. Yet to such schemes, traditional religionists of many stripes raise objections.

### ABORTION

A careful study in Europe by eminent physicians found that abortion during the first three months of pregnancy, induced by an experienced doctor in a hospital, involved "far" less medical risks to the mother than those accompanying full-term pregnancy and delivery. The operation is dangerous only when performed by the incompetent and/or under unfavorable circumstances. In cultures where the whole social and ethical system supports abortion, guilt is not notable. If the culture gives legal approval to abortion, this fact will itself reduce the feeling of having done something wrong.

The view that life is an either-or matter, something which does not exist in sperm and ovum but exists full-fledged once the two join, cannot be supported from contemporary science. And early church fathers can be cited as holding that life did not begin until several months after conception.

I believe that abortion should be categorically available to any woman who wants it at least during the first three months of pregnancy. Humanistic ethics may demand more than a passive acceptance of such views; they may demand active opposition to and conflict with those who, on other sincere ethical grounds, block the availability of abortion. Those who do not wish to have or perform abortions should not be forced by others, but neither should those who wish to have or perform them be denied this alternative. This is especially true in view of the population crisis and the enormous potential of abortion for population control, as demonstrated in Japan.

### Out of Marriage

Although the focus in the second half of this paper will be on premarital contraception in the teens and early twenties, much of what is said applies also to contraception in adultery. Also, the term "premarital" implies that marriage will later occur; *permanently* unmarried, widowed, separated, or divorced individuals also have intercourse, and these relations may involve contraception. Premarital intercourse, conception, abortion, birth, and contraception are occurring on a significant scale among Western youth; our focus below is on the ethics of premarital contraception.

## THE SOCIAL CONTEXT

The American student lives in a society where premarital intercourse is made logistically convenient by the absence of parents and servants from the home, by automobiles, motels, anonymity, free time, the no-chaperone system, and by a host of other factors. Internal controls are often equally lax; organized religion plays a largely ornamental role; values are heterogeneous, relative, and unclear. There is a duplicity in sex standards, so that parents who condemn high school intercourse are often involved in extramarital affairs. It would be interesting to tabulate the proportion of readers whose sex relations had been confined to the marriage bed. Popular media frequently glamorize sex out of wedlock. Many youths experience positive social pressures to have intercourse, added to biological pressures which are relatively forceful at their age. Prolonged education and other factors postpone marriage age.

But there is a horror of premarital conception and birth, at least in the middle class. The same two-faced society that snickers at premarital sex looks cold, pious, accusing, or the other way if pregnancy occurs. In the lower classes, condemnation is less likely to be wholehearted, and sometimes is mere lip service to norms of higher-status groups. Some unmarried students want pregnancy—to hurt parents, shame the sexual companion, force marriage, gain status with peers, and the like. But for most Americans premarital conception is perceived as extremely undesirable.

Granted permissiveness toward premarital sex intimacies joined with strong penalties for pregnancy, couples seek some adjustment, especially in the middle class. Adjustments include "semi-intercourse" and contraception. Petting to climax, sleeping together nude without intercourse, and "technical virginity" based on hairline definitions have much to recommend them. They not only avoid pregnancy (if limits are successfully imposed), but reduce guilt and preserve self-esteem among the many who regard full intercourse as more wicked. Also, they may result in great sexual satisfaction for the woman. Within marriage where many husbands quickly demand their "rights" and insist on quick, sometimes nervous, "on-and-off" intercourse, wives often lack sexual satisfactions that could be produced by more foreplay and patience. Among inexperienced teenagers, males may be especially quick and females especially slow. But the unmarried suitor, forced to rely on seductive skills rather than conjugal duty to get his mate's cooperation, may be much more attentive than a husband. And since many women (married or single) can achieve orgasm only through finger-genital or mouth-genital contacts anyway, petting to climax may be more sexually enjoyable for many unmarried women than the forbidden "full enjoyment." Despite these advantages, it would be naïve to hope to "sell" the unmarried *en masse* on petting to climax as a substitute for intercourse, making contraception unnecessary.

Contraception fits with a technical society where gadgets abound and taking drugs for innumerable reasons is common. Contraceptives, especially those of the newest style, have status in some groups. Like cigarettes, automobiles, and marijuana, birth-control pills or loops can symbolize adulthood. Condoms need never be used, but only carried around, to create awe.

### ENCOURAGING PREMARITAL SEX?

A recurrent question is whether knowledge and/or availability of contraception merely keeps down pregnancy among those who would be having intercourse anyway, or whether it encourages an increase in premarital sex relations. This question was discussed in several articles in the April, 1966, *Journal of Sex Research* but with little data. Schofield's research is distinctive in that the interviews were with random samples of British youth from different social class and age groups. Half of the "sexually experienced" boys and 70% of the girls had felt real fears of pregnancy at some times. Nevertheless, the majority of the experienced girls reported that they "neither took precautions themselves, nor insisted upon their partners' using any contraceptive method." Schofield's "experienced" sample did not know more about contraception than the others. Although this one study does not prove that an increase in contraceptive availability will not produce some increase in premarital sex, it does document squarely that *lack* of contraceptive information and supplies, and fear of pregnancy, will not necessarily prevent premarital intercourse.

Studies showing a correlation, over time, between contraceptive availability and volume of premarital sex would simply demonstrate the old truism that correlation does not prove causation. What is needed is an experimental study in which one group or community was given a concentrated program of premarital contraceptive information and/or supplies, and compared with controls. Dependent variables should include not only measures of volume of premarital sex but of premarital conceptions. Some would regard this as a highly dangerous experiment using "our impressionable youth as human guinea pigs." But the idea is not so far-fetched, especially if it concentrated on pregnancy-prone groups. The March 8, 1967, newsletter of Planned Parenthood–World Population described a program in Baltimore involving 2,000 teen-agers from slum neighborhoods shown to be prone to out-of-wedlock conceptions. "In some instances, if parents agree, contraception will be begun at a very early age. Teen-age programs are afoot in . . . other cities." It would appear that these projects need only control groups and some attention to experimental design to constitute research such as we have suggested above. In 1968, Planned Parenthood–World Population adopted a policy of making contraception available to any women of any age who wanted it.

PENALTIES OF "GETTING CAUGHT"

The penalties of pregnancy, especially to middle-class girls, are well known by common sense. In the white non-prison sample of the Kinsey studies, 89% of the pregnancies to single women reportedly ended in induced abortion, in contrast to 17% for married women. Although this sample is open to much criticism, abortion is a major "way out" among pregnant single girls. Even those who argue that abortion is often preferable to continuing the pregnancy will readily agree that it is only the "lesser of two evils" and still poses many problems in our culture.

When the pregnancy continues, a degree of social ostracism often results. Whether the child is kept or given for adoption, guilt often remains for years. If the child is kept, anger and guilt felt toward him may wreck the mother-child relationship.

Forced marriages are not desirable ones. Even when income and social class are controlled as carefully as possible, studies show that divorce is more likely, and the economic well-being of the couple is less, when the first pregnancy was premarital.

### IS PREMARITAL CONTRACEPTION ETHICAL?

Questions of morality can be phrased into three questions, asking 1) whether it is immoral to have premarital conceptions, 2) whether it is immoral to have premarital sex, and 3) whether avoiding premarital pregnancy would "offset" a certain increase in volume of premarital sex, if it occurred. On the first question, we regard premarital conceptions as immoral and unethical in cultures that frown on them. In the aforementioned newsletter of Planned Parenthood, the organization's president, Dr. Alan Guttmacher, opined that when sex relations do occur out of wedlock they "must be protected by effective contraception," and failure to use such protection "is the grossest form of sexual immorality and irresponsibility. . . ." We agree.

Our second question, whether premarital intercourse is immoral, is discussed elsewhere in this collection of papers. Our own view is that premarital intercoure is sometimes good, helpful, and desirable, and sometimes bad, harmful, and tragic —depending on each of the two individuals involved and on many specific circumstances. In our view the taboos on premarital sex arose, historically, because pregnancy out of wedlock created problems for family organization, inheritance patterns, etc. Near-perfect contraception will change this, so that taboos on premarital intercourse are logical anachronisms. (The same logic might apply to incest and to some extent to adultery.) But taboos on premarital intercourse are supported by other cultural factors now, and will not be quick to disappear, even with perfect contraception. In the meantime, contraception is not perfect and there are many real penalties on premarital sex.

In discussions of the ethics of premarital sex, the adult discussants may be influenced by their own not-too-conscious problems. Advocacy of premarital sex may be a vicarious way to achieve the liberty one would currently like, or wishes one had had as a youth. Crusades against premarital sex may involve overreaction against one's own desires. Youths are sometimes very perceptive when they accuse adults of being jealous, and it is not only celibate priests who may be open to such a charge.

If an increase in premarital intercourse is not, on balance, undesirable, then there is no cause to oppose the spread of contraceptives among the unmarried even if intercourse will thereby be increased. But let us assume, for purposes of discussion and because many would make this assumption, that an increase in premarital intercourse in a given community is undesirable. Let us further assume a condition which has *not* been demonstrated by research: that making contraceptive information and/or supplies available may lead to some increase in premarital sex, but will result in a net decrease in premarital conceptions. Would one then be justified in advocating premarital contraception? For many people the answer would depend on how much increase was expected in intercourse, and how much decrease in pregnancy. Research has not quantified these variables. The answer would also depend on judgment about the relative morality of premarital intercourse and pregnancy, and these are matters rooted in values and religious beliefs. The writer has been working with a research instrument that asks respondents the number of "extra" net premarital unions, if any, which might be "justified," in respondents' thinking, by the prevention of one unwanted conception.

There is often a respect for the status quo, and the latter is confused with "nature" or even "the will of God." As a result it may seem that acting, doing, and changing involve responsibility—because they interfere with the "natural" status quo—whereas doing nothing involves no responsibility. Encouraging premarital contraception interferes with the status quo, but *not* encouraging it may also be a decision which should be responsibly made.

In 1965, a modified probability sample of the United States population—over 3,000 respondents—was asked, "Do you believe that information about birth control ought to be easily available to any single adult person who wants it?" Half the respondents said "Yes," and seven percent were not sure. "Yes" answers were given by 39%, 51%, and 63% of those with grade school, high school, and more education, respectively; and 43% of Catholic and 52% of non-Catholic respondents. It appears that considerable proportions of Americans do not regard it as necessarily immoral to encourage premarital contraception. Of course the question not only specified "adult" but spoke of those "who want it," with the possible implication that they were already engaged in sex relations. A parallel study in 1967 showed similar patterns.

METHODS AND DIFFICULTIES FOR THE UNMARRIED

Pohlman discussed methods of contraception especially suited to or difficult for the unmarried, and some of the special psychological problems they have in practicing contraception. Among more conservative youth, to make contraceptive plans is to admit to oneself an intention that may seem sinful. To be "swept off one's feet" when the moon is full requires but a weak moment, and can be explained as sudden passion. But planning may mean living with a knowledge of premeditation of sin. The same individual may experience repeated cycles of uncontracepted sex relations, repentance, resolutions never to "sin" again, and backsliding. Hence it would seem that among those having premarital sex, the individuals feeling most guilty would be least likely to use contraception! We have some unpublished data consistent with this hypothesis, although the sample is not adequate to test it properly.

Kirkendall found that, in general, college couples who had more sustained friendships and attachments to each other were more liable to use contraception. Apparently there was greater risk of pregnancy to those women who had less basis for expecting fathers of any resulting children to marry them!

Premarital sex is often sporadic and unpredictable. In such cases oral contraceptives are using a shotgun to kill a mouse—an expensive shotgun and one that may risk harm to very young women whose skeletal development is not complete. For medical reasons, intra-uterine devices are also not well suited to the unmarried bed. The condom is the one method that provides some protection against venereal disease—albeit imperfect protection—and this is especially important to the unmarried. Condoms can be purchased from vending machines without embarrassing personal conversations with authority figures; this gives them a key role in premarital contraception. If used, condoms are highly effective in preventing conception. But since, unlike pills and loops, they require annoying interruptions at the moment of sexual arousal when judgment is poor, and they interfere with physical enjoyment, in many cases they will not be used. No presently perfected methods are ideal, and for the unmarried the "best" method depends on personal tastes and circumstances, including the frequency and regularity of intercourse.

For many unmarried couples the ideal contraceptive method would be one that could be decided upon and used *after* a woman has, perhaps with no premeditation, had intercourse. There has been some research on a possible "morning after" or "missed-period" pill. Any method that does not have to be used until *after* intercourse has advantages. If a woman could wait until she discovered pregnancy before taking "retrocontraceptives," she might be more strongly motivated, and physicians and parents and society more willing, to do what was necessary to get the pills into the woman. To secure and take medication "just in case" might seem less imperative and justifiable to all involved. Whether or not retrocontraceptives—if perfected—would be classified as abortion and hence condemned is not clear.

### ROLE OF SCHOOLS AND COLLEGES

Pohlman has discussed the role of American public high schools and junior high schools in premarital contraception. The average public high school cannot encourage premarital contraception in any open way. (Some adventurous schools, especially in areas with high risk of premarital pregnancy, should experiment with programs.) But the very fact of including discussions of contraception in classes gives some encouragement to premarital contraception, even though information is labeled as "for marriage only." When students bring problems and decisions to counselors or other school personnel for *individual* discussions, premarital contraception can be mentioned when it appears that they are engaging in intercourse or about to start. Schools can refer students to physicians and other agencies where contraceptive information and supplies can be dispensed. In public and private colleges and universities, the conflict over whether to provide contraceptive information and supplies through the health center is fairly well known; ethical principles involved have been covered above.

Public-school administrators are subject to the realities of community pressures, including those from organized religion. Perhaps the decisive question is the balance between concern over premarital pregnancy and concern over teaching children "bad" things. There is often a general perception that "all moral people" are opposed to premarital sex, abortion, and the encouragement of premarital contraception. Religious and other groups refer to these generalized perceptions, and the school cannot be unresponsive. To arm itself with information, San Joaquin County in California did a countywide study in which students and teachers of various school levels, and specific professional and other groups of adults, were asked whether each of a list of very specific "sex education" topics (including contraception) should be taught in public schools and if so at what grade level. Data were analyzed both by types of respondents and specific town or community within the county. If such a survey shows that most respondents in a given town favor the teaching of a particular topic, this can at least silence noisy critics when they claim they have the majority supporting them in opposing such training.

### *Summary*

Unwanted children and avalanching population growth are such grave problems that it is a matter of high ethical priority to struggle to stop them. And to fail—by neglect, avoidance, or default—is wickedly immoral in view of its consequences for future generations, so wickedly immoral as to dwarf adultery, theft, and murder. Since "unnatural" contraception, abortion, sterilization, and massive financial incentives for those who keep families small are all promising ways to avoid births, it is ethical to work to remove the legal and social blocks to these. Of course this must be done with diplomacy and a respect for those whose ethical systems make them feel otherwise. But at some point these value systems clash head on, and it may become a matter of ethics for the humanist to do what he can, by whatever means are truly effective, to see that people who want abortion (for example) are not thwarted from getting it by those with traditional ethical scruples.

Since the cultural context permits and even encourages premarital intercourse, while penalizing premarital pregnancy, premarital contraception is an extremely important topic. For those who are engaging in premarital intercourse, contraception is an ethical responsibility and failure to use it seems grossly immoral. More complex are ethical judgments about the provision of contraceptive information supplied to unmarried people in a community in general, through schools, health centers, and youth agencies. It is often believed that such steps, though they may cut down premarital pregnancy, will increase premarital intercourse.

This belief has not been adequately checked with research, although it is clear that fear of pregnancy and absence of contraceptives are not sufficient to prevent premarital intercourse. Even if one assumes for argument that availability of contraception increases fornication in a community on the average, those who do not view this increase as undesirable experience no ethical conflict. But those who regard such an increase as bad may struggle with the question of whether a reduction in premarital pregnancies is sufficient to "justify" some increase in premarital intercourse. Some methods of contraception are especially suited to or difficult for the unmarried, who experience certain special psychological problems in practicing contraception.

# 15. Population Control and Personal Freedom— Are They Compatible?

ALICE TAYLOR DAY

The twentieth century may well be remembered as the last period in which man could reproduce without regard for the social consequences of his behavior. Few developments in history have so challenged the ability of man to live harmoniously within his social and physical environments as has the unprecedented increase of his own species. Recognition of the penalties of unlimited reproduction is leading increasingly to the demand that action be taken to alter the ruinous course of present demographic trends. The rising pressure for action is reflected in the expansion of programs to influence reproductive behavior, and in the growing discussion of broad questions about population policy itself. The important question is now no longer whether man should curtail his excess reproduction, but how best to induce him to do so. The urgency of the problem is even more pronounced in view of Pope Paul's Encyclical, "On Human Life."

## Replacement or Expansion?

Two leading American demographers have recently offered different views about the means necessary to end the current population expansion. Differences in their outlooks can be traced to their differing judgments about the adequacy of current family-planning programs to effect a genuine long-term decline in population growth. Asserting that action programs now under way are successfully bringing birth rates under control, Donald Bogue claims that within the brief span of five years a change amounting to "a social revolution" has taken place both in the acceptance of the need for birth control and in the growth of knowledge and research activities concerning the techniques of effective family planning. Crediting organized family-planning programs with most of the declines in the birth rate in Korea, Pakistan, Taiwan, and Colombia, he goes on to say that, considering the rapid pace of "fertility control" over the past few years, ". . . it is quite reasonable to assume that the world population crisis is a phenomenon of the twentieth century, and will be largely if not entirely a matter of history when humanity moves into the twenty-first century."

Kingsley Davis is much less sanguine. Even if we accept the judgment that the next few decades will witness the rapid adoption of contraception all over the world, there are firm grounds, he believes, for skepticism about whether the widespread use of family planning will signal an end to the population explosion. He notes first that despite the enthusiasm about the spread of family planning, birth rates in many underdeveloped countries are rising, not falling. Moreover, he continues, the responsibility of family-planning campaigns for falling birth rates in particular areas may well have been exaggerated, for in many such instances birth rates were beginning to decline well before family-planning campaigns were under way. Declining fertility could be attributed, therefore, at least as much to the influence of social change and modernization as to the introduction of birth control.

In fact, claims Davis, talk about "population control" or "fertility control" in connection with family-planning programs is misleading. Such programs make no attempt to influence the factors actually determining levels of reproduction. The aim is, instead, to enable individual couples to bear the number of children they want when they want them. Any program designed to enable parents to have no more than the number of children they want can reduce a population's growth rate only if couples have been having more children than they want to have. Though such conditions of excess childbearing seem to exist in many (if not all) underdeveloped countries, the numbers of children desired are well above those needed for replacement only. In the developed countries, moreover, recent studies of reproductive motivation show that the numbers of children couples say they want are frequently *above* those they actually have. So far as is known, there is no population—whether in an underdeveloped or a developed country—whose childbearing aspirations are currently low enough to halt population increase. The prevention of unwanted births (the actual result of a successful family-planning program) could still leave a rapid rate of population growth.

### Needed: A Change in Attitude

Extension of control over childbearing to individuals is obviously an important preliminary to population control, but it is only a preliminary. To effect a substantial decline in growth rates there must also be a fundamental change in the size of the families couples want. Present action programs avoid persuading couples to reduce their desire for children. Family planning is urged as a means to improve personal family interests: the health of the mother and the quality of the children born. The demographic results of such programs are at the best ambiguous. Appeals to control reproduction couched in terms of personal interests may reduce high-order birth in the short run, but the long-run consequences may be to encourage couples to bear more children as their economic and social fortunes improve. Once couples possess the means to plan their families, a crucial question still remains: What, in fact, influences a couple's decision to have a given number of children; and where population limitation is clearly indicated, what are the attributes of that social setting that will prompt couples to have no more than the number needed to replace themselves?

By failing to come to terms with this question, warns Davis, we are evading the real issue of population policy, "which is how to give societies the number of children they need." Demographic history has demonstrated repeatedly that the family-building habits of couples are almost totally uninfluenced by demographic considerations. In European countries the biggest advances in the spread of family limitation came in the 20's and 30's against a background of official alarm about the possibility of underpopulation. During the 1960's, in many of these same countries, the three-or-four-child family has been gaining in popularity, particularly among certain higher socio-economic groups, and this at a time of increasing public concern with the threat of overpopulation. Projection of the average family size of 2.6 recently given as "ideal" by a sample of newly married British couples would lead in two centuries to a United Kingdom population of 400 million, a number 10 times the 40 million proposed at the 1966 Conference of the British Association for the Advancement of Science as the maximum those densely settled islands could sustain at reasonably comfortable levels of living. The gap between private behavior and public needs becomes even more obvious when we realize that to achieve that figure of 40 million the British population would have to experience an actual decline over the next two centuries to three-fourths of its present size.

Clearly, individual assessments of the number of children conducive to family welfare do not necessarily add up to a population size conducive to collective welfare. Demographic man, making isolated personal choices about his family size, is ill-suited to create demographic conditions beneficial to himself and his progeny. Ultimately, genuine control over population would require a judicious arrangement of the socio-cultural context in which family formation takes place along lines that would promote the family whose size is most congruent with social needs.

Before specific measures to meet this challenge can be intelligently considered, we must have clearly in mind what it is we hope to achieve by a cessation of population increase. We must remember that population control is itself only a means to broader human goals. The ultimate goal of population control is survival of the human species. Any rate of population increase would eventually exhaust the earth as a human habitat. But suppose for a moment that (though they have not yet done so) developments in the provision of food, clothing, and shelter did manage to keep abreast of today's population increases. Would a world of, say, 20 to 30 billion be fit for human life? Under conditions of such high density, human behavior of all kinds would have to be rigidly controlled. Spontaneity could not be permitted; individual variation would have to be virtually nil. What is at stake here is no less than the survival of human society as we know it.

Fortunately, such an extreme is quite improbable demographically. Before an age of encapsulated man could become reality, the pressure of human numbers would so depress levels of living that mortality would rise to preindustrial heights. Population would cease to grow because mankind would no longer exercise control over death.

Much more pertinent to our present concern is the immediate threat of population growth to conditions of life that are essential to the fulfillment of goals sought by the 3.5 billion people who already inhabit the earth. Such goals as health, longevity, material well-being, the rule of law, and the orderly settlement of conflicts are generally preferred to their opposites by men everywhere, regardless of the particular social setting in which they live. The attainment of these goals is, in fact, coming to be recognized as requisite to the pursuit of most other individual interests—intellectual, spiritual, and esthetic. Underlying the agitation for population control is the growing conviction that, above all else, the continued addition of human numbers diminishes the capacity of society to provide those conditions that serve individual interests and offer the greatest possibilities for the full development of human faculties.

At the most general level the means chosen to control human reproduction must be consistent with the goal of promoting the kinds of social conditions that are hospitable to human development and the satisfaction of individual interests. So far, instructing parents about how to plan the number of their children to coincide with their personal family interests has been relied upon as the only policy consistent with this goal. But, as we have suggested, the family-planning approach to population policy, while it advances individual interests in the short run, will be self-defeating in the long run (and not so very long at that) if it fails to accomplish that reduction of conditions of life throughout the world. To what avail is nurturing the family if the individual members of the family are unable to satisfy their needs for good health, education, employment, and recreation? In short, it may be necessary to alter the traditional emphasis on the family in order to safeguard the individual from deterioration of the social conditions through which most of his goals as both a human and a social being must be met.

## Possible Solutions

A value choice of this sort seems to underline Davis' admonition that what is required to halt population growth is not family planning as such, but rather, "selective restructuring of the family in relation to the rest of society." To this end Davis proposes two broad changes in present family systems: 1) raising the age at marriage, and 2) encouraging further limitation of births within marriage. Although some of the measures he proposes to spur change in these directions are in the nature of inducements to refrain from childbearing, the general tenor of his proposals is decidedly negative. The majority of them involve the imposition of some kind of restraint and hardship not only on family life but on all individuals in the society. Davis himself acknowledges this in noting:

A realistic proposal for a government policy of lowering the birth rate reads like a catalogue of horrors: squeeze consumers through taxation and inflation; make housing very scarce by limiting construction; force wives and mothers to work outside the home to offset the inadequacy of male wages, yet provide few child-care facilities; encourage migration to the city by paying low wages in the country and providing few rural jobs; increase congestion in cities by starving the transit system; increase personal insecurity by encouraging conditions that produce unemployment and haphazard political arrests.

But as a long-term policy of population control, would these measures be any more effective than the extension of current family-planning programs? The adequacy of such measures, imposed by themselves, seems, in fact, to be open to question on two counts: 1) Many of these measures are patently inconsistent with the basic aim of improving conditions of life, and 2) In the absence of pertinent research, their consequences for population growth are by no means clear. Such measures, for example, as "increasing congestion in cities" or "increasing personal insecurity by encouraging conditions that produce unemployment and haphazard political arrests" (while undoubtedly included by Davis to highlight the barrenness of current ideas about how to encourage a limitation of childbearing), would obviously in the long run promote certain of the very conditions that population control is designed to alleviate. Moreover, a policy of indirect repression (i.e., limiting the supply of housing and squeezing consumers) might have quite different consequences for the birth rates of successive age groups. Major fluctuations in family size very likely occur more as a response to changes in social conditions than as a response to any particular elements in the social situation. What one age group experiences as a change may be taken for granted as facts of life by those who follow. Given the breathing space afforded by the lower reproductivity of their parents, succeeding age groups might be encouraged—unless different and even more stringent measures were applied—to have larger families than did their ancestors.

Actually, even the short-run consequences of all such specific measures is uncertain. One of the difficulties in devising a national policy for lowering the birth rate is that specific measures may have quite different consequences for the childbearing of different groups. The effectiveness of specific measures for lowering family size would vary with the social setting in which they were applied and the needs met by childbearing for couples in different socio-economic categories. Depending on the social context, for example, increasing childcare facilities to encourage women to take jobs after bearing one or two children might be a more effective (as well as a less repressive) policy than denying women access to the possibilities of leaving their children in competent hands (which could discourage them from pursuing interests outside the family). For a great many women in the United States, facilities for the care of preschool children are now so rudimentary that this indirect method of influencing family size may be considered to be already in effect.

In fact, the conditions Davis enumerates already exist for a large minority of the American population. The Negro migrants to American metropolitan centers (and to a lesser extent the urban poor of all description) are daily subjected to such "horrors"; and, indeed, the birth rate of urban Negroes is substantially lower than that of their rural counterparts. Though the burden of blighted living conditions falls heaviest on the Negro and the poor, Americans from all social strata are increasingly experiencing the weight of certain of Davis' measures: the congestion of cities, higher taxes and inflation, and increased personal insecurity. It is hard to avoid the conclusion that this spreading of hardship may have some bearing on the fact that American fertility rates have been steadily declining since 1957. It is such evidence as this—piecemeal observation of the economic and social conditions that have in the past accompanied intervals of low birth rates—that, in the absence of systematic sociological and demographic research on the matter, demographers have been obligated to use in support of their contention that only a repressive population policy will be effective. Certainly, in historical perspective, the lowest birth rates appear to have been associated with periods of rapid changes and conditions that contribute to general insecurity, such as economic depression, housing shortages, migration to cities, and economic and political instability of the sort found today in certain Eastern European countries—predominately Catholic countries, by the way—which have the lowest birth rates in the world.

But does this necessarily mean that to be effective a program of population control must be coercive, or, as a minimum, draw its provisions extensively from Davis' "catalogue of horrors"? Or is it possible that potential parents might choose to have small families as a response, instead, to a healthy adjustment to their surroundings, and confidence that their lives can be rewarding without resorting to childbearing in excess of the number necessary for replacement? Whether limitation of childbearing to the necessary degree could indeed come about as such a positive response, and what the conditions are that would bring it about and maintain it, should become the target of intensive research, supported generously as contributing information about population policy of the most practical kind.

## Substitutes for Childbearing

If population policy is to emphasize inducements for limiting reproduction rather than sanctions against parenthood, it is necessary, first, to have a clear understanding of the rewards now presumed to be secured through childbearing. Given the apparent preference for more than two children among populations in which birth control is widely practiced, the question we must ask is why the desire for families of moderate size remains so durable? As a start, we suggest that children be viewed as a source of satisfaction of personal interests, rather than regarded chiefly in terms of the costs they represent to their parents. What, then, are the interests served by childbearing among the different groups in the population, and can alternatives be provided that would reduce dependence on children as a means of satisfying these interests? Specific inducements to limit childbearing may have to be geared to the needs of couples in particular social environments; but any policy designed to have more than a random, short-term influence on demographic behavior would have to consider as well the effect on family building of more general socio-cultural conditions. To suggest that the meaning of childbearing for the Negro urban mother on welfare might be somewhat different from that for the white wife of a business executive living in suburbia is not to diminish the importance to family size of influences these two may have in common. Both, by reason of their residence in the same country, are exposed to certain of the same general cultural themes and social arrangements. Both, by reason of their common humanity, presumably seek to satisfy through childbearing certain of the same general interests: support (psychological if not financial) in periods of crisis and old age, interest and variety, meaningful activities to fill in time, self-esteem and a sense of unique contribution, a shield against loneliness.

In line with the purpose of seeking positive measures to curtail reproduction we suggest that one way to reduce incentives to childbearing might be to increase the opportunities for finding these rewards in situations outside the family. This is not a new idea. The provision of financial security in old age and expanding educational and occupational opportunities for women have already been proposed as measures to lower fertility. But there are many other measures that might at once increase the individual's scope for satisfying his interests and at the same time lower fertility by reducing his dependence on marriage and childbearing. Such changes as improving public transportation to community facilities, increasing the access of urban populations to outdoor recreation, providing more opportunities for people of all ages to engage in socially useful activities, in increasing opportunities for adults to have meaningful relationships with children other than their own could all conceivably have this effect—in addition, of course, to enlarging access to a variety of birth-control techniques. Some have proposed the establishment of a permanent national service corps, the ostensible purpose of which would be to alleviate pressing domestic needs—from the tutoring of educationally disadvantaged children to the beautification of public places, and even the maintenance of clean public toilets. If such a program could offer genuinely attractive provisions for such interests as a satisfying social life for single individuals, a respite from routine work, accessible employment for married women, productive activities for the elderly, a chance for urbanites to spend time in the country, it could have important indirect consequences for repressing fertility. Among other things, it could provide an alternative to early marriage, and also reduce the temptation to resort to childbearing for want of other meaningful options.

In the long run, assuming that the demographic and social conditions found today in industrialized countries (i.e., low death rates, early and near-universal marriage, and high material levels of living) eventually spread throughout the world, stability in population size could be maintained, short of coercion, only in a social climate in which the family of three children was considered large. I suggest that as a minimum, there are two conditions necessary to achieve this favorable predisposition to the replacement-sized family: 1) much greater accessibility to effective means of limiting births and 2) much greater concern for the well-being of each individual at all stages of life. The relation of the first to a reduction in births is clear; the second is as yet only a hunch. If adults are to be content with a long life relieved by the diversion of but few of their own children, they must have confidence in their own and their children's chances to fulfill themselves in whatever terms the society defines as worthwhile. I suggest that a more solid foundation for the small-family system is a population policy designed to foster attractive alternatives to marriage and childbearing rather than a policy aimed at increasing the already substantial burdens of everyday living. Such a policy would also be more consistent with human needs and human goals. Surely, there may be limits to the effectiveness of indirect repression in reducing childbearing. Though low fertility has in the past been associated with insecurity and hardship, excess childbearing seems actually to thrive most in a context of indifference to human potential. The population policy that stifles human interests may well boomerang by enhancing the role of the family as a source of security and personal intimacy. To avoid this impasse, much research is needed to determine both the needs that are presumed to be met by childbearing and the measures that would provide real substitutes for childbearing in meeting these needs. At this transitional stage in our attitudes toward population control, what is needed is a bold sense of the future, in terms of both the sort of demographic and social conditions we can expect and the part man should play in shaping demographic behavior to realize more nearly his individual and collective goals.

## 16. Sterilization— Accepting the Irrevocable

### GARRETT HARDIN

*In the initial stages of planning for this book a decision was made to include Dr. Garrett Hardin's chapter "Abortion —or Compulsory Pregnancy," published in the May, 1968 issue of the* Journal of Marriage and the Family. *In the meantime abortion laws in a number of states have changed, legalized abortion is now more available than it was.*

*Recently New York replaced its 142-year-old abortion law with one permitting a doctor to perform an abortion up to the sixth month of pregnancy for any reason decided on by doctor and patient together. In Washington, D.C., a recent federal judge's ruling against the extant 69-year-old abortion law has similarly had the effect of liberalizing abortion practice. Currently, the National Association for the Repeal of Abortion Laws is considering establishing an abortion clinic open to women from all over the country. Now there are only about three deaths per 100,000 cases of hospital-performed abortions as compared to about 20 deaths for each 100,000 live births. The element of grave danger to the mother's life no longer exists. Clearly, the trend is set, the pattern of freedom is emerging, and the general situation has changed materially in a relatively short time.*

*In a society that has adequate sterilization measures at its disposal, that has effective birth-control technology available, it is not usually defensible to use abortion as a regular means to control population. Since the thrust of our concern in Part VII has been to explore humanistic approaches to population control, we have decided to examine, instead of abortion, the use of sterilization to help stave off the real possibilities of over-population in the near future.*

*Although such currently popular population theorists as Paul Ehrlich* (The Population Bomb) *continue to forecast doom, we as humanists must take all possible action in pursuit of more rational population policies. The next large-scale attack will no doubt bear down heavily on sterilization for those who wish to solve the current dilemma of being able to live active sex lives without contributing to the crushing world problem of over-population.*

THE EDITORS

In many respects the best method of birth control is sterilization. It is the surest method; and although it requires a surgical operation, in the long run it is by far the cheapest method of birth control. Let's see what is involved.

In the male, sterilization is produced by cutting the vas deferens on each side. After being cut, each end of each vas deferens is folded over on itself and securely tied. Usually a short section of the "vas" is removed. The operation is called a vasectomy (literally, "removal of vas"). By this operation the possibility of spermatozoa making the journey through the vas deferens to the outside is prevented. Since the vas deferens tubes lie free in the scrotum (which hangs loosely from the male body) the operation is a very simple one which can be performed under local anesthesia. It is painless or almost so. It takes only a few minutes. The patient then can get up and go about his business.

At least the operation *can* be very simple and inexpensive. It can also be built up into a small dramatic production— several days in the hospital, a regular operating room, numerous attendants and considerable expense. In the name of "first-rate medicine" it can be made virtually unavailable to the poor. The importance of availability is illustrated by an experience in India in 1967.

Seeking to curb population growth, Indian authorities set up an information booth in the main railway station in Bom-

bay where they persuaded passing men to sign up for sterilization at a hospital. But only five per cent of those who signed
the book ever turned up at the hospital.

One day one of the clients put his finger on the trouble.
"If this operation is as simple as you try to make out," he
asked, "why do you have to go to a hospital to have it done?"
The director of the project got the point and set up a simple
operating theatre in a shed that had a floor space of only
four by six feet. Soon they were doing four operations an hour
on suburbanites traveling to or from work. The operating
shed was often in use until one o'clock in the morning.

In the female, sterilization is a somewhat more complicated operation. The object is the same: to keep the female
reproductive cells (eggs) from traveling from the gonad
(ovary) to a place where they can encounter reproductive
cells from the male. But the tubes down which the eggs pass
—the oviducts or Fallopian tubes—are harder to get at. There
are two ways to do this.

In the older operation, called a *tubectomy,* the abdominal
wall is opened and each Fallopian tube is tied ("ligated")
twice and cut between the two ligatures. "Tying the tubes"
is about as serious and expensive as the removal of an ap-
pendix. Under modern medical conditions, both operations are
quite easy; but the hospitalization required does run the expense up a bit. For a few days after the birth of a child, the
oviducts are unusually easy to get at. Sterilization performed
at this time is less expensive, and does not require any days
spent in the hospital beyond what the woman would spend
after having a child anyway. So most female sterilizations are
performed right after childbirth.

Another method of closing the passage of the Fallopian
tubes has recently been perfected. A flexible instrument is
introduced through the vagina and the uterus and into each
of the Fallopian tubes in turn. With this instrument, the in-
terior of the tube is electrically "cauterized" (mildly damaged
by heat). In response to this damage scar tissue soon forms,
sealing the tube closed, thus preventing the passage of eggs
down the tube, or spermatozoa up it. The almost microscopic
eggs whose passage is thus blocked simply disintegrate a few
days after escaping from the ovary, without any effect on the
woman who produces them. The cauterization can be done in
a doctor's office; hospitalization is not required.

If sterilization is the best of all methods of birth control, why is it not used oftener? The answer is well-known: because it is irrevocable. Unlike condom, diaphragm or pill, it cannot be alternately used and not used. Most people quite naturally think hard before taking an irrevocable step of any sort.

However, it should be pointed out, as the English law professor Glanville Williams put the matter: "After all, if tubal ligation is irrevocable so is the birth of an unwanted child."

Is it really irrevocable? Not quite. For example, in the male the free ends of the cut vas deferens can be surgically reconnected. With luck, the cut ends will heal together and the passageway will be open and continuous again. It can be easily appreciated that such an operation requires a great deal of skill—much more than the small amount of skill required to cut the tubes in the first place. Unless the technique of the surgeon is very good, scar tissue will form and plug the opening of the reconnected tubes.

When the "reverse operation" was first performed, surgeons reported only 5 to 10 per cent success. In recent years, success has been approaching the 90 per cent figure. But the operation is expensive; it costs about 20 times as much as a vasectomy.

What is needed is a method of sterilization that is simply and inexpensively reversible. To date, this problem has not been solved. About a generation ago some sterilizations were done by X-radiating the scrotum of a male. When the proper dose is used, the male becomes sterile for 6 to 12 months. There is an extremely serious criticism to be made of this operation, however. In the process of damaging the sperm-forming cells of the gonads, X-rays change them genetically. When the sperm-forming cells recover from the X-ray effect, they recover in changed form. After X-radiation, sperm-forming cells produce mutated sperm cells in higher frequency than they did before. That is, an X-radiated male is more likely to produce defective children than is a non-X-radiated male. Plainly this method of sterilization is so undesirable that it should not be tolerated. It has, in fact, been abandoned in the United States.

Another possible way of bringing about a reversible sterilization is being worked on now. Using dogs, it has been found that the cutting of the vas deferens can be avoided if a suitable plastic substance is injected into each vas deferens. This substance forms an impassable blockade to sperm cells. Later, it can be removed. A fine hypodermic needle is thrust through the wall of the vas deferens and the plastic is drawn out. The reverse operation in this case is very simple, and should be cheap. However, it takes a long time to bring medical research to a successful conclusion. It may be some time before this method is available for use on human beings. And, of course, there may turn out to be some reason why it should not be used. We will just have to wait and see.

For the present, it is probably better to think of sterilization as an almost irrevocable operation. Proceeding on this basis, what are the advantages and disadvantages of sterilization, as compared with its alternatives?

First of all, the possibility of failure should be kept in mind. In the case of the female, failure is almost unknown. Among males, it is rare, but more frequent. Most commonly the failure of male sterilization occurs because the physician has neglected to warn his patient of one very important fact. Cutting and tying the vas deferens prevents spermatozoa newly formed in the testes from traversing the length of the tubes. But there are already some spermatozoa on the wrong side of the cut, in the seminal vesicle, for example. These sperms will be released in sexual intercourse, and there may be enough for several weeks. So for about a month, the sterilized male should assume he is fertile and should take contraceptive precautions as usual. It is advisable that he have a physician make a microscopic examination of his semen after a few weeks; contraception should not be discontinued until after the semen examination is negative.

In a small percentage of cases—much less than one per cent—the sterilization operation fails to work entirely in the male. The failures that have been recorded in the medical literature are really rather mysterious. It's hard to see how a competent physician could fail to perform a successful operation. Perhaps a few physicians are incompetent. Or perhaps Nature is very clever (and a bit of a practical joker!).

Are there any undesirable side effects of sterilization? *Only if you think there should be!* The thing that men are afraid of is that the operation will diminish their sexual abilities. This is because the operation is a rather new one and is often confused with the millennia-old operation of castration. In castration the gonads are removed. Once they are removed, no more spermatozoa are produced. But also: no male hormones are produced either. Because of this, sexual activity is reduced to a very low level, perhaps even to zero. The operation of castration has been feared for thousands of years, and rightly.

But sterilization is quite different. Although the release of spermatozoa is completely prevented, the male hormones continue to be produced and secreted into the blood stream in normal amounts. Even the amount of semen produced is not noticeably affected. Only one five-hundredth of the volume of the semen is sperm cells. It takes a microscopic examination of the semen to show that anything is missing in the sterilized man.

Similarly, in the female, tying the tubes merely prevents the escape of the eggs, and has no influence whatsoever on the elaboration of female hormones. Sterilization in either sex should then have no effect whatsoever on sexual activity.

What are the facts? To answer this question, a large number of married couples were studied in Japan. One or the other of the partners had been sterilized some years previously. Each couple was asked whether sexual activity had been affected by the operation. In 68 per cent of the cases, they reported *No*. This fits in with our theory. But among the rest, 3.5 per cent of the couples said that sexual activity had been depressed, while 28.5 per cent said that it had increased as a result of the operation. How can we explain these results?

Explanation is easy. First, let's take the 28.5 per cent who reported increased sexual activity. Any woman who has been married for a number of years can tell you that the fear of pregnancy hangs like a sword of Damocles above her head. Married men feel this danger somewhat, though usually not so keenly. Fear interferes with sexual spontaneity, with achieving the "total mutual abandon" that everyone regards as desirable. Once their fear of pregnancy is reduced to zero, many married couples find that their sexual activity is significantly increased.

What about the 3.5 per cent of the couples who said that their sexual activity was depressed? Does this mean that

sterilization is a sort of castration after all? Not at all—
*unless one thinks it is.* The man or a woman who picks up
incorrect ideas in early life may not later be able to free
himself entirely from his unjustified fears. Even after hearing
a competent explanation, he may have a residual feeling that
sterilization is something like castration, that a sterilized man,
for example, has lost something of his "manhood." Anxiety
naturally interferes with sexual performance. Such, no doubt,
is the explanation of the small percentage of people who
report unwanted side effects from sterilization.

This is, of course, another example of the "self-fulfilling
prophecy" that was discussed earlier. The results of the
operation of sterilization are strongly influenced by the expectations of the person operated on. This means that the
physician who performs such an operation has a strong obligation to see to it that his patient has the very best expectations. In practice, this means that the physician should
not even mention the small possibility that the effects might
be undesirable; rather he should emphasize the positive aspects, namely that there is a good chance that the person's
sexual life will be increased in intensity and enjoyment. We
cannot escape the consequences of self-fulfilling prophecies, so
we might as well use them to make our lives as enjoyable as
possible.

By 1969, voluntary sterilization was legal in every state
of the Union except Utah. A Gallup poll has shown that
two-thirds of the American people approve of sterilization
as a method of birth control. No records are kept of the
number of operations performed, but it is estimated that
something like two million Americans now alive have been
sterilized for contraceptive reasons. It is also estimated that
more than 100,000 men and women undergo voluntary
sterilization each year. So this is not a rare operation; and it
is undoubtedly becoming commoner.

It would be still more common if it were not for the
reluctance of many doctors to perform, or even to recommend, the operation. Some of them think it is illegal, or
that a patient might later change his mind and sue the
doctor. Their fears are unfounded. It is standard procedure
to get not only the patient but his or her spouse to sign
the "release" for the operation, on the legal grounds that

the reproductive abilities somehow "belong" to both partners of a marriage. Legally, such a release is all a doctor needs. The reluctance of many doctors to cooperate with his patients seems to be but one more legacy of the tabooridden Victorian age. A determined patient often has to approach several physicians before he finds one who has outgrown the sexually repressive ideas of yesteryear.

It should be realized, however, that there are some subsidiary psychological problems connected with voluntary sterilization. Picture a young couple in their thirties and happily married. They have had, say, two children, and think that this is all they want to have. In the past they have resorted to contraception intermittently. But since they don't want any more children, they are now considering sterilization. At this point a very "sticky" question arises: Who should get sterilized? The man or his wife?

If the couple decides on sterilization before the birth of what they want to be their last child, they may easily agree that the woman should be sterilized, because the sterilization operation can be combined with childbirth. If they reach their decision after this time, they may decide that the male should be sterilized, because this operation costs less. Economics may dictate the solution. But there is a difficulty, a skeleton in the closet, so to speak. Something they may find it difficult to talk about.

They have had all the children they want. But suppose, through some unusual accident—a fire, or an airplane accident, or who knows what—one or all of these children were to be lost? How would they feel then about having had an irrevocable operation performed? This possibility, remote as it is, makes them hesitate to resort to the irrevocable.

There is yet one more thing they may be hesitant to talk about. This is the possibility of divorce. If they get divorced, and if they remarry, they might well want to have more children. That is, the divorced and remarried woman might want to have more children by her new husband; or the divorced and remarried man might want to have children by his new wife. Given the existence of divorce and remarriage, these possibilities are not remote. And divorce is not so rare an event that one should rule it out of consideration.

But the trouble is, how can they consider it? How can they bring up the possibility? A couple may have a real and understandable reluctance to mention this possibility. Subconsciously, they recognize the reality of self-fulfilling prophecies. Subconsciously, they may feel that it would be bad luck to admit the *possibility* of divorce; they feel it might endanger the continuance of their marriage.

They may or they may not be correct in their subconscious estimation of the dangers. That isn't the point. The point is that such subconscious estimations do occur and frequently prevent frank discussion between husband and wife. Because of this, many people who might otherwise welcome sterilization reject it *without discussion* and continue using contraception during all the fertile years of their marriage. Were it not for these subconscious fears, sterilization would no doubt be resorted to much oftener than it is.

If and when a simple method of reversible sterilization is worked out, the whole picture will no doubt change. But for the present that is the way matters stand.

# Epilogue

LESTER A. KIRKENDALL

At this point we close our volume, *The New Sexual Revolution*. We cannot in any sense, however, feel that the last word has been said. Mainly we have raised issues relating to sexual changes and developments, hopefully within the context of "humanism." Since these are human issues which are influenced by cultural forces, they will forever be requiring reexamination and reassessment. Furthermore the application of humanistic concepts to human sexuality is only just beginning. In these closing remarks I should like to tie these concepts more closely to human sexuality.

The humanist believes, as I see it, that the authority which influences him in his decision-making is derived from an understanding of the nature of man, and of what is necessary if man is to find adequate satisfaction in living his individual and social life. As Dr. Kurtz says in his preface, "any limitations that emerge must emerge from within human experience; not be forced on people from without. Also they must be appropriate to the needs and desires of human beings."

The humanist supports the authority derived from the processes of rational and systematic inquiry. From the humanistic point of view, man has made his own problem; if solutions are to be found he must find them. He is the architect of both his triumphs and his defeats. There is no supernatural, no transcendental authority to which man can look for help and intervention. Humanism also rests upon certain basic assumptions about the nature of man. Of course, we have much yet to learn about man and his nature, whether we are speaking from a philosophical, biological, psychological, or a social background.

Yet I think it safe to say that such division as I have just mentioned—philosophical, biological, psychological, social—is unsound if we attempt to consider any one of these aspects of man's nature and that alone. Man really functions as a unitary organism, and each aspect of his being affects other aspects as well. Since man is a social animal, his nature demands satisfying associations in which he can feel secure and within which he can reveal himself, finding and giving acceptance. He finds his deepest satisfactions and his profoundest miseries in his close association with others.

Those who have read this book will know that sex is much more than a physical experience; it is a social experience as well which ministers in various ways to the needs and desires of men. When sexuality is examined within the framework of humanism we find that beyond sex lie still more issues—many of them commonly regarded as non-sexual.

Sexuality is a part of the complete human being and affects his relationships with others. Dr. Kurtz in his Preface was referring to this point when he wrote that the sexual revolution was "basically a *humanist* revolution." He might have added that if it is not a humanist revolution it is not basically a sexual revolution.

Since man is so dependent upon others for his fulfillment and since sex is a part of the nature of each person, no sexual revolution can exist unless it concerns itself with reassessment and reevaluation of human relationships.

Man must then involve himself with questions such as these: How does he tie his sexuality to love; how does he relate it to his aggressive impulses? How does sexual expression affect his total productive achievement? How does it differ from youth to old age, and across and within sex lines? Is there a sharp dividing line that separates sex from non-sex? How are intimacy, eroticism, and sensory awareness related to sexuality? How are responsibility and enjoyment shared in sexual encounters? Will the future cause us to turn more, or less, to traditional sexuality? How does man deal with sex in a sharply specialized, repressive society as compared with one which is open and gives him an opportunity to develop all his potentialities? These questions must be asked if we are to experience a genuine humanistic sexual revolution. These are the questions, it seems to me, which led McLuhan and Leonard to comment, "Sex as we now think of it may soon be dead."

Our authors have argued throughout that sex contributes greatly to the fulfillment of mankind, but we also know that man has many aspirations and a plethora of needs. These must all be harmonized and reconciled.

The satisfaction of man's sexual needs brings greatest fulfillment when associated with a love both given and received, and when man feels he is most productive and useful in his social environment. Sexual fulfillment will not come with the development of a single pattern of sexual behavior. It must be associated with the entirety of one's life and interrelationships.

Youth, for example, have long discussed whether premarital intercourse weakens or strengthens a relationship. Burgess and Wallin[1] stimulated this discussion in their book, *Engagement and Marriage*. They asked eighty-one men and seventy-four women, all engaged, if they felt their experience in premarital intercourse strengthened or weakened their relationships. Some 92.6 per cent of the men and 90.6 per cent of the women felt it did, and only 1.2 per cent of the men and and 5.4 per cent of the women thought the sexual experience had weakened relationships. The others noted no effect.

Commenting on their own findings, Burgess and Wallin wrote

This finding could be construed as testimony for the beneficial consequences of premarital relations, but with some reservations. First, couples who refrained from having premarital intercourse were not asked whether not doing so strengthened or weakened their relationship. They might have reported unanimously that their relationships had been strengthened by their restraint.

Such a finding could be interpreted as signifying one of two things: (a) that both groups are rationalizing or (b) that given the characteristics, expectations, and standards of those who have intercourse the experience strengthens their relationships, and, similarly, that given the standards of the continent couples the cooperative effort of couple members to refrain from sex relations strengthens their union.

In my own investigations[2] I asked my subjects if premarital sexual intercourse had strengthened or weakened their relationships. I reached the second conclusion of Burgess and Wallin cited above. Those who rejected intercourse also agreed that its rejection strengthened their relationship. What occurs is that some deeply affectionate couples have, through the investment of time and mutual devotion, built a relationship which is significant to them, and one in which they have developed mutual respect and a deep appreciation of each other. Some of these couples, who are relatively free from the customary inhibitions about sexual participation, may then experience intercourse without damage to their total relationship. I use the expression "without damage" in preference to "strengthening," for it seemed to me that in practically all instances "non-damaging" intercourse occurred in relationships which were already so strong in their own right that intercourse, *per se*, did not have much to offer toward strengthening them.

It is important in understanding the role of any form of sexual expression in strengthening or weakening a relationship to avoid fastening our attention upon sex, or assuming that it is the determining factor. We need to be concerned much more broadly with the whole relationship and the various factors and circumstances which make it meaningful, or destroy its meaning.

Masters and Johnson in their research made the same point in regard to marriage. Their first book, *Human Sexual Response*,[3] concentrated heavily on clinical findings in the field of physiological data. They reported medical findings which recorded the physiological responses of men and women to various forms of sexual stimulation in their laboratories. In their second book, *Human Sexual Inadequacy*,[4] they have turned strongly toward their counseling program, thus emphasizing their concern with the emotional and psychological aspects of sexual adjustment. Physiological knowledge still provides an invaluable source of insight, but their emphasis now is on partnership and mutual interaction. They comment that the marriage itself is the patient, that there is no such thing as an uninvolved partner in the marital bed. Here again we see the interplay between clinical knowledge of sex and its physical and emotional aspects. Counselors make constant use of this insight in their therapeutic activities.

Whether or not there is a sexual revolution is a matter of debate and constant disagreement. As we have noted, Dr. Kurtz has said that a sexual revolution must be "basically a *humanist* revolution." Now we must ask what this means. One might suspect there is less a humanistic sexual revolution than the potentiality for one. Descriptions of sexual revolution are usually in taxonomic terms—who did what to whom and when? If there is to be a genuine humanistic revolution we must put into practice what we already know about sex as an integral part of human life. This means a deep concern with those processes through which human beings interact and relate to one another sexually and otherwise.

The question was asked earlier, "What is the relationship of sex to love?" The situation ethicist says that love, and only love, is the overriding factor in human relations decision-making. No other consideration can supersede it. Love, or at least mutual respect, is clearly basic to a humanistic sexual revolution, yet we must go still farther in defining what we mean by these terms. What constitutes love and mutual respect must be spelled out; their characteristic elements considered. The place of empathy, motivation, compassion, genuine communication, methods of building and maintaining trust and similar factors must be clarified. Humanism does not disavow the quality of love, but seeks to place love and its components in the setting of a relationship.

A similar question arises when we consider the association of sex with intimacy. Dr. Whitehurst in his Introduction writes "What we all say we want is fully-developed intimacy with significant others, but what we actually achieve is highly superficial and stilted forms of interaction with others. Real intimacy is much more than sexual and probably the most rare of all human experiences." Intimacy, he suggests, is the more inclusive factor. We often get the reversal of this reflected in our vocabulary. Thus we say of a couple known to be sexually involved that "they have been intimate." Perhaps there was no intimacy at all; only the proximity of bodies.

In my lecture work in the past several years I have used a set of slides which show closeness and physical embrace in many forms—a mother nursing her child, parents romping with children, older married couples touching each other fondly, touch used to comfort, reassure, and relieve despair, adolescent boys embracing, couples in positions which might suggest coitus, touch showing joy and appreciation. One of the most perceptive responses to the slides came from a woman who said, "These pictures leave me wondering! Is there a sharp line between intimacy and sex in male-female, female-female, or male-male relationships? Where does one leave off and the other begin? Can they ever be completely divorced or separated?"

I think she had quite clearly identified what is involved in the integration of intimacy, a perception which many of us never achieve. We are so fearful of our capacity to control sex that in many of our relationships we regard intimacy as threatening and feel that unless we are careful it will get us into trouble.

Openness is a highly important quality here also. Not the glib openness flowing from the mass media, but the highly sensitive openness which in our personal relationships makes it possible for one person to reveal himself honestly to another. This kind of openness is a major concern of those humanist youth discussed by the Salisburys in their chapter. Their discussion also made it clear that "instant" intimacy is chimerical and unrealistic; intimacy comes with increasing trust, empathy, and faithfulness.

With this approach the whole question of chastity may be seen in a new context. The delegates to the World Council of Churches in Uppsala, Sweden, in 1968 were confronted with a document which argued that with modern methods of preventing conception it may become very common for unmarried couples to live together. The paper argued also that chastity is more than abstinence from intercourse. It argued that chastity is surely "concerned with the way love is expressed, with qualities of tenderness and responsibility which not only restrain people in their personal relations but also sustain husband and wife in a life-long commitment to each other." Harvey Cox,[5] another theologian, writes "The [sexual] question however, now becomes one of taste and discrimination rather than of censorship and prohibition."

As a last illustration let us look at the purposes and motives with which sex may be used. We constantly speak of the exploitation which comes through the use of sex. The double standard, which has been mentioned by several of our authors, is a common example of an exploitation sanctioned by culture. We ordinarily suggest that the double standard works to the detriment of women. They are not granted as much sexual freedom as men; and sanctions against women who violate accepted patterns are more severe.

What is usually overlooked is that the double standard works to the detriment of men as well. The double standard requires men to approach women in a deceitful way; the man cannot come out openly and say what his intentions are. Thus he is led to see those women who trust and respond to him as naïve and unsophisticated. Like the highly successful financial con man, he comes to regard all his victims as suckers. In relationships in which he hopes to find permanence and fidelity he is constantly plagued by the doubts and uncertainties which his past associations have aroused.

The double standard has also had the effect of providing rigid, unnatural roles for both men and women. Men, in our culture, have been expected to forego all sentimentality and tenderness in emotional expression; the interest in sex was mainly physical, and a measure of masculinity. Women were expected to be demure and uninterested in sex; their role was subordinate to man. Some writers comment on the disappearance of the double standard. It has changed in some respects, but if we are to have a genuinely *humanistic* sexual revolution much has yet to be done to provide equality and mutual respect in male-female relationships.

Exploitation is often more direct. Males will cynically use females for their own private titilation; women will seek to use sex, or the promise of it, as a method of entrapment. Certainly hostilities and aggressions are often worked out through sex. Semantics reflect many of the antagonisms which manifest themselves in sex. Males speak of "screwing" or "laying" a girl; the girl may become a "cunt," the man a "prick." And so in humanizing sex we are forced back to both cultural factors which influence us, and to our motives, conscious and subconscious.

Counselors who work with people on personal problems often say that the sexual problems posed for them today are different from those formerly brought by persons who were struggling with their childhood repressions and inhibitions. Many of their present patients complain that sexual experience has little or no meaning for them—"It doesn't mean much," "It didn't live up to expectations." These people have almost undoubtedly lost the meaning of love, intimacy, and closeness

—most probably the meaning of life itself. Humanism, in order to restore meaning to sex, must concentrate, not solely on sex, but in helping human beings to find meaning and zest in life itself.

## Notes to Epilogue

1. Ernest W. Burgess and Paul Wallin, *Engagement and Marriage*. Philadelphia: J. B. Lippincott, 1953.
2. Lester Kirkendall, *Premarital Intercourse and Interpersonal Relationships*. New York: Julian Press, 1961.
3. William H. Masters and Virginia E. Johnson, *Human Sexual Responses*. Boston: Little, Brown and Co., 1966.
4. William H. Masters and Virginia E. Johnson, *Human Sexual Inadequacy*. Boston: Little, Brown and Co., 1970.
5. John C. Wynn, ed., *Sexual Ethics and Christian Responsibility*. In a chapter "Sexuality and Responsibility: A New Phase" by Harvey G. Cox.

# Bibliography

Atkinson, Ronald, *Sexual Morality*. New York: Harcourt, Brace & World, 1965.

Barnes, Harry Elmer, *Society in Transition*. New York: Prentice-Hall, 1939.

Baker, Luther G., Jr., "The Personal and Social Adjustment of the Never-Married Woman," *Journal of Marriage and the Family*, August, 1968.

Bell, Robert R., *Marriage and Family Interaction*. New York: Dorsey, 1967.

Bell, Robert R., *Premarital Sex in a Changing Society*. New York: Prentice-Hall, 1966.

Blood, Robert O., *Marriage*. 2nd ed., New York: Free Press, 1969.

Bossard, James H., *Marriage and the Child*. Philadelphia: University of Pennsylvania Press, 1940.

Brown, Helen Gurley, *Sex and the Single Girl*. New York: Popular Library, 1961.

Cassara, Beverly (ed.), *American Women: The Changing Image*. Boston: Beacon, 1962.

Cavan, Ruth, *The American Family*. New York: Thomas Y. Crowell Co., 1969.

Christinsen, H. T. and C. R. Carpenter, "Value Discrepancies Regarding Premarital Coitus," *American Sociological Review* XXVII, 1962.

Christinsen, Harold T., *Handbook of Marriage and the Family*. Chicago: Rand McNally & Co., 1964.

Cole, William Graham, *Sex in Christianity and Psychoanalysis*. New York: Oxford, 1955.

Cuber, John F. and Peggy B. Harroff, *Sex and The Significant Americans*. Baltimore: Penguin, 1966.

Daly, Mary, *The Church and the Second Sex*. New York: Harper & Row, 1968.

Duvall, Evelyn M., *Why Wait Till Marriage?* New York: Association Press, 1966.

Edwardes, Allen, *The Jewel in the Lotus*. New York: Julian, 1964.

Ehrmann, Winston, *Premarital Dating Behavior*. New York: Henry Holt, 1959.

Ellis, Albert, *If This Be Sexual Heresy. . . .* New York: Lyle Stuart, 1966.

————, *Reason and Emotion in Psychotherapy*. New York: Lyle Stuart, 1962.

————, *Sex Without Guilt*. New York: Lyle Stuart, 1965.

————, "Sexual Promiscuity in America," *The Annals,* vol. 378, July, 1968.

————, *Suppressed: Seven Key Essays Publishers Dared Not Print*. Chicago: New Classics House, 1965.

Ellis, Albert, and Robert A. Harper, *A Guide to Successful Marriage*. New York: Lyle Stuart, 1968.

Ellis, Albert, with Janet Wolfe and Sandra Moseley, *How to Prevent Your Child from Becoming a Neurotic Adult*. New York: Crown, 1966.

Erikson, Eric, *Childhood and Society*. New York: Norton, 1963.

Farson, Richard D., *et al., The Future of the Family*. New York: Family Service Association of America, 1969.

Ferkiss, V., *Technological Man*. New York: Braziller, 1969.

Fisher, Charles, Joseph Gross and Joseph Zuch, "Cycle of Penile Erection Synchronous with Dreaming (REM) Sleep," *Archives of General Psychiatry* XII, 29, 1965.

Fletcher, Joseph, *Moral Responsibility: Situation Ethics at Work*. Philadelphia: The Westminster Press, 1967.

Foote, Nelson, "Sex as Play," *Social Problems,* 1 (April 1954), pp. 159-163.

Ford, C. S. and Frank A. Beach, *Patterns of Sexual Behavior*. New York: Harper, 1951.

Frank, Lawrence K., *The Conduct of Sex*. New York: Grove Press Inc., 1963.

Friedan, Betty, *The Feminine Mystique*. New York: Dell Publishing Co., 1963.

Fryer, Peter, *Mrs. Grundy: Studies in English Prudery*. New York: London House and Maxwell, 1963.

Fromm, Erich, *The Art of Loving*. New York: Bantam, 1963.

————, *Escape from Freedom*. New York: Avon, 1968.

————, *The Revolution of Hope: Toward a Humanized Technology*. New York: Bantam Books, 1968.

Frumkin, Robert M., "Early English and American Sex Customs," *The Encyclopedia of Sexual Behavior*. Ed. by Albert

Ellis and Albert Abarbanel. New York: Hawthorn, Vol. I, 1961.

Gagnon, John H., William Simon (eds.). *Sexual Deviance*. New York: Harper and Row, 1967.

Gebhard, Paul H., John H. Gagnon, Wardell B. Pomeroy, Cornelia V. Christenson, *Sex Offenders: An Analysis of Types*. New York: Harper and Row, 1965.

Girvetz, Harry, *et al.*, *Science, Folklore and Philosophy*. New York: Harper and Row, 1966.

Guyon, Rene, *Sex Life and Sex Ethics*. London: John Lane, The Bodley Head, 1933.

Greenwald, Harold, *The Call Girl*. New York: Ballantine Books, 1958.

Hadden, Jeffrey K. and Borgatta, Marie L., *Marriage and the Family: A Comprehensive Reader*. Itasca, Ill.: F. E. Peacock, 1969.

Hegeler, Sten and Inge, *An ABZ of Love*. New York: Medical Press, 1963.

Hoffman, Martin, *The Gay World*. New York: Basic Books, 1968.

Holloway, Mark, *Heaven's on Earth*. New York: Dover edition, 1966.

Hunt, Morton M., *The Affair: A Portrait of Extra-Marital Love in Contemporary America*. Cleveland: The World Publishing Company, 1969.

_____, *The Natural History of Love*. New York: Alfred A. Knopf, 1959.

Johnson, Cecil E., *Sex and Human Relationships*. Columbus, Ohio: Charles E. Merrill Publishing Co., 1970.

Karacan, I., D. R. Goodenough, A. Shapiro, and Stephen Starker, "Erection Cycle During Sleep in Relation to Dream Anxiety," *Archives of General Psychiatry* XV, 183, 1966.

Kinsey, Alfred C. *et al.*, *Sexual Behavior in the Human Female*. New York: Pocket Books, 1967.

_____, *Sexual Behavior in the Human Male*. Philadelphia: W. B. Saunders Co., 1948.

Kirkendall, Lester A., *Premarital Intercourse and Interpersonal Relationships*. New York: Julian Press, 1961.

Knowles, Horace, ed., *Gentlemen, Scholars and Scoundrels*. New York: Harper, 1958.

Landis, Judson T., and Mary G., *Building a Successful Marriage*. Englewood Cliffs, N.J.: Prentice-Hall, 1963.

Lederer, W. J., and D. D. Jackson, *The Mirages of Marriage*. New York: Norton, 1968.

Levi-Strauss, Claude, *A World on the Wane*. New York: Criterion Books, 1961.

Lewinsohn, Richard, *A History of Sexual Customs*. New York: Bell, 1958.

Lilly, J. C. and J. T. Shurley, "Experiments in Maximum Achievable Physical Isolation with Water Suspension of Intact Healthy Persons," *Psychophysiological Aspects of Space*. New York: Columbia University Press, 1961.

Mace, David and Vera, *The Soviet Family*. Garden City, New York: Doubleday, 1963.

Malinowski, Bronislaw, *Sex and Repression in Savage Society*. Cleveland and New York: World Publishing Company, 1961.

Mann, William Edward, "Sexual Standards and Trends in Sweden," *Journal of Sex Research*, August 1967.

Maslow, A. H. *Motivation and Personality*. New York: Harper, 1954.

_____, *Psychology of Science*. New York: Macmillan, 1966.

_____, *Toward a Psychology of Being*. New York: D. Van Nostrand Co., 1964.

Masters, R. E. L. *Forbidden Sexual Behavior and Morality*. New York: Matrix House, 1966.

Masters, William H. and Virginia E. Johnson, *Human Sexual Inadequacy*. Boston: Little Brown & Co., 1970.

_____, *Human Sexual Response*. Boston: Little, Brown & Co. 1966.

Mead, Margaret, *Coming of Age in Samoa*. New York: Dell, 1967.

_____, *Male and Female*. New York: William Morrow, 1949.

Marmor, Judd, ed., *Sexual Inversion*. New York: Basic Books, 1965.

Money, J., J. G. Hampson and J. L. Hampson, "Imprinting and the Establishment of Gender Role," *Archives of Neurology and Psychiatry*, LXXVII, 333, 1957.

Montagu, Ashley. *Man Observed*. New York: G. P. Putnam's Sons, 1968.

_____, *On Being Human*. New York: Hawthorn, 1966.

Murdock, George P., *Social Structure*. New York: Macmillan, 1949.

Neubeck, Gerhard. *Extra Marital Relations*. Englewood Cliffs, N. J.: Prentice-Hall Inc., 1969.

Nordhoff, C. *Communistic Societies of the U.S.* New York: Dover, 1967.

Packard, Vance. *The Sexual Wilderness*. New York: McKay, 1968.

Pangborn, Cyrus R. "Sex and the Single Standard," *Christian Century*, May 17, 1967.

Pannor, Reuben, *et al. The Unmarried Father*. New York: National Council on Illegitimacy, 1968.

Pohlman, E. *The Psychology of Birth Planning.* Cambridge, Mass.: Schenkman, 1969.

Pollak, Otto, and Alfred S. Friedman, eds., *Family Dynamics and Female Sexual Delinquency.* Palo Alto: Science & Behavior Books Inc., 1969.

Rainwater, L., K. Weinstein. *and the poor gèt children.* New York: Quadrangle Books, 1960.

Reiss, I. L. *Premarital Sexual Standards in America.* New York: The Free Press, 1960.

Rimmer, Robert H. *The Harrad Experiment,* Los Angeles: Sherbourne, 1966.

_____, *The Rebellion of Yale Marratt.* New York: New American Library, 1968.

Resner, Robert G. *Show Me the Good Parts: The Reader's Guide to Sex in Literature.* New York: Citadel, 1964.

Rossi, Alice S. "Abortion Laws and Their Victims," *Trans-action,* 3 (September-October 1966), p. 7.

Roy, Rustum and Della. *Honest Sex.* New York: New American Library, 1968.

Rubin, Isadore. *Sexual Life after Sixty.* New York: Basic Books, 1965.

Rubin, Isadore, and Lester A. Kirkendall, (eds.) *Sex in the Adolescent Years.* New York: Association Press, 1968.

Sagarin, Edward, Donald E. J. MacNamara. *Problems of Sex Behavior.* New York: Thomas Y. Crowell Company, 1968.

Schofield, M. *The Sexual Behavior of Young People.* London: Longmans, Green, 1965.

Scott, George Ryley, *Curious Customs of Sex and Marriage.* New York: Key, 1960.

Shaw, Maude R., *The Threefold Cord.* London: Gollancz, 1947.

Skinner, B. F., *Walden II.* New York: Macmillan, 1948.

Spock, Benjamin, *Baby and Child Care.* New York: Pocket Books, 1968.

Sprey, Jetse. "On the Institutionalization of Sexuality," *Journal of Marriage and the Family,* 31 (August 1969), pp. 432-440.

Stephens, William N., *The Family in Cross-Cultural Perspective,* New York: Holt, Rinehart & Winston, 1963.

Stokes, Walter R., "Modern View of Masturbation," Vol. 27, 1961. "Sex Fantasies in Marriage," Vol. 29, 1963. "How to Handle Children's Masturbation," Vol 32, 1965. "Sex in Sleep and Dreams," Vol. 34, 1967. *Sexology.*

Sumner, William Graham, *Folkways.* New York: New American Library, reprinted 1960.

Taylor, Gordon Rattray. *The Biological Time Bomb.* New York: The World Publishing Co., 1968.

Udry, J. Richard, *The Social Context of Marriage.* New York: J. B. Lippincott, 1966.

Ungersma, Aaron J. *Escape from Phoniness*. Philadelphia: The Westminster Press.

Watson, Richard A. and Patty Jo, *Man and Nature: An Anthropological Essay on Human Ecology*. New York: Harcourt, Brace and World, 1969.

Watts, Alan, *The Book*. New York: Pantheon, 1966.

Wheeler, Stanton, "Sex Offenses," *Law and Contemporary Problems*, XXV, 1960.

Winick, Charles. *The New People: Desexualization in American Life*. New York: Pegasus, 1968.

# Notes on Contributors

WESLEY J. ADAMS is Assistant Professor of Family Life at Central Washington State College. He is a member of American Association of Marriage Counselors and the National Association of Social Workers. He holds a Ph.D. from Oregon State University. Among his publications are: *The Marriage of Minors: An Unsuccessful Attempt to Help Them,* and *Clients, Counselors, and Agencies—Ingredients of a Myth?*

LUTHER G. BAKER, JR., has a Ph.D. from Oregon State University in Family Life and Human Development. He is a Professor of Family Life and chairman of the Department of Home Economics, Central Washington State College, Ellensburg, Washington. He is active in the National Council on Family Relations, American Home Economics Association, and Pacific Northwest Council on Family Planning. His publications include articles in the *Journal of Marriage and the Family* and *The Family Coordinator.*

DONALD J. CANTOR is a practicing attorney in Hartford. A graduate of Harvard Law School (1959), he has published in the *Atlantic Monthly, The Humanist,* and other journals on homosexuality, divorce, narcotics, and other topics.

ALICE TAYLOR DAY is currently a lecturer in Urban Sociology at Albertus Magnus College. She is the mother of two children. She and her husband, Lincoln H. Day, are co-authors of *Too Many Americans* (1964), a book that deals with the effects of population growth in the United States. Mrs. Day has also published articles on population in the *Journal of Marriage and the Family, Parents Magazine, Columbia University Forum,* and elsewhere.

ALBERT ELLIS is the executive director of the Institute for Rational Living and the Director of Clinical Services for the Institute for Advanced Study in Rational Psychotherapy. He is 'the author of over 250 articles and of 26 books, including *Sex Without Guilt, The Art and Science of Love, The Encyclopedia of Sexual Behavior, A Guide to Rational Living,* and *Reason and Emotion in Psychotherapy*

GARRETT HARDIN, PH.D., is Professor of Human Ecology at University of California, Santa Barbara. He is actively engaged in abortion reform activities and in population studies. He is author of *Biology: Its Principles and Implications; Nature and Man's Fate; Population, Evolution and Birth Control; Science, Conflict and Society;* and the essay *The Tragedy of the Commons.*

LESTER A. KIRKENDALL has been constantly associated with interpersonal relationships and with sex-education programs throughout his life as a public school and college teacher. He is closely associated with SIECUS and AASEC. Of late years he has lectured throughout the country and contributed widely to the literature. He is also a member of the Publications Committee of *The Humanist.* One of his best-known books is *Premarital Intercourse and Interpersonal Relationships.* From 1949 to 1969 he was a professor of family life at Oregon State University.

PAUL KURTZ is editor of *The Humanist* and Professor of Philosophy at the State University of New York at Buffalo. He is the author of *Decision and the Condition of Man* and *Moral Problems in Contemporary Society,* among other works.

EDWARD POHLMAN has published *The Psychology of Birth Planning* and 40 professional articles. Two monographs in press deal respectively with children and incentives in birth planning, and they spring from two years' research in India, supported by the Carolina Population Center. Dr. Pohlman has been consultant to the World Health Organization and the National Institute of Child Health and Human Development, holds a Ph.D. in psychology from Ohio State University, and is Professor at the University of the Pacific.

DELLA M. ROY is married to Rustum Roy and is the mother of three teenage sons. She is Associate Professor of Materials Science, The Pennsylvania State University, University Park, Pa. She holds a Ph.D. degree (1952) from Penn State. She co-authored, with her husband, the book *Honest Sex* (1968).

RUSTUM ROY was born and educated in India. He graduated with bachelor's and master's degrees in Chemistry from Patna

University, and obtained his Ph.D. from The Pennsylvania State University in 1948. He has been on the faculty of The Pennsylvania State University since 1950 and is now Professor of The Solid State, and Director of the intercollege, interdisciplinary Materials Research Laboratory. Professor Roy is an experimental solid-state chemist, and the author of some 300 scientific papers, and the recipient of various professional awards. Dr. Roy is a member of the (Pennsylvania) Governor's Science Advisory Committee, Chairman of its Materials Advisory Panel, and active in its "New Cities" panel. He is a member of the National Research Council, and has served on various committees of the National Academy of Sciences.

EDWARD SAGARIN received his Ph.D. in Sociology from New York University in 1966. He is presently Assistant Professor of Sociology at City College of New York and is vice-president of the American Society of Criminology. His most recent book is *Odd Man In: Societies of Deviates in America* (1969).

FRANCES FERTIG SALISBURY received her B.A. in English Literature from San Jose State College in 1964. She was Research Assistant in the Department of Continuing Education at the University of California San Francisco Medical Center from 1964 to 1967, and Instructor in the New College of San Jose State College from 1969 to the present. With her husband, W. W. Salisbury II, she co-authored "The Myth of Alienation and Teenage Drug Use: Coming of Age in Mass Society," *California School Health*, Vol. 4 No. 1, Part 1, Winter, 1968, pp. 29-39.

WINFIELD W. SALISBURY II is Associate Professor of Sociology at San Jose State College in California. He received his Ph.D. in Sociology from the University of Iowa (1963). He was an N.I.M.H. Post-Doctoral Fellow at U.C., Berkeley, in 1965-66. He is a social psychologist, his theoretical interest being symbolic interaction and the self-image. He has published articles on self-conceptions, sociology of youth and group therapies and the expansion of consciousness.

DR. LEON SALZMAN is Professor of Psychiatry and Director of Psychoanalytic Medicine at Tulane University Medical School. He is Past President of the American Academy of Psychoanalysis and a member of the American Psychoanalytic Association. He is the author of over seventy articles in psychiatry and psychoanalysis and three books including *Developments in Psychoanalysis* and *Obsessive Personality*.

HERB SEAL is an instructor in Anthropology and Sociology at Los Angeles Trade Technical College.

WALTER R. STOKES, LL.B., M.D., is a psychiatrist and marriage counselor. He is a lecturer on sex education at the University of Miami. He is the author of *Modern Pattern for Marriage* (1948); *Married Love in Today's World* (1962); a contributor to several other books and author of many articles in professional journals. He is a Fellow of the American Psychiatric Association, and a member of the American Association of Marriage Counselors and Society for the Scientific Study of Sex. Mr. Stokes is on the editorial board of *Sexology Magazine*.

ROBERT N. WHITEHURST received his Ph.D. in Sociology from Purdue University (1963). He has taught at Bowling Green State University, Indiana University, Fort Wayne, and currently is Associate Professor of Sociology at the University of Windsor, Ontario. He is a member of the American Association of Marriage Counselors and has contributed articles to periodicals on marriage-adjustment, extra-marital sex, and youth and social change in the context of marriage. He is presently doing research on the women's liberation movement in Canada.

CHARLES WINICK is professor of Sociology at the City College of the City University of New York. He is the author of a forth-coming study of prostitution in America and of *The New People: Desexualization in American Life* (1968). He previously taught at Columbia, MIT, University of Rochester, and the Postgraduate Center for Mental Health.